The Sovereignty and Supremacy of King Jesus

Bowing to the
Gracious Despot

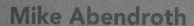

Mike Abendroth

DayOne

© Day One Publications 2011
First printed 2011

ISBN 978–1–84625–267–9

British Library Cataloguing in Publication Data available

Published by Day One Publications
Ryelands Road, Leominster, HR6 8NZ
☎ 01568 613 740 FAX 01568 611 473
email—sales@dayone.co.uk
web site—www.dayone.co.uk
North American—e-mail—sales@dayonebookstore.com
North American—web site—www.dayonebookstore.com

Cover design by Wayne McMaster
Printed in the United States of America

Commendations

In a world that has trivialized and domesticated Jesus, this book offers a startling but profoundly necessary exhortation: Bow to the despotic rule of King Jesus. Jesus is your friend, but he's also your King. As you read this book, you'll learn what a great comfort that is. Mike Abendroth writes with insight, conviction, and humor—all from a pastor's heart.

Stephen J. Nichols, Research Professor of Christianity and Culture, Lancaster Bible College, Lancaster, PA, USA, and author, Jesus Made in America

There is a reason why believers call on Jesus as their "Lord and Savior." Christ is the most blessed of all despots, and He is right to demand the complete submission of His people. Yet ours is a generation that desires a Savior who is less than Lord. Mike Abendroth has done a wonderful service by setting forth the kingly demands of our Lord Jesus in all their gospel sweetness. Here is hard truth that heals! Here is a surrender that liberates! Read this book and start living in the power of the gospel for a transformed life.

Richard D. Phillips, Senior Minister, Second Presbyterian Church, Greenville, SC, USA

You are holding what is destined to be one of the worst-selling books of all time. There are a plethora of books describing Jesus as friend because they sell. There are very few books that describe Jesus as King. It's about time that a book is written and published to balance the scales of our understanding of our God. Evangelicals need to read this book.

Todd Friel, host of Wretched Radio and Wretched TV

The modern-day pseudo-sophisticates who attempt to craft a 21st-century culture featuring the autonomy of individuals who rule their own lives have blindly overlooked one basic fact of life—Jesus Christ in heaven and on earth has always been, and will forever be, "King of kings and Lord of lords" (1 Tim. 6:15; Rev. 17:14; 19:16). Scripture unmistakably, frequently, and compellingly presents Christ's kingship in a timeless, omnicultural, and obligatory sense. Mike Abendroth's courageous portrayal of King Jesus can bring light and life to a

Commendations

dead and dark generation which futilely exchanges the eternal glory of God for the bankrupt, alleged grandeur of humanity. This volume captures the profound sense of Jesus' kingship, which makes it a must-read for all Christians and for those seeking to know the regal reality of life eternal in the kingdom of God.

Richard Mayhue, Th.D., Executive Vice-President and Dean, The Master's Seminary, Sun Valley, CA, USA

Mike Abendroth rightly reminds us that our relationship with God is not a democracy but a monarchy. God's reign over all is good news, for his Lordship is the basis of our salvation and our only hope for the promise of a new creation. Abendroth regularly and helpfully unpacks the pastoral and personal implications of God's Lordship over all.

Thomas R. Schreiner, James Buchanan Harrison Professor of New Testament Interpretation, The Southern Baptist Theological Seminary, Louisville, KY, USA

I wholeheartedly endorse this book and strongly encourage you to carefully read its message. Mark up its pages. Devour its truths. Share it with others. Use it as an evangelistic tool. Draw from it to preach. Use it to teach small-group Bible studies. You will find this book to be an invaluable resource.

Steven J. Lawson, Senior Pastor, Christ Fellowship Baptist Church, Mobile, AL, USA

To W. Robert Godfrey,

who first opened my eyes to the truth

about God the King!

Dedication

Now to the King eternal, immortal, invisible, the only God,

be honor and glory forever and ever. Amen.

1 Timothy 1:17

I am a man who has received only the cream off the top of God's blessings: from experiencing the best seminary education in the world (The Master's Seminary and The Southern Baptist Theological Seminary), sitting under the best pastor/preacher alive today (John MacArthur, Jr.), marrying the most godly and beautiful person I know (Kimberly), living with the four children who fill my life to the brim with joy (Hayley, Luke, Maddie, and Gracie), ministering alongside superb elders (Steve Cooley, Dave Jeffries, and Pradeep Tilak), working with a godly publishing company which values righteousness over retail sales (Day One), to pastoring a church that would make most pastors green with envy (Bethlehem Bible Church, West Boylston, MA)—I am a very blessed man. Each of these gifts has been granted to me directly from the hand of the great King, Jesus Christ. Thank you, Lord Jesus. You are a "gracious despot"! SDG.

My sincere gratitude also goes out to Sheryl Caissie, for her assistance, Ray Johnson, for his constant encouragement, and Suzanne Mitchell and Jim Holmes at Day One, for their leadership in bringing this book to fruition.

Mike Abendroth graduated from The Master's Seminary (M. Div.) in 1996 and became the pastor of Bethlehem Bible Church, West Boylston, MA in 1997. He received his Doctorate of Ministry in Expository Preaching at the Southern Baptist Theological Seminary in 2006. Mike has been married to Kimberly since 1989 and they have three daughters, Hayley, Maddie, and Gracie, and one son, Luke. Mike has been preaching expository sermons on a weekly basis since 1992. One of his passions is training men to teach the Bible expositionally; his doctoral dissertation title was "Training Laymen to Teach the Bible Expositionally." He is the author of *Jesus Christ: the Prince of Preachers* (Day One, 2008) and he is heard daily on No Compromise Radio (nocompromiseradio.com).

Contents

Contents

The foundational truth of all Christian theology is that bedrock doctrine of all doctrines: the sovereignty of God over the entire universe. Here is the towering reality that soars above all theology, the Mount Everest of all truth, namely, that God is God, not merely in name, but in full reality. Divine sovereignty means that God is enthroned in the heavens and is working all things after the counsel of His eternal will. That is to say, God is causing all things to work together for the glory of His name and for the good of His people.

To be sure, God *alone* is sovereign. Satan certainly is not, though some Christians act as though he is. Neither are both God *and* Satan jointly sovereign. Nor is man in control. Nor are God *and* man. Neither are circumstances or blind fate controlling human history. Rather, God exclusively is ruling over the universe. This means that God does as He pleases, *when* He pleases, *where* He pleases, *how* He pleases, and *with whom* He pleases. This truth must be the first article of our doctrinal creed and the chief cornerstone of our confession—that God *is*, and that the God who *is* is the God who *reigns*.

The sovereignty of God, A. W. Pink writes, is "the Godness of God." In other words, the supreme authority of God is what uniquely distinguishes God as God. He is "the only Sovereign, the King of kings and Lord of lords" (1 Tim. 6:15). Every other biblical truth must be brought into tight alignment with the chief cornerstone. All other doctrines must rest squarely upon this solid rock.

There is a second truth that is closely aligned with the sovereignty of God: the deity of Jesus Christ. The Bible unmistakably asserts that Jesus Christ is God. This means that Jesus is *Lord*. He is absolutely sovereign over all. Now seated at the right hand of God, the exalted Jesus possesses all authority in heaven and earth, by which He is building His church, overturning circumstances, and converting His enemies. The Lordship of Christ means that Jesus is the Supreme Head over all. Therefore, all who would enter His kingdom must submit to Him and acknowledge His right to rule their lives.

These two truths—the sovereignty of God and the Lordship of Jesus Christ—are the twin pillars that soundly uphold the Christian faith. And they are the dual doctrines featured in this book by Mike Abendroth.

Could any focus be more central to the Christian faith than this? Abendroth has done the church a great service by skillfully writing this important work. The entire thrust of this book is to present the absolute sovereignty and supreme authority of the Lord Jesus Christ. At the same time, this work shows what must be the life-changing effect of this lofty truth.

Today, we desperately need the sovereignty of Christ—what Abendroth calls "the Kingship of Christ"— to be emphasized. In this present hour, Christ's Lordship is being marginalized. Sadly, this glory is being veiled in the minds of the world. But, worse, this preeminent rule is being masked in countless churches and pulpits. In response, this book presents in clear, convincing fashion the non-negotiable truth of the unrivaled Lordship and irresistible authority of our Lord Jesus Christ. This watershed issue directly affects the entire life of the church, defining its evangelism, worship, preaching, obedience, and prayer. In addition, the kingship of Christ is essential in understanding other foundational doctrines, such as the eternal decree of God and His sovereign election.

I wholeheartedly endorse this book and strongly encourage you to carefully read its message. Mark up its pages. Devour its truths. Share it with others. Use it as an evangelistic tool. Draw from it to preach. Use it to teach small-group Bible studies. You will find this book to be an invaluable resource.

Steven J. Lawson
Senior Pastor
Christ Fellowship Baptist Church
Mobile, Alabama, USA

God. Yes, that's right—God. An interesting word to begin a book, you say? I consider it a strategically placed jump-start. Abruptness often serves as a starter fluid for the engines of our minds. The word "God" acts as a propellant to spark the engines of our imaginations. Another book starts in this similarly shocking fashion: "In the beginning, God ..."

What thoughts or concepts flood your mind when you think of the meaning of the word "God"? When you think of God, how long does it take you to think of the word "king"? If you are like most Westerners, it may take a long time, if you even associate the word. Why is this?

A. W. Tozer is correct when he says, "What comes into your mind when you think about God is the most important thing about you."[1] In light of Tozer's statement, I ask you again, "If you were required to explain who God is, how long would it take you to portray God as King?" My supposition is that you might commence by describing God's attributes and perfections (which is not wrong) and then, after some coaching, get around to relating His divine titles such as Savior and Lord (which also is not wrong). You might even unfold God's total sovereignty and divine decrees. But have we as evangelicals lost the concept that "God is King"? I think so. What if we asked that same question of a person who lived 2,000 years ago in the land of Israel? Likely the response time to arrive at "God is King" would be much shorter.

To complicate matters more, even if you did use the word "king" to describe God, it would probably hold little meaning today. Would your definition of "king" thoroughly or only vaguely represent God as a Near Eastern monarch in biblical times?

Results from Internet search engines reflect what is popularly believed and they are therefore insightful tools when trying to determine what a culture thinks and does. I decided to search "God King" and I found articles about Good King Wenceslas and H. G. Wells' book *God the Invisible King*; one search even produced "Hulk Hogan talks about God on *Larry King Live*." I wish I were kidding! A quick search of the Bible yields completely different conclusions. "King" is used in the New King James Version 2,237 times in an astounding 1,801 verses. Kings were part of everyday life for the people of the Bible (in both the Old and the New

Preface

Testaments). To the original readers of the Bible, kings were so common that the concept of monarchy was akin to that of breathing air—regular and taken for granted. The people hoped for a good, righteous, strong, and wise king, but they *knew* they would have a king reign over them. There were no alternative hierarchies.

In this book I hope to address a twofold problem. First, most Christians do not consider (at least initially) God as any type of monarch. Second, when they do, they think about current monarchies that are usually weak (like a constitutional king) within democracies (Great Britain, for example), instead of reflecting on the utter Lordship of God, the ultimate King. Put simply, I want you to biblically embrace God as King. It is difficult to think outside of our own time, culture, and environment, but we must do so in order to grasp God as He ought to be understood. I hope this book fills the gap in modern literature and thinking. In it, we will examine God as King, and many of the practical ramifications of that truth.

Note

1 **A. W. Tozer,** *The Knowledge of the Holy* (San Francisco: Harper & Row, 1961), 1.

How Is This Book Organized?

There are two parts to this book. Part 1 shows that the God of the Bible (both the Old Testament and the New Testament) is revealed as a King. In other words, God requires that we think about Him as "King" because that is how He has revealed Himself in His own Word. These chapters are self-explanatory and attempt to condense the biblical data in a few short chapters so that you will be convinced of the important truth that "God is a King." Part 2 describes the implications derived from Part 1. Put in the form of an exhortation, "Your life cannot stay the same if you understand God as King." Since ideas have consequences, Part 2 elucidates the ramifications of the eternal verity that "God is a King."

The chapters found in Part 2 are supplemented by simple and clear discussion questions or points of application. These are designed to promote further consideration of a particular aspect of God's Monarchy and are suitable for group discussions, family worship, home Bible studies, or Sunday-school classes. Each chapter also concludes with a hymn, some well known and others less recognizable, but which all extol God as King. I trust that each hymn will assist you in proclaiming this truth. Furthermore, these songs reinforce the fact that the universal church has always recognized God as the divine Monarch. I want you to sing this truth!

I remember that, each time my wife was pregnant, I became suddenly much more aware of other ladies who were with child. They were seemingly everywhere, multiplying, in my mind, like proverbial rabbits. There were actually no greater number of pregnant women walking the streets of Los Angeles, but I was more in tune with, and aware of, their existence. May this book similarly help you see God as King everywhere in the Word and in the great hymns of the faith. May you become more aware of the truth that God is King.

What Is the Premise of This Book?

Since the Bible regularly represents God as a King, it behooves the church, in every generation and culture, to understand God as the Monarch. Christians should endeavor to think of God only as He has revealed Himself in Scripture. Grasping the concept "God is King" will radically change every aspect of the lives of all Christians, both their thought lives and their deeds. Christianity was meant to be lived under the banner of "Jesus is the King of kings."

What Are the Goals of This Book?

What is your favorite form of government? By the end of the book, I hope that your favorite regime type will be neither a democracy nor a republic, but a Monarchy. Whether Democrat or Republican, Labour or Conservative, all Christians must ultimately appreciate, and live under, God's Monarchy. Have you considered the two root words that form the English word "monarch"? The word *mon* (or *mono*) means "one" or "alone," and *arch* means "rule." God alone is the universe's Ruler! There is only one Ruler of the universe. In Hebrew, He is the *melech ha'olam*, the King of the universe. Would you want it any other way? Is it truly desirable to be governed only by human rulers, chance, serendipity, or evolution? I hope this book will force you to admire, respect, and obey the Monarchy of the One God, who is the Father, the Son, and the Holy Spirit.

To a much lesser degree, I hope that you also become so fascinated by this neglected subject that you resolve to study kings, royalty, and monarchies. I wish that you, following my example, would search out throne rooms as you travel on holiday, admire earthly kings' crowns, and inject an enthusiasm into those around you for the things of imperial rule. My family loves to find judgment halls, throne rooms, thrones, and other royal regalia as we travel!

Who Will Benefit from This Book?

Everyone can benefit from this book—believers and unbelievers, new Christians and mature Christians. Anyone who wants to know who God is and know Him better will find nuggets about God as King.

FOR UNBELIEVERS

This book is perfect if you are not a Christian. Why? Because it introduces God in a manner that is far from superficial. Unbelievers often hear about God's attributes, like love and mercy, and His characteristics and titles, like "Savior," but they rarely hear about God as King due to the "overselling" of the "positive" aspects of God (i.e. those aspects that are "uncontroversial" or not "harsh") at the expense of the truth of the God who made the heavens and the earth. Yet all unbelievers must have sufficient knowledge of the object of their needed faith, that is, the triune God. In this book, I will introduce you to many of the essential facts about God as described by Himself in the Bible. This particular aspect of God—supreme Ruler and King—lends itself to our allegiance, submission, and repentance. There is only one God and King, and that means that all other gods are impostors, frauds, and charlatans. My prayer is that if you are an unbeliever, you will better understand the God who must be your object of worship.

The Kingship of God displayed in His Word, which is quoted throughout this book, demands the soul of each and every reader. I trust that you will bow in repentant submission to Jesus Christ the Lord, to the glory of God the Father, the King.

FOR BELIEVERS

As Abraham Kuyper gave the inaugural address to the Free University of Amsterdam in 1880, he made this shocking statement: "There is not a square inch in the whole domain of human existence over which Christ, who is sovereign over all, does not cry: 'Mine!'"[1] Every Christian needs to be reminded of this ruling Christ, the King.

I hope that this book will aid the new, recently converted Christian. I often approach ministry from the standpoint of "I will teach Christians under my care the ideas and topics that I wished someone had taught me!" In God's sovereign plan, the concept of King and Monarch was not initially introduced to me. But now, since I know of its importance, I want to infect everyone I know with the wonderful virus that must invade every Christian's mind—that God is King. May there be no inoculation from this blessed fact.

I trust that this book will also be used to encourage mature Christians. Even you can be bolstered in your view of God when you properly comprehend Him as King. This doctrine is like a legal steroid for the soul.

Perhaps you are thinking that this subject is not that important, or is even irrelevant. You might respond with "I already think properly" or "I do not really need much help in this area." "Frankly," you might add, "my marriage is falling apart, so I have more critical matters in my life." Fair enough; I take that challenge. I dare you to read this book and to determine whether you find yourself contemplating the greatness of the King more often than you find yourself despairing over your marital troubles. I dare you to read this book and then keep God as King and the problems in your marriage in two separate and unrelated compartments. The more you yield to God as King, the more self-sacrificial you will be in your marriage.

Finally, I intend this book to be used as a guide for those who disciple and train others about the Word of God. The study points at the end of each chapter in Part 2 are suitable for homework, follow-up, and discussions.

"God Is My King"

For a royal hymn/song teaser, consider Bach's first cantata. It should whet your hymn appetite. Even though he was a brand-new organist at Mühlhausen, Bach there penned his first and only published cantata called, of all things, *Gott ist mein König* ("God Is My King," BWV 71). I love the idea and I love the name of the cantata. Interestingly, the church board thought that Bach's style was not respectful. In any case, *Gott ist mein König* was printed on February 4, 1708 and a sample of its lyrics shows utter respect for God the King:

God, my King,
Thy might confessing,
Ever will I bless thy name;
Day by day thy throne addressing,
Still will I thy praise proclaim.

Time Capsules, Hermeneutics, and Faux Pas

Kings today are usually much different compared with kings who lived during Bible times. Since God is often called "King," all Bible students should train their minds to think of kings with the biblical background and import, and to attempt to avoid the unhealthy practice of seeing the Bible with the eyes of a Westerner living in the twenty-first century. There is no valor in acting like theological ostriches, with our heads in the sand of our own culture, oblivious to the realm of the Bible.

In Bible days, kings were a fact of life. Subjects might hate their monarchs or they might love them, but they could not ignore them and treat them as if they did not exist. If, in a word-association game, you said "king" to a person 2,000–4,000 years ago, that person's response would be dramatically different from ours today. During the biblical time period, people would have responded with words like "sovereign," "lord," "powerful," and "benevolent." In America today, the same word-association exercise would generate responses that included the nickname of a professional basketball team in Sacramento, a card game that culminates in drinking alcohol, a nickname for the basketball player Lebron James, or a media designation for Michael Jackson (or Elvis Presley: take your generational choice)—and the popular-culture list goes on.

Curt Daniel illustrates the dire need of correcting these common and modern misconceptions as he explains the difference between modern monarchs and God Himself:

There are still a few monarchies left on earth, such as in Great Britain. However, there is a great difference. The Queen of England reigns, but she doesn't rule. She has authority but no power. She is really just a titular monarch, one in name only. But the Lord is "king of kings" and "the only potentate." He both reigns and rules. He rules over all, for He created all and governs all. Some kings have men as slaves, but God is a King who has kings as slaves.[2]

We are so removed from the biblical concept of monarchies that we must acknowledge the need for properly interpreting such cross-cultural differences. For instance, did you know that, throughout time, many kings have been worshipped by their subjects, hence the term "divine king"? These powerful kings were considered to be god-like and therefore led both the local governmental and the religious institutions in the land. *Divine* kings have included Japanese and Chinese emperors, pharaohs from Egypt, Mayan and Inca leaders, and even the Dalai Lamas of Tibet, as well as the better-known divine emperors in Ancient Rome. These imperial forms of worship, often called *cults*, were the order of the day in many Eastern cultures. They were the norm, not the exception. Ask a person on the street today what an imperial cult is and you might receive an answer about a polygamy sect or some brain-washing group in the country, but you would not get a historically accurate answer about dynasties that were hailed as deities. In the UK, the average person would better understand what a king is, but the interpretation would be that of a king neutered of his absolute power and sovereignty and limited by a constitution.

The Cultural Context Unlocks Proper Bible Interpretation

When reading the Bible, what enters your mind when you read about meat sacrificed to idols, the value of a denarius, double blessings for the firstborn, fig-trees, and mustard seeds, or "girding up your loins"[3]? All these examples need to be understood properly and culturally. Should not the same philosophy be used when we discuss kings? What about when God is called "King"? How do we interpret these cultural issues?

Biblical interpretation would be easy if we could only get into a time machine and travel back to the Middle East in the days of Moses or Jesus! Since we cannot achieve time travel, what is a Bible student supposed to do to rightly understand the authorial intent of the Scriptures? Answer: study hermeneutics. Hermeneutics, most simply stated, is the science and art of biblical interpretation. Hermeneutics factors in the differences of time, culture, language, geography, and a whole host of other variables that would normally prevent someone from obtaining a thorough and complete knowledge of another society. Hermeneutics allows people today to rightly comprehend ancient literature, in our case, the Bible.

When a deep-sea scuba diver ascends too quickly from too deep a depth, he or she gets what is commonly called "the bends." As the pressure in the body decreases, nitrogen bubbles form in the body and the diver gets decompression sickness. Physical bends causes itching skin, rashes, joint pain, paralysis, and even death. Spiritual bends, a common malady caused by ignoring authorial intent, results in misinterpretation, eisegesis (reading something into the text), false totality transfers,[4] and a host of other errors that are worse than physical turmoil because God's Word and glory are at stake. Decompression stops are mandatory after a long or deep dive in the ocean. Hermeneutical decompression, stopping long enough to sort out what the author means by what he says, is absolutely necessary because of the extensive fissure between our culture and the culture of the Bible. It is not good to read the Bible too quickly, without sufficient time spent adjusting to the alien culture and/or historical depths, or you will get spiritual nitrogen bubbles that distort the meaning of the King's message.

The goal of hermeneutics is to determine authorial intent. What did God the Holy Spirit move the human authors to say? What did God mean when He had them write? All Bible readers must study diligently to figure out the actual authorial intent in the passage they are reading. Proper biblical understanding is not optional. It is both mandatory and indispensable. Scholar Roy Zuck agrees: "Cultural matters are not niceties we may search out if we have the time but which we may ignore under the pressure of time and circumstances. They are indispensable for the accurate understanding of Holy Scripture."⁵ All Bible readers must be proactively seeking a proper understanding of what the Bible meant when it was written. Zuck goes on to say,

Understanding the Bible properly requires that we clear our minds of all ideas, opinions, and systems of our own day and attempt to put ourselves into the times and surroundings of the Apostles and Prophets who wrote. To the extent that we seek to transport ourselves into the historical situation of the Bible writers and disengage ourselves from our own cultures, to that extent the likelihood of our being more accurate in interpreting the Bible increases.⁶

When we travel to a different country, especially a country that speaks a different language, we need to be prepared. If we are not ready, we will experience culture shock and bewilderment. Sadly, we Americans are notorious for seeing other cultures through our own cultural contact lenses, hence the term "ugly American." Yet it is impossible to visit, live in, and appreciate another country and its culture if we wrongly interpret it. Reading America into another culture or place is "traveler's eisegesis." Immeasurably worse would be to read something into the Bible that does not exist. Bernard Ramm agrees:

There is also the culture-gap between our times and Biblical times which the translator and interpreter must bridge. Culture, in the anthropological sense, is all the ways and means, material and social, whereby a given people carry on their existence. Until we can recreate and understand the cultural patterns of the various Biblical periods we will be handicapped in our understanding of the fuller meaning of Scripture.[7]

Do not read anything into the Bible, but study the Bible to extract what it originally meant.

In our day, primacy is placed on the reader's perspective and not on the author's intent. Students are wrongly taught to dismiss the original intention of the text and to dive deeply into the dark abysses of themselves, asking questions like "What does this book mean to *me*?" Secular philosophy, fueled by Jacques Derrida's deconstruction technique, assaults the traditional view of authorial intent. Derrida did not believe that any text's meaning was fixed and unchanging; rather he thought that it ebbed and flowed with the reader.[8] Postmodernism promotes and rejoices in the dismissal of what the author actually meant when he or she wrote. Since God is the Author of Scripture, the first and only question must be, "What did God mean when He wrote this?" Anything less (or more) will distort the truth and will fall prey to wrongly handling the Holy Scriptures. Virkler lambasts this common error as he says lamentingly, "Unless we have a knowledge of the writer's background, supplied through historical–cultural and contextual analysis, our tendency is to interpret his writings by asking, 'What does this mean to me?' rather than 'What did this mean to the original author?'"[9] Do you do this?

Study Assignment

Two whole books in the Bible are about kings. Before you keep reading this book, read 1 and 2 Kings. The culture of the day in Bible times was steeped in kings, and you need to be also. People we read about in the Bible lived under kings, and you can get a taste of that normal life as you read 1 and 2 Kings. There are forty-seven packed chapters that beckon you to realize the reality of living under monarchs. My proposition is this: put this book down until this assignment is complete; and remember: no cheating.

Notes

1 Quoted by **James Edward McGoldrick,** "Every Inch for Christ: Abraham Kuyper on the Reform of the Church," in *Reformation & Revival Journal*, Fall 1994, 91–99.

2 **Curt D. Daniel,** *The History and Theology of Calvinism* (Springfield, IL: Reformed Bible Church, 2003), 176.

3 A common biblical expression suggesting alertness and a readiness for action (i.e. 1 Peter 1:13, KJV). A modern-day equivalent would be "roll up your sleeves."

4 "In biblical interpretation, this refers to the illegitimate transfer of a word's total possible meaning, with all its variations and nuances, and forcing them all into a particular context." Cited by **William Dicks,** "Illegitimate Totality Transfer," August 6, 2008, at Just Thinking: williamdicks.blogspot.com.

5 **Roy B. Zuck,** *Basic Biblical Interpretation* (Colorado Springs: David C. Cook, 2002), 80.

6 Ibid. 77.

7 **Bernard Ramm,** *Protestant Biblical Interpretation* (Grand Rapids: Baker, 1970), 5.

8 **Patricia Sullivan,** "Jacques Derrida Dies; Deconstructionist Philosopher," *The Washington Post*, October 10, 2004; at: washingtonpost.com.

9 **Henry A. Virkler,** *Hermeneutics: Principles and Processes of Biblical Interpretation* (Grand Rapids: Baker, 1981), 78.

Kingmakers

"Kingmaker" is an odd word. What is a kingmaker? Who are kingmakers, and what do they do? Most people do not use words like "kingmaker" today, nor do they even understand it.

Originally, kingmakers, for all practical purposes, decided who the next king was going to be (and, conversely, who he was not going to be). In the fifteenth century in England, Richard Neville, Earl of Warwick, was known as Warwick the Kingmaker because of his considerable political influence. In our modern times, there are not too many actual kings, so the word "kingmaker" has had to adapt in order to stay alive. For example, kingmakers today are the movers and shakers in the political realm. It is said that James Farley was the man behind the election of Franklin D. Roosevelt. Farley was a kingmaker.

While the word "kingmaker" was not used in Bible times, the role existed. Do you remember Samuel? God used him as the first kingmaker (in the literal sense of the word). Scripture says, "So the LORD said to Samuel, 'Heed their voice, and make them a king.' And Samuel said to the men of Israel, 'Every man go to his city'" (1 Sam. 8:22, NKJV).

In biblical history, the magi functioned as the Persian version of kingmakers (see Matthew 2:1–12 for the visit of the wise men, or magi, and how they effectively "made," or, to be more biblical, recognized, Jesus as King). These men were part of a secret society that operated behind the scenes of the kingdom. In the New Testament, the magi disturbed Herod the king when he found out that the kingmakers were on their way to identify the new king, Jesus. Herod fully understood the magis' function: men who would put their seal of approval on the new king. They were kingmakers.

Why have I called this section of the book "Kingmakers"? First, because the chapters it contains include language associated with royalty. Second, because, just as kingmakers decided who the next king would be (or, at least, had a major influence in the decision), so this section uses Scripture itself, revelation from God, to make the case (or simply to remind us and reaffirm) that God must be thought of as King. In other words, the purpose of Part 1 is to establish in our minds and hearts, through the Word of God, that God is a King. God wants us to think about Him as the Monarch. Anything less is man-centered idolatry. My goal is for you to recognize this fundamental concept of Bible truth. Tragically, many never even consider God as King today.

This task is difficult, not due to a lack of data, but because of the problem of deciding what to leave out. The biblical data relating to God as King is immense and readily accessible. Anyone with a Bible and a concordance can rapidly collate all the data and be appropriately impressed with the repeated and common theme of God as King. In this section, I intend to use the Word of God to state clearly, so that there is no room for any ambiguity, that God is a King. To be more precise, God is *the* King.

Jesus Christ Is a Despot

When Shakespeare penned Juliet's famous words "What's in a name? That which we call a rose by any other name would smell as sweet," he intended Juliet to convince Romeo to abandon all his formal ties to his family, since they were warring with Juliet's family. Juliet pressed upon Romeo, who was from the family of Montague, that he himself was the person she loved, not Romeo *of Montague*, a name which contained so much unnecessary baggage of family name, relatives, and past disagreement with her family. In response, Romeo, with Esau-like travesty, deliberately turned his back on his name, essentially denying his father, and was content to be known simply as Juliet's lover.

Could there be anything more tragic? Yes; a far greater tragedy occurs regularly in Christianity. It is the calamity that has many believers promoting a view of God that is divorced from that found in the Bible. Like Juliet, they are content to let peace, warm feelings, or pragmatism win the day. After all, the God of the Bible comes with a ferocity that unsettles many and upsets a myriad of apple carts.

In our day, people are attempting to protect God from what the Bible says about Him. For example, many Christian books speak of God using paraphrased interpretations of the Bible like *The Message* because these nonliteral "Bibles" dull the stark transcendence of God. For their publishers and readers, the sign posted states, "No sharp edges, please." In a culture where many evangelicals want to park their theological cars on the pavement of "God is so crazy about me," some biblical words are too jagged and cutting to use in the company of polite, sophisticated people. "Despot" is certainly one of these words. When did you last hear the phrase "Jesus is a Despot"? Well, He is.

Does language like this cause you to cringe? Let's face it: words like this are not common parlance for the twenty-first-century Christian. Perhaps an atheist or someone criticizing the Christian faith would use them, but evangelicals rarely call God a Despot.

Phrases like "Jesus is a Despot" tend to invoke visceral reactions. To

Chapter 1

many, "Jesus is a Despot" are veritable fighting words. Are thoughts of God as Despot actually blasphemous? For certain, this chapter's title is mentally provocative and is like a goad or sharp cowboy spur driven into the ribs of a horse, or, in this case, into you.

I will never forget when I first read that God was jealous. I could not wrap my mind around that concept. It seemed so foreign, so unlike God (and, from a natural, fallen perspective, it is). I immediately grabbed the only resource available to me that addressed my problem: *Baker's Dictionary of Theology*.[1] In a brilliant article, the author confirmed my worst nightmare: God is jealous. Really jealous. Repeatedly jealous. Righteously jealous. Gradually, I submitted to the clear revelation of Scripture, and the Holy Spirit sealed this marvelous truth in my mind. God and His Word were not the source of the problem; that was within my finite and fallen mind, and in the way I had always associated sinful and unbiblical thoughts with the word "jealous." I needed my sinful thoughts sanded down so that they could be contoured to match what God said plainly in His Word. It is the same with this concept of "despot." I intend to rivet the truth that Jesus is a Despot into your mind and have you accept it into your theological grid. I want you to affirm these words of Curt Daniel:

The universe is not a democracy. God's authority is not based on a majority vote. Nor is it an oligarchy, or shared authority, much less anarchy. No, God is the undisputed King of all ... God is a totalitarian despot, but a holy one. Now, to the non-Reformed ear, these words sound severe and unbecoming of God. "What, is God a cruel despot like Adolf Hitler? Is He a totalitarian dictator like Idi Amin? Is he an unquestioned potentate like Stalin?"[2]

No, God is not like them. Remember that God's sovereignty is a holy sovereignty. Nevertheless, He is still a King with unlimited authority in Himself over all people and things.[3]

Four Cushions to Help Absorb the Initial Shock
To alleviate any initial fears and to allow you to more quickly get over the shock to your system, let us look at four clarifications that will serve as

spiritual shock absorbers. These four facts should help muffle the troubling sound of the theological implications of God as Despot. Just as modern automobiles come complete with air bags designed to minimize damage in a collision, so the following discussion will help ease most of the stress associated with considering God as an absolute Ruler. A reaction similar to that experienced when fingernails are scratched over a chalkboard need not result when we associate the word "despot" with God. As you will soon see, the Bible itself uses the concept of "despot" to describe God's Lordship. Facts being facts, the sooner we can learn to face them, the sooner we will think biblically.

THE ORIGIN OF THE WORD "DESPOT" REMOVES THE NEGATIVE CONNOTATION

The initial negative reaction can be tempered by being reminded of the very real differences between the Greek, Hebrew, and English language definitions of "despot." The English word comes from the Greek *despotes*. The English word is itself broken down into *des* and *pot*. *Des* is short for *domos* ("house"; hence "domicile") and *pot* is short for *potentate* ("lord" or "ruler"). Thus, "despot" literally means "house ruler" or "house lord" (lord of the house or master of the household). Certainly, every Bible student would concur with the great creed "Jesus is Lord" (Phil. 2:11), so why would anyone fuss and fume over "Jesus is Potentate"? Why is there an unenthusiastic reaction to "Jesus is a Despot"?

The answer is obvious. In history, "despot" has most commonly been used for ogre-like leaders who have controlled their people completely and ruthlessly. A great example of an ancient despot would be any of the pharaohs of Egypt.

As time passed, the words "tyrannical" and "despot" began to be regularly linked together, like a ball and tether. For example, the modern-day English dictionary meaning of "despot" is "a ruler with absolute power and authority [or] a person exercising power tyrannically."[4] It is fascinating that the most common usage of this word today defaults to that second, negative definition; it is important to study words in their historical contexts.

Chapter 1

FAMILIARITY WITH THE BIBLICAL GREEK REVEALS THE TRUE DESPOT-LIKE CHARACTER OF CHRIST

The second and closely related contributor to the problem with seeing God as Despot is found in the distance between the English language and the Greek New Testament. For reasons unknown to us, Bible translators preferred to translate the Greek word for "despot" in a nonliteral fashion. While many words, such as the Greek for "baptism," are strictly transliterated, "despot" cannot be found in any English translation that I know of. Yet the Greek text reveals Jesus Christ as something far greater than a viceroy, grand duke, archduke, duke, count, tsar, or baron. He is not portrayed as a president, nor is He shown to be a prime minister. The entire corpus of Holy Scripture portrays Jesus Christ of Nazareth as the God who towers over, and rules over, all—including pharaohs, chieftains, kaisers, khans, shahs, and sultans. Jesus is the King. Jesus is the Despot. And the Greek Bible does not hide from that fact.

When studying a word in the Bible, it is important to go further than simply perusing a couple of English dictionaries. If you don't know Hebrew and biblical Greek, find a resource that does and start there.

DON'T LET THE PREVALENT CULTURE OF INDEPENDENCE IN WESTERN GOVERNMENT, CULTURE, AND SOCIETY INHIBIT YOUR UNDERSTANDING

The third aid to facilitating scriptural thinking is to honestly reflect upon our origin and who we are. It is very difficult for fish to think about life outside the aquarium; likewise it is complicated for us to look at our culture and life externally and objectively, but we must.

The concepts of freedom and independence ring loudly and truly for almost every Westerner today (and most Easterners too). Arguably, the trinity of autonomy, self-determination, and choice is at the top of the charts for the majority of people in the world today. Curt Daniel brilliantly portrays the reaction of today's culture when it figures out that God is King and therefore culture is not, as it once thought, autonomous. He says that the doctrine of the utter sovereignty of God

... sounds harsh to our Western ears, we who are so accustomed to democracy. But let's go deeper. Why do men resist this great truth? It is this: it strikes them to their very being that God is God, not them. And men want to be little gods (Gen. 3:5). There is, therefore, something about the sovereignty of God that sticks in the craw of sinful man. Note that I said "sinful" man, for the holy angels and redeemed men in heaven have no trouble with this truth whatsoever. On the contrary, they rejoice in it daily. But sinful worms called "men" here below rebel against it.[5]

Sinful men and women vehemently insist that there must be no external or internal restriction placed upon them. They are like wild stallions refusing both bit and bridle; such independence is clearly a manifestation of the pride of fallen man. Man wants no powerful authority figure exerting influence upon the pursuit of life, liberty, and happiness. Our Western heritage and American culture contribute to our distaste of anything but democracy, as we chant, "One man, one vote. No taxation without representation."

The US Declaration of Independence triumphantly bellows, "We hold these truths to be self-evident, that all men are created equal, that they are endowed by their Creator with certain unalienable Rights, that among these are Life, Liberty and the pursuit of Happiness." But when was the last time you read the entire Declaration of Independence? I would wager that you have forgotten these words:

But when a long train of abuses and usurpations, pursuing invariably the same Object evinces a design to reduce them under absolute *Despotism*, it is their right, it is their duty, to throw off such Government, and to provide new Guards for their future security.—Such has been the patient sufferance of these Colonies; and such is now the necessity which constrains them to alter their former Systems of Government. The history of the present King of Great Britain is a history of repeated injuries and usurpations, all having in direct object the establishment of an absolute Tyranny over these States [emphasis added].[6]

Despotism is something most Westerners are conditioned to run from, flee from, and, frankly, topple. This aggressive reaction reminds me of the body's reflex action when the doctor softly hits your knee with a rubber mallet. Man's reflex is to downplay the rule of God while simultaneously exalting his own autonomy. Yet, eerily, John Hancock penned these closing words of the Declaration: "And for the support of this Declaration, with a firm reliance on the protection of Divine Providence, we mutually pledge to each other our Lives, our Fortunes, and our sacred Honor."[7] It sounds as if our forefathers were running from the realm of one despot into that of another! How surreal it would be if Hancock had written, "And for the support of this Declaration, with a firm reliance on the protection of the Divine *Despot*, we mutually pledge to each other our Lives, our Fortunes, and our sacred Honor"! The authors of the Declaration were not undermining God by calling Him the "Divine Providence"; rather, they were stating a fact, a fact that would give the citizens hope, trust, and confidence. The biblical concept of despot should be just as encouraging as the biblical truth of providence.

It behooves us to recognize the culture of independence in which we are living (and in which we have been incubated) and how it can, and probably does, detrimentally affect us.

THE PRIDE OF MAN CONTRIBUTES TO THE DISDAIN OF DESPOTS

Inextricably connected to the previous point is the fact that man's pride handicaps his understanding of God as Despot. God made man in His likeness and image. In a very real sense, Adam resembled his Creator as he exercised sovereignty over creation. Adam, as image-bearer, acted sovereignly. Sadly, after the Fall, everything was sinfully distorted. Young boys still reflect God's image as they play army games in the sandbox, deciding who is evil, who is strongest, who lives, who dies, and who wins the war; but there are aspects of fallen image-bearers that are not so cute. Divine sovereignty to the prideful man means that he, the creation, is not the one most highly exalted. Man hates having another King to contend with, and he rebels.

The pride of man, and his disdain for God's rule, can be heard in the words spoken by Sirhan Sirhan just after he shot Senator Robert Kennedy: "They can gas me, but I am famous; I have achieved in one day what it took Robert Kennedy all his life to do."[8] The murder of a potential president is heinous, but it is a small infraction compared with the spiritual treason prideful man executes as he attempts to overthrow God's government and laud himself. As R. C. Sproul said, "Sin is cosmic treason."[9]

Man's pride blurs his vision and gives him a skewed view of himself, and, more tragically, of God the King. Reflection upon Ella Wheeler Wilcox's poem would benefit all created beings:

You cannot put one little star in motion,
You cannot shape one single forest leaf,
nor fling a mountain up, nor sink an ocean,
presumptuous pigmy, large with unbelief!
You cannot bring one dawn of regal splendor,
nor bid the day to shadowy twilight fall,
nor send the pale moon forth with radiance tender;
and dare you doubt the One who has done it all?[10]

We should no longer be shocked to think of Jesus as a Despot, as long as we are thinking etymologically and biblically. Let's look at five biblical "exhibits" that reinforce the actuality of God as Despot. Whether we take them separately or together, we should have no further need to wonder if Jesus is a Despot, biblically speaking. Notice how each biblical example yields wonderful insight into the nature and character of God.

Exhibit 1: Jude 3–4

The epistle of Jude, to use terrorism language, profiles false teachers and describes how they, with great subterfuge, infiltrate the church. Second Peter told its first readers that this infiltration would happen in the future, but already, just as God predicted, false teachers had cunningly and covertly slipped into the church, bent on total destruction. Like their father, the devil, these wicked and base offspring were satisfied with nothing less than the defamation of God Himself. They were jealous for their own glory and were ruthless enough to understand that stealth is the wisest vehicle for entrance into the bride of Christ and her sacred fellowship.

Jude, the half-brother of Jesus, had hoped to write to his readers about God's salvation. He initially planned on discussing it and probably reveling in it. Humanly speaking, the Christian church nearly had another book hailing the matchless mercy of Jesus Christ, possibly an epistle similar to Romans in its amplification of God's righteousness. However, God the Holy Spirit interrupted Jude and moved him to valiantly vie for the Christian faith, the faith that was unchanging and eternally and irrevocably fixed. The book of Jude is a brilliant call to arms for the Christian, and it is strategically placed just before the Revelation of Jesus Christ.

See if you can find the word that, according to the Greek, should really be translated "despot":

Beloved, while I was making every effort to write you about our common salvation, I felt the necessity to write to you appealing that you contend earnestly for the faith which was once for all handed down to the saints. For certain persons have crept in unnoticed, those who were long beforehand marked out for this condemnation, ungodly persons who turn the grace of our God into licentiousness and deny our only Master and Lord, Jesus Christ.

If you thought that "Master" is a translation of the Greek for "despot," you would be right (this is too easy)! The actual Greek word is *despotan*. Jude calls Jesus our Despot to highlight the devilish depths to which the false teachers go in their attempted usurpation. Jesus the Lord, and absolute Sovereign, is blatantly renounced by the ungodly false teachers. How do they do this? By twisting grace into licentiousness.

Interlopers have a creed. Lacking the real gospel, they feel free to change the sanctifying gospel for a religion of irreverence and loose living. Heretics vainly attempt to excuse their immorality in ways similar to those of atheists, but they disguise it with polite and suitable religious vocabulary. If they really believed that Jesus was Lord and Despot (Master), they would behave in a way commensurate with that fact, because servants are to obey their masters. Since they want unbridled living as their god, however, they need to mentally construct a god who is less than Master and Despot. False teachers crash the gates of the church and spout half-truths about the Person and work of Jesus Christ, trying to minimize and restrict His complete rule so that they can live the way they want to live (and heap up followers who also like sin but still want to name the name of Christ).

Acting like believers, intruders editorially cut and paste biblical truth to fit their own selfish ends. The result is a faith that more resembles science fiction than biblical truth. Thankfully, God knows, sees, and overrules all their satanic shenanigans. Such apostasy is doomed before it is started. God has written down this condemnation beforehand and will mete out a severe punishment that befits this capital crime. Trespassing on God's sovereignty might prove initially profitable (earning power, wealth, and prestige), but sinful impostors will one day be forced to receive the awful judgment from the Master, Jesus Christ.

Do you believe that Jesus is a Master and a Despot? If you believe the Bible, you must affirm that Jesus has total authority and is the supreme Ruler. Knowledge like this should help suppress any desires to follow charlatans and shams who try to dislocate God's grace in an attempt to live licentiously. Thankfully, Jesus is Lord and Master over sinful and false pastors who spout heretical doctrines so that people will follow them.

"Master" is found in a parallel passage, 2 Peter 2:1–3. The exact same Greek word found in Jude 4, *despotan*, is used in verse 1:

But false prophets also arose among the people, just as there will also be false teachers among you, who will secretly introduce destructive heresies, even denying the Master who bought them, bringing swift destruction upon themselves. Many will follow their sensuality, and because of them the way of the truth will be maligned; and in their greed they will exploit you with false words; their judgment from long ago is not idle, and their destruction is not asleep.

Lying prophets are ghastly when they come from any nation, but when they have their roots in Israel, a nation redeemed from the land of Egypt, it is the supreme felony against God. Jewish teachers stood in a long lineage of men and women who were physically redeemed out of Egypt. Of all people on the planet, Jewish teachers should have known better because of all the temporal and spiritual blessings their nation had received. Peter is expressing utter dismay at Jewish false prophets. They are especially condemned because God had "bought them," that is redeemed them out of Egypt. The apostle lambasts these false-doctrine smugglers as they sinfully import and export damning lies with the ferocity seen on the floor of the New York Stock Exchange as the opening bell rings.

Unlike in Jude 4, the focus of "Master" in 2 Peter 2 is not specifically Jesus Christ. The term refers generally to the God who saved Israel from Egypt.[11] God delivered (bought) a nation from the clutches of Pharaoh and was now repaid with a bevy of false teachers looking to attract followers after themselves. Peter warns his readers of the trouble that is looming. Destructive heresies escort people straight to their damning doom. Thankfully, the Master and Lord knows these people and will soon return to dish out appropriate vengeance.

Below are several other verses describing Jesus as a Despot, but how many more verses would we need to answer the question "Biblically speaking, is Jesus Christ a Despot?" We must be committed to thinking about God as He has revealed Himself in the canon of Scripture. Evangelicals are, by definition, committed to only one source of revelation: the Bible. Just as a sprinter must stay within the prescribed lanes to qualify for the finish, so the Christian confines his or her mind to the lanes of Scripture—that is, with the book of Genesis on one side and the book of Revelation on the other. Anything else is grounds for disqualification as a runner in the race of sanctification. The Scriptures clearly teach that Jesus is the supreme Ruler and that He exerts divine power over the entire world and beyond.

Words have many meanings. The specific meaning of a word must be determined by context and syntax. Unlike the Amplified Bible (which includes every definition of each word, regardless of context), we are not forced to import every single meaning into a word. Just because the definition of "despot" contains a pejorative meaning, it is not incumbent upon the reader to import that meaning—especially when it is used of the Messiah! Jesus never uses His power in an unfair or cruel fashion, so the derogatory part of the definition cannot apply. The pejorative portion of "despot" must not be foisted upon Jesus as if He were some resented, indecisive, human monarch like the French king Louis XVI.

Jesus, thankfully, is the Lord and powerful Master of the Universe. Jesus is God. His Monarchy is absolute and universal. Far from being that of a sinful and selfish tyrant, Christ's despotism stems from His character of goodness, graciousness, righteousness, and holiness.

Exhibit 2: Acts 4

In Acts 4, Luke records,

When they had been released, they went to their own companions and reported all that the chief priests and the elders had said to them. And when they heard this, they lifted their voices to God with one accord and said, "O *Lord*, it is You who made the heaven and the earth and the sea, and all that is in them, who by the Holy Spirit, through the mouth of our father David Your servant, said,
'Why did the Gentiles rage,
And the peoples devise futile things?
The kings of the earth took their stand,
And the rulers were gathered together
Against the Lord and against His Christ.'
For truly in this city there were gathered together against Your holy servant Jesus, whom You anointed, both Herod and Pontius Pilate, along with the Gentiles and the peoples of Israel, to do whatever Your hand and Your purpose predestined to occur."

(Acts 4:23–28[12])

With an emphatic "You," the Lord is extolled as the all-powerful and sovereign Creator (v. 24). The Greek declares that the Despot (*despotes*) made the heavens and the earth through the Holy Spirit! The Christians boldly beseech the Lord, quoting the Messianic Psalm 2. They call upon the all-powerful Sovereign. He surely has the resources and dominion to grant their requests. The evidence is mounting.

Exhibit 3: Revelation 6

The exiled apostle John provides our third Despot example, saying,

When the Lamb broke the fifth seal, I saw underneath the altar the souls of those who had been slain because of the word of God, and because of the testimony which they had maintained; and they cried out with a loud voice, saying, "How long, O *Lord*, holy and true, will You refrain from judging and avenging our blood on those who dwell on the earth?" And there was given to each of them a white robe; and they were told that they should rest for a little while longer, until the number of their fellow servants and their brethren who were to be killed even as they had been, would be completed also.

(Rev. 6:9–11)

The NET correctly translates "O Lord" in verse 10 as "Sovereign Master." The Greek word is transliterated as *despotes*. Why would faithful martyrs cry out in united voice, "How long, O Despot?" They appealed to the absolute rule and reign of the only One who would be able to avenge their blood. It is God's prerogative to judge and to pay back. Who else is able to accomplish such a feat? This holy King and Judge would properly and adequately retaliate on their behalf. Far from being some kind of genocidal, Pol-Pot-type tyrant, this Despot is holy and true. He righteously reigns and should be the object of all the saints' prayers—even yours! If the martyrs can trust the King in a horrendous situation like the tribulation, how much more can we confidently rely upon the Sovereign Master, the Despot!

Exhibit 4: 2 Timothy 2

What does Timothy teach us about God in the following verses?

> Now in a large house there are not only gold and silver vessels, but also vessels of wood and of earthenware, and some to honor and some to dishonor. Therefore, if anyone cleanses himself from these things, he will be a vessel for honor, sanctified, useful to the *Master*, prepared for every good work. (2 Tim. 2:20–21)

The Greek word *despotes* is used in verse 21. God, the holy Despot and Master, employs cleansed vessels. Translating this as "Master" is so much better than "Lord" because it gives the reader an inkling that the Greek word used is not *kurios*. Even if you believe that *kurios* and *despotes* have the exact same meaning (which is not the case), it is helpful to know when the Greek New Testament uses one or the other. God Himself wants you to know this; otherwise He would have had His apostles write *kurios* or *despotes* consistently. Paul's illustration in this letter is driving this point home: God's people run from iniquity (v. 19). Just as the master of a household uses proper tools to get the job finished, so too God, as Master and Despot, employs holy and pure lives for His gospel work.

Household masters own some vessels (such as household jars, tools, containers, and dishes) that are for special occasions and purposes; these are used for honor. Other vessels are relegated to common and menial use (such as privy pots); these are used for dishonor. Timothy and every other Christian leader or layperson should strive to be used by the divine Despot for noble and honoring purposes.

Exhibit 5: Luke 2

Lastly, God is seen as a Despot in chapter 2 of Luke:

And there was a man in Jerusalem whose name was Simeon; and this man was righteous and devout, looking for the consolation of Israel; and the Holy Spirit was upon him. And it had been revealed to him by the Holy Spirit that he would not see death before he had seen the Lord's Christ. And he came in the Spirit into the temple; and when the parents brought in the child Jesus, to carry out for Him the custom of the Law, then he took Him into his arms, and blessed God, and said,
"Now *Lord*, You are releasing Your bond-servant to depart in peace,
According to Your word;
For my eyes have seen Your salvation,
Which You have prepared in the presence of all peoples,
A light of revelation to the Gentiles,
And the glory of Your people Israel." And His father and mother were amazed at the things which were being said about Him. And Simeon blessed them and said to Mary His mother, "Behold, this Child is appointed for the fall and rise of many in Israel, and for a sign to be opposed—and a sword will pierce even your own soul—to the end that thoughts from many hearts may be revealed."   (Luke 2:25–35)

Based on typical English translations, most readers would never see the importance of the word "Lord." They would assume that the original word is no different from the regular use of *kurios*. Yet here God the Holy Spirit intends the Greek word *despotes* to be understood. What fine distinction does the Author want the reader to grasp? In this passage, there is a reason to consider God as the authoritative Master who rules the world. The NIV translation is to be commended for translating this word as "Sovereign Lord," prompting the reader to ask, "Why these words?" The answer Paul would give (2 Tim. 2:20–21) is that God owns and controls all things, including people (referred to as "vessels").

Won't you praise God, the Despot, with Simeon? Exalt the King who reigns over life and death! Speak well of the God who sovereignly brings all prophecies to pass! Do not let language like this disturb you. Biblical language is not meant to act like a small rock in your shoe or stick in your craw, but, instead, to magnify your praise and give you a reason for joy in a world of sin.

Summary

The next time you read your Bible and run across the word "Master" or "Lord," you might want to stop and check the original text. The introductions to most Bibles tell the readers how *Adonai*, *Yahweh*, and *Elohim* are translated, yet do not reveal when the original language denotes the meaning of "Despot."

As you ponder the nature of God, make certain that you think of "Despot" as the most powerful Ruler, not as some vindictive tyrant. Void your mind of simple notions of human emperors and Byzantine princes, and focus on what God means by what He has said in Scripture. This will ensure that your mind does not drift toward thoughts of political powers or statehoods.

God's universe has no room for majorities, oligarchies, or democracies. God created the universe and it is His alone to govern. Thankfully, the Lord of lords is benevolent and gracious in the ruling of His totalitarian regime. God is a Despot, or, to use the Latin, He is *dominus*! Unlike the Emperors of Trebizond, who became rulers by inheritance, cunning, or popular vote, Jesus was never awarded this position for His services or given this title by mortal man. Instead, the God-Man is Despot by His eternal nature, essence, and Word.

Hymn

Rejoice, the Lord is King! Your Lord and King adore;
Mortals, give thanks and sing, and triumph evermore;
Lift up your heart, lift up your voice;
Rejoice, again I say, rejoice!

Jesus, the Savior, reigns, the God of truth and love;
When He had purged our stains He took His seat above;

Lift up your heart, lift up your voice;
Rejoice, again I say, rejoice!

His kingdom cannot fail, He rules o'er earth and Heav'n,
The keys of death and hell are to our Jesus giv'n;
Lift up your heart, lift up your voice;
Rejoice, again I say, rejoice!

He sits at God's right hand till all His foes submit,
And bow to His command, and fall beneath His feet:
Lift up your heart, lift up your voice;
Rejoice, again I say, rejoice!

He all His foes shall quell, shall all our sins destroy,
And every bosom swell with pure seraphic joy;
Lift up your heart, lift up your voice,
Rejoice, again I say, rejoice!

Rejoice in glorious hope! Jesus the Judge shall come,
And take His servants up to their eternal home.
We soon shall hear th'archangel's voice;
The trump of God shall sound, rejoice!   (Charles Wesley, 1744)

Notes

1 **Walter E. Elwell** (ed.), *Baker's Dictionary of Theology* (Grand Rapids: Baker, 1996); available under "Dictionaries" at: biblestudytools.com. Accessed November 2010.
2 **Curt D. Daniel,** *The History and Theology of Calvinism* (Springfield, IL: Reformed Bible Church, 2003), 229.
3 I cannot overemphasize how valuable Curt Daniel's work is for all serious students of the Bible.
4 "Despot," at *Merriam-Webster* online: merriam-webster.com. Accessed November 2010.
5 **Daniel,** *History and Theology of Calvinism*, 228.
6 "The Unanimous Declaration of the Thirteen United States of America," July 4, 1776; cited at: ushistory.org. Accessed November 2010.

7 Ibid.

8 Cited at "The Study of Assassination," at: assassinology.org. Accessed November 2010.

9 **R. C. Sproul,** *The Holiness of God* (Wheaton, IL: Tyndale, 1985), 115–116.

10 Ella Wheeler Wilcox, "Presumption," at: readbookonline.net. Accessed February 2011.

11 Second Peter's general reference to God is actually confirmed to be Jesus via Jude 4. Blum says, "The focal point of their error was christological; they were 'denying the sovereign Lord who bought them.' The sovereign Lord (*despotes*) is Christ … as in the parallel in Jude 4" (**Edwin Blum,** "2 Peter," in *Hebrews–Revelation*, vol. 12 of **Frank E. Gaebelein** and **J. D. Douglas** (eds.), *The Expositor's Bible Commentary* (CD-ROM; Grand Rapids: Zondervan, 1984).

12 Emphasis in all Scripture quotations is mine.

The Decree of the King

Introduction

While the President of the United States can issue executive orders and Congress can pass legislation, only kings can pronounce edicts and decrees. In the world of consensus and majority rule, words like "edict" and "decree" seem odd and out of place, yet they must be embraced in the world of monarchies and kings.

Living in republics and democracies yields certain advantages, but these methods of governing (with power residing in the population) have made it harder for the typical Western man or woman to understand the daily lives of the majority of Bible characters. Why? Because kings controlled the landscape of most of the Bible, and these monarchs did not take surveys, defer to the judicial or legislative branches, or concern themselves with polls and voting booths. They ruled with as much authority as their power, usually military, would allow. When a king wanted to direct the people, institute new laws, or change the direction of his country, he would simply speak the words. Remember the saying "Your words are my command"? The words of law might be recorded in a certain scroll, sealed by a signet ring, proclaimed by a herald, or formalized in another unique cultural fashion, but they were to be obeyed. Negotiation and debate were not viable options—if you wanted to live. Kings, and kings alone, had the authority to make the rules of law. Their decisions were absolutely binding.

Our word "decree" is derived from the Latin *decretum*, from *decerno*, which means "I judge." The superior one, the king, declared new law with the effect of a judgment—the king's judgment. Remember King Ahasuerus and his decree? "When the king's edict which he will make is heard throughout all his kingdom, great as it is, then all women will give honor to their husbands, great and small" (Esth. 1:20). The word that the NASB translates as "edict" in this verse is given as "decree" in other Bible translations. Ahasuerus gave an order that the entire kingdom had to obey. The Hebrew word behind "edict" is *pitgam*, which is a Persian loanword for "decree."[1] The king's announcement had the force of immediate law or judgment. His decision was both compulsory and authoritative. To use an ancient slogan signifying the law's irreversibility and irrevocability, the king's new commandment was as binding as "the law of the Medes and Persians."

As much as I like the theologian James P. Boyce, he seems to be too apologetic when he initially discusses "decree," saying, "The term 'decree' is liable to some misapprehension and objection, because it conveys the idea of an edict, or of some compulsory determination."[2] What else would it be? A suggestion? A hope? A wish? A prayer? No; a decree was an edict from the king. Both Old and New Testament readers would have sharply disagreed with Boyce. Consider that human kings would regularly issue decrees such as "Pay more taxes," "Join the military for five years," and even "Send your young daughters to join my harem." If the king was kind and good, his decrees would be the same, but if he was evil and wicked, those in his kingdom would suffer the brunt of his evil decrees. Why? Because his word was law.

Why Is the Decree of God Important?

The notion that God, as the ultimate King, has a decree is misunderstood. My goal is to get you familiar with hearing and seeing the word "decree," understanding its meaning, and being comfortable reading and hearing it, as God, the King, expects. Since understanding God and His decree is essential to knowing the mind of God so that He can be properly obeyed, worshipped, and followed, the sooner you accept the fact that God has a decree, the better off you will be. Strangely, the decree of God, although an essential aspect of Christianity, is rarely discussed. The decrees of human kings are widely disseminated and followed—or else. Why the eerie silence in our contemporary churches regarding the decree of God? Let's examine the biblical notion of the decree of God and why it is an important concept.

Once we accept this notion of God's decree, more questions arise. Since God is seen in Scripture as a King, does He have several decrees or just one? What are His decrees, or what is His decree? What does the Bible say specifically concerning His plans, decrees, and purposes?

Have you ever thought, "I wonder what my husband/wife is thinking?"

Did you know that God has allowed us to know what He is thinking? A correct grasp of the decree of God will dramatically increase your praise, wonder, and awe. It will propel you toward greater appreciation of the God who is, without His revelation, completely beyond finding out. Historically, people have greatly benefited by knowing the mind of their king. How much more would it benefit Christians today to seize, with understanding, the mind of God *the* King?

Either God created things for a certain end or He did not. Since God is omniscient and omnipotent, He is always able to ensure the complete accomplishment of His purpose. And His purpose is called His *decree*. Boyce is right when he emphatically pronounces, "In the creation, preservation, and government of the world, God must have had a plan, and that plan must have been just, wise and holy, tending both to his own glory and the happiness of his creatures."[3] It would be total insanity for God to create something and have no plan for it. Creation without purpose sounds more like something Frankenstein would have been involved in. Far from the deist's notion of God, the God revealed in Scripture controls and rules with purpose. He is a hands-on Ruler and is, in a positive way, the micromanager of every atom in the universe.

A Definition of "Decree"

A. W. Pink plainly describes God's decree as "His purpose or determination with respect to future things."[4] *The Westminster Shorter Catechism* is slightly more expansive, saying, "The decrees of God are His eternal purpose, according to the counsel of His will, whereby, for His own glory, He hath foreordained whatsoever comes to pass."[5]

To round out our understanding, let's examine six aspects of God's decree: God has one decree; and it is free, wise, effectual, all-encompassing, and eternal.

God the King Has One Decree

The most incredible aspect of the noun "decree" in the "decree of God" is its grammatical number. Shockingly and surprisingly, the Bible consistently uses the singular when speaking of God's decree. In other words, the Bible proclaims that the divine King has one, and only one, decree. In God's supreme mind, there are no plan Bs, no ifs and buts, and no what-ifs. God has no flowchart tracing human history that contains lines and arrows pointing in lots of crazy, different directions. More than that, He certainly does not have a plan that is in need of an eraser so that He can make changes to His edict when the unexpected happens. God never needs any correction fluid! If God were a chess player strategizing against human history, He would never hear "check" (or "checkmate," for that matter) from humanity. Succession of thought is too human for God.

Those who travel on the sea, venture off on moon exploration, or climb Mount Everest must have plans to allow for unexpected emergencies. Not so with God. God's decree is fixed, eternal, unchanging, and *singular*; therefore, nothing can arise that God does not ordain or know. God's plan cannot even get better (not even by one iota) because it is already the wisest it could be, and it stems from a perfect God who has a perfect mind. When was the last time you made plans at work or for a vacation and then changed them due to an unforeseen circumstance? As winds are prone to change velocity and direction, so too are man's plans prone to be amended, altered, and modified. However, God's singular plan is immutably ideal and faultless.

Think about it. God, who has never learned and can never learn anything, has one singular, unified plan. Don't skip over this thought too quickly. Robert Dabney expresses this unity of God's mind in this way: "It is one act of the divine mind; and not many."[6] Human kings and their decision-making processes are the polar opposite of God with His infinite plan. Even the phrase "decision-making process" should not be used when describing the mind of God. There is no need for processing, sorting, or evaluating. Notice the singular nouns referring to God's plan or purpose in the following verses:

Also we have obtained an inheritance, having been predestined according to His *purpose* who works all things after the counsel of His will.   (Eph. 1:11)

This was in accordance with the eternal *purpose* which He carried out in Christ Jesus our Lord.   (Eph. 3:11)

And we know that God causes all things to work together for good to those who love God, to those who are called according to His *purpose*. (Rom. 8:28)

Declaring the end from the beginning, and from ancient times things which have not been done, saying, "My *purpose* will be established, and I will accomplish all My good pleasure ..." (Isa. 46:10)

Finite human planning needs regular amending because these plans are always affected by uncontrollable outside forces. Furthermore, no person arranges his or her plans as one simultaneous work. There is no greater difference between God and man than on this point. Dabney compares human and divine planning in this way: "As His natural knowledge is all immediate and cotemporaneous, not successive, like ours, and His comprehension of it all infinitely complete always, His purpose founded thereon, must be a single, all comprehensive and simultaneous act."7

Has it ever occurred to you that to think of the plural "decrees" is not the best way to ponder the mind of God? Doesn't a singular "decree" clearly demarcate God from all other kings? In all candor, no human being can wrap his or her mind around this kind of God. God and His singular decree are humanly unfathomable and wondrously mind-blowing.

The Decree of God Is Free

Imagine all the people in a king's court who would have personal agendas for the king. The king's mother would certainly influence him. The military leader's opinion would need to be sought and valued. The king would regularly take secret straw polls of the people in his kingdom so that he would know how far he could push his agenda and figure out the "temperature" of his subjects. With God, however, this type of thinking is categorically wrong. God is free from all external influence, opinions, and pressure.

The decree of God is utterly liberated from every would-be external compeller. God selected, planned, purposed, and then declared, simply and only based on His own independent choice. Whatever He decided goes. God experiences no peer pressure because He has no peers—literally.

This makes complete sense only when we remember that before there was a beginning, God alone existed. Who gave input or advice to the triune God when He was by Himself? Therefore, God decreed the universe and all history just as He alone saw fit. Pink affirms this truth, stating, "God was alone when He made His decrees, and His determinations were influenced by no external cause. He was free to decree or not to decree, and to decree one thing and not another. This liberty we must ascribe to Him who is supreme, independent, and sovereign in all His doings."[8] The London Baptist Confession of 1689 simply states that God is not bound by any external influence:

God hath decreed in himself, from all eternity, by the most wise and holy counsel of His own will, freely and unchangeably, all things, whatsoever comes to pass; yet so as thereby is God neither the author of sin nor hath fellowship with any therein; nor is violence offered to the will of the creature, nor yet is the liberty or contingency of second causes taken away, but rather established; in which appears His wisdom in disposing all things, and power and faithfulness in accomplishing his decree.[9]

I ask with Isaiah,

Who has directed the Spirit of the LORD,
Or as His counselor has informed Him?
With whom did He consult and who gave Him understanding?
And who taught Him in the path of justice and taught Him knowledge
And informed Him of the way of understanding?   (Isa. 40:13–14)

God is totally free. His is the only will in the universe that is totally free (every other will in the universe is subject to sin or Satan, and to God Himself). God does what He wants simply because He so chooses. Pink, in his blunt yet biblical way, says, "God does as He pleases, only as He pleases, always as He pleases."[10] Read the following verses that stress that God does what is well-pleasing in His sight, with no external compulsion:

For I know that the LORD is great
And that our Lord is above all gods.
Whatever the LORD pleases, He does,
In heaven and in earth, in the seas and in all deeps.   (Ps. 135:5–6)

But He is unique and who can turn Him?
And what His soul desires, that He does. (Job 23:13)

All the inhabitants of the earth are accounted as nothing,
But He does according to His will in the host of heaven
And among the inhabitants of earth;
And no one can ward off His hand
Or say to Him, "What have You done?" (Dan. 4:35)

But our God is in the heavens;
He does whatever He pleases. (Ps. 115:3)

If something "blows your mind" it stimulates amazement and awe. The concept of the decree of God provokes this kind of response. God's free and sovereign decree serves as a kind of rocket-fuel booster for praise. God is God by name, but also by His mind and purpose.

Any theological position that allows man's total freedom quickly and radically hurls us into theological quicksand. Think about the following quote: "[God] does not purpose or dispose everything that happens … This means, of course, that at times his plans and purposes are thwarted … Even God's ultimate purpose that all persons will acknowledge him as Lord seems to be unrealized."[11] Is this true? The concept of the free decree of God obliterates such nonsense (at best) and shows it to be blasphemy (at worst). Call me old fashioned, but I prefer the inspired words of Paul the apostle: "Also we have obtained an inheritance, having been predestined according to His purpose who works all things after the counsel of His will" (Eph. 1:11).

God works only as He pleases, and as often as He pleases. He works things after the counsel of no one else's will. God does not do anything that does not please Him.

The Decree of God Is Wise

Through the centuries, kings have made disastrous blunders. They have miscalculated, acted rashly, and reacted pridefully to a myriad of situations and circumstances. To be more precise, all human kings, because of original sin and their own sin, have regularly failed to act wisely. Kings need groups of wise counselors to facilitate their decision-making. They call upon others so that they can see every side of an issue or problem. Since a king's decision will affect many, great caution is needed in reaching it.

God needs zero external knowledge or revelation because "with Him are wisdom and might; to Him belong counsel and understanding" (Job 12:13). God is, by nature and essence, all-wise and all-knowing. Theologian James P. Boyce strategically adds "wise" in his definition of decree "as that just, wise, and holy purpose or plan by which eternally, and within himself, he determines all things whatsoever that come to pass."[12]

God does not merely know what will happen in the future—He planned every second of history. Since He knows every detail of history, and how the particulars fit together, God's absolute wisdom helps to ensure that His plan will be consummated, and consummated to His liking.

What is wisdom? Tozer classifies it in a way that leads us to ponder the decree of God:

Wisdom, among other things, is the ability to devise perfect ends and to achieve those ends by the most perfect means. It sees the end from the beginning, so there can be no need to guess or conjecture. Wisdom sees everything in focus, each in proper relation to all, and is thus able to work toward predestined goals with flawless precision.[13]

Packer similarly highlights God's innate wisdom and His manifestation of His wisdom, pronouncing, "Wisdom is the power to see, and the inclination to choose, the best and highest goal, together with the surest means of attaining it. Wisdom is, in fact, the practical side of moral goodness. As such, it is found in its fullness only in God. He alone is naturally and entirely and invariably wise."[14] Repeatedly, God's Word screams forth His wisdom:

Do you not know? Have you not heard?
The Everlasting God, the LORD, the Creator of the ends of the earth
Does not become weary or tired.
His understanding is inscrutable.   (Isa. 40:28)

Oh, the depth of the riches both of the wisdom and knowledge of God! How unsearchable are His judgments and unfathomable His ways!   (Rom. 11:33)

Behold, God is mighty but does not despise any;
He is mighty in strength of understanding.   (Job 36:5)

Great is our Lord and abundant in strength;
His understanding is infinite.   (Ps. 147:5)

To the only wise God, through Jesus Christ, be the glory forever. Amen. (Rom. 16:27)

Daniel said,
"Let the name of God be blessed forever and ever,
For wisdom and power belong to Him.
It is He who changes the times and the epochs;
He removes kings and establishes kings;
He gives wisdom to wise men
And knowledge to men of understanding."   (Dan. 2:20–21)

Since God is all-wise, it doesn't stretch the imagination to affirm that God knows all the best outcomes and the clear-cut means to achieve these outcomes. God, as the Master Architect, has designed a faultless blueprint. Grudem and Dabney, respectively, offer antiphonal affirmations of God's wise planning:

God's wisdom means that God always chooses the best goals and the best means to those goals. This definition goes beyond the idea of God knowing all things and specifies that God's decisions about what he will do are always wise decisions: that is, they always will bring about the best results (from God's ultimate perspective), and they will bring about those results through the best possible means.[15]

… God's knowledge was always perfect … He finds out nothing new, to become the occasion of a new plan. His wisdom was always perfect, to give Him the same guidance in selecting means and ends. His power was always infinite, to prevent any failure, or successful resistance, which would cause Him to resort to new expedients. His character is immutable; so that He will not causelessly change His own mind. There is therefore nothing to account for any addition to His original plan.[16]

Many describe wisdom as applied knowledge. Such a concise definition is perfectly appropriate to God's decree.

The Decree of God Is Effectual

Frustration. Incompletion. Incapability. Words like these describe the results of many of the most grandiose edicts of kings throughout the ages. They have had world-changing plans, but they did not have the resources to bring their purposes and laws to fruition. "God, accordingly, is not like men. Men conduct experiments, but God carries out a plan."[17] That quote nicely reveals the Grand-Canyon-like difference between the effectual decree of God and the impudent plans of man, as do the writings of the prophets:

I know that You can do all things,
And that no purpose of Yours can be thwarted.   (Job 42:2)

The LORD of hosts has sworn saying, "Surely, just as I have intended so it has happened, and just as I have planned so it will stand."   (Isa. 14:24)

God knows whether something will occur in the future. He knows this because He has purposed to cause it to happen. If something God purposed did not actually happen as He planned it, His knowledge would be faulty and He would actually be deceived and misled. But God the King has no theories or hypotheses regarding the universe and what exactly will happen: He knows that His plans will happen and He accomplishes them by His omnipotent right hand. God's unlimited power enables Him to achieve mission-accomplished status for every detail in His decree. Only a smarter and more powerful being would be able to thwart God's plans, but no such being exists.

God's decree is effectual in that it accomplishes all of its intention, but it is also effectual in that it relates to every detail in the universe. There are no rogue protons, neutrons, or electrons in God's world.

The decrees of God relate to all future things without exception: whatever is done in time, was foreordained before time began. God's purpose was concerned with everything, whether great or small, whether good or evil ... God's decree is as comprehensive as His government, extending to all creatures and all events. It was concerned about our life and death; about our state in time, and our state in eternity. As God works all things after the counsel of His own will, we learn from His works what His counsel is (was), as we judge of an architect's plan by inspecting the building which was erected under his directions.[18]

Rabbi Kushner said, "God wants the righteous to live peaceful, happy lives, but sometimes even He can't bring that about. It is too difficult even for God to keep cruelty and chaos from claiming their innocent victims."[19] What a tragic and gross error when pontificating about God and His character! God's decree is not conditional.

The LORD nullifies the counsel of the nations;
He frustrates the plans of the peoples.
The counsel of the LORD stands forever,
The plans of His heart from generation to generation.   (Ps. 33:10–11).

The Decree of God Is All-Encompassing

One can visualize a king telling his Army General the battle plan, advising his Secretary of Agriculture of the rationing plan, and instructing his other leaders in the particulars of his decree; yet throughout the time of man, forgetfulness and an inability to see all sides of an issue have led to the fall of many an empire. Finite man is, by definition, restricted. He cannot view the future, and therefore he cannot have an all-encompassing decree.

Dabney saw the universality of God's decree, explaining it this way: "The decree is universal, embracing absolutely all creatures, and all their actions ... If then we prove that God has a perfect foreknowledge of all future events, we shall have virtually proved that He has foreordained them."[20]

Scripture says that God works "all things after the counsel of His will" (Eph. 1:11). His will is all-embracing. Consider the extent of God's decree:

He made from one man every nation of mankind to live on all the face of the earth, having determined their appointed times and the boundaries of their habitation.

(Acts 17:26)

The lot is cast into the lap,
But its every decision is from the LORD. (Prov. 16:33)

Are not two sparrows sold for a cent? And yet not one of them will fall to the ground apart from your Father. But the very hairs of your head are all numbered.

(Matt. 10:29–30)

Small or large, important or trivial, temporal or eternal: all things are enveloped by God's decree. Every person, place, thing, and event was, is, and will be under the comprehensive government of God. The alternative would be demoralizing if true. If sinful man were the author of his own destiny and plans, I am quite confident that there would be no world today. The sinfulness of sin would have raped and pillaged every corner of the universe, and man would have destroyed every image-bearer he could get hold of.

Thankfully, there is no room for Lady Luck in God's universe. Nor is there any need to "knock on wood." If God has decreed something, we could knock down a redwood tree with a bulldozer and God's mind would not be altered. We can also feel free to walk under ladders, cross the paths of black cats, and sit in seat 13 on airplanes.

The Decree of God Is Eternal

Kings are born, kings die, and the process is repeated. Because kings are not eternal, neither are their edicts. Conversely, since God is eternal and immutable, so is His decree. While concepts like this tax the mind, they also expand the mind to rightly view God. Boyce concurs, saying,

Therefore his thoughts, and purpose, and plan must be eternal. The fact also that his knowledge is infinite, and cannot be increased, forbids the forming of plans in time, which, as they become known to him, would add to that knowledge. It is also to be remembered that the plan must precede its execution, but as time began with that execution, the plan must not have been formed in time, and must be eternal.[21]

Deductive learning does not apply to God the King. As the infinite Monarch of the world, He knows all eternally, and His comprehension is perpetual. God's decree does not grow or change over time (even for the better), because His decree was perfectly established in eternity. Once again, in Ephesians 3:11, Paul calls God's decree "the eternal purpose," signifying that God's arrangement was not planned in time; rather, according to O'Brien, it "can be traced back to his everlasting purpose."[22] Pink elaborates upon God's plans:

To suppose any of them to be made in time, is to suppose that some new occasion has occurred, some unforeseen event or combination of circumstances has arisen, which has induced the Most High to form a new resolution. This would argue that the knowledge of the deity is limited, and that He is growing wiser in the progress of time—which would be horrible blasphemy. No man who believes that the Divine understanding is infinite, comprehending the past, the present, and the future, will ever assent to the erroneous doctrine of temporal decrees. God is not ignorant of future events which will be executed by human volitions; He has foretold them in innumerable instances, and prophecy is but the manifestation of His eternal prescience.[23]

We must be careful not to attempt to imprison the eternal mind of God in the jail of human thinking. God's mind is infinite. God instantly and immediately knows all knowledge, and He knows it without ever thinking successively. God does not need any RAM; His mind is infinite. As Curt Daniel says, "The universe has been pre-programmed,"[24] but its programmer is divine and infinite, and therefore does not need to think consecutively in steps and stages. God the King's decree contains the past, the present, and the future.

What kind of pressure would this present to God to get the decree initially correct—perfectly correct? Absolutely none. Literally, *no single thing* can deviate or go awry, because, if it did, God's name and character would be impugned. If God's eternal decree were even slightly out of kilter, God would no longer be faithful and trustworthy; frankly, He would not be God.

All history is interrelated and irrevocably linked together in a seamless, organic fashion. When we study history, we must guard against thinking that history is strictly linear or even cyclical. Historian Arnold Toynbee espoused the "cycle-of-history" view, and he wanted God's historical pattern to be broken. This reminds me of the Tower of Babel and mankind trying to become as great as God. Vanity of vanities! The Bible says, without compromise, "Known unto God are all His works, from the beginning of the world" (Acts 15:18, KJV).

Don't fall prey to what is known as "The Theory of Middle Knowledge." God's decree is so rough and jagged that many have attempted to smooth it out by the doctrine of *scientia media*, or mediate knowledge, hoping to make God more "user-friendly." The concept of Middle Knowledge is closer to Greek philosophy than it is to biblical theology. Richard Muller defined this aberration as "a conditional and consequent knowledge of future contingents by which God knows of an event because of its occurrence … Such events are outside of the divine willing."[25] God is never needy and reliant upon the sinful and finite will of man for His decree to be actualized. Furthermore, God is not accurately defined by "process theologians" who yield a god who needs to learn as the future unfolds. God is perfect; therefore, His knowledge is also perfect. God is eternal; therefore, His decree is eternal.

Aren't you glad that Clark Pinnock is categorically wrong when he boldly asserts,

What we detect … is not some dark predestinarian decree operating behind the scenes making sure everything works out right. What we do encounter is the freedom of God to respond, positively and negatively, to man's freedom. God weaves into his plan for history the significant choices that we make. History is not a computer printout of programmed decisions set long before by an all-determining Deity. It is much more like a dialogue between the Father and his human respondents.[26]

For some, perhaps, Pinnock's god is more palatable and easy to swallow, theologically speaking, but he is not the God of Scripture. God is not an Epicurean, nor is He accurately described by Epicureans or Pinnockians.

If our salvation depended on a king of random history, dependent upon fallen man's will, or based upon anything outside the eternal decree of

God, we would all be doomed. But God never had to look down the corridors of time. The eternal decree of God prohibits the use of such God-debasing and man-glorifying language. Think of God's eternal decree as you read these verses:

You were not redeemed with perishable things like silver or gold from your futile way of life inherited from your forefathers, but with precious blood, as of a lamb unblemished and spotless, the blood of Christ. For He was foreknown before the foundation of the world, but has appeared in these last times for [your] sake.

(1 Peter 1:18–20)

But we should always give thanks to God for you, brethren beloved by the Lord, because God has chosen you from the beginning for salvation through sanctification by the Spirit and faith in the truth.

(2 Thes. 2:13)

[God] has saved us and called us with a holy calling, not according to our works, but according to His own purpose and grace which was granted us in Christ Jesus from all eternity.

(2 Tim. 1:9)

Summary

Can you spot some of our six descriptions of the decree of God in the following wonderful poem?

Lord of glory—eternal King!
Let us to Him our worship bring.
Righteous and pure are His decrees,
Standing sure for eternity.
For naught can ever stay His hand,
He will complete His purposed plan!
His decrees are all sure and true,
By grace imparted unto you
That you may know the Upward Way
That leads to God's eternal day.

(Mona A. Fetter[27])

Society today is fascinated by what-if scenarios. People like to view the history of the world with different glasses that yield different outcomes of times past. Modern literature is flooded with a new genre of what-if books. A hybrid between fiction (the events did not actually happen) and non-fiction (much is based on actual historical events leading up to the author's what-if scenario), this genre captures the public's imagination.

The book *What If? The World's Foremost Military Historians Imagine What Might Have Been* has a compelling first sentence: "What if Sennacherib, king of Assyria, had conquered Jerusalem in 701 B.C. when he led his imperial army against a coalition of Egyptian, Phoenician, Philistine, and Jewish enemies, and handily defeated them all?"[28] Interesting, yes, but possible—no. Why? Because "alternative history" is a misnomer in theology-speak.

Such recent books unfolding other possibilities are fascinating, but they are, in actuality, basic science fiction. Other titles include *What Ifs? of American History*; *What If? 2: Eminent Historians Imagine What Might Have Been*; *What Might Have Been: Imaginary History from Twelve Leading Historians*; *The Best Alternate History Stories of the 20th Century*; *Roads Not Taken: Tales of Alternate History*; *If the South Had Won the Civil War*; and *Virtual History: Alternatives and Counterfactuals*.

Science fiction is a better category for these so-called history books. Why the fascination with alternative, faux history? Shouldn't it be the other way round? We should be most fascinated by the fact that there are no what-ifs with God.

Hymn

Sovereign Ruler of the skies!
Ever gracious, ever wise;
All our times are in thy hand,
All events at thy command.

His decree who formed the earth
Fixed my first and second birth;
Parents, native place, and time,
All appointed were by him.

He that formed me in the womb,
He shall guide me to the tomb;
All my times shall ever be
Ordered by his wise decree.

Times of sickness; times of health;
Times of penury and wealth;
Times of trial and of grief;
Times of triumph and relief.

Times the tempter's power to prove;
Times to taste the Savior's love;
All must come, and last, and end,
As shall please my heavenly Friend.

(John Ryland, 1753–1825)

Notes

1 פתם in **R. Laird Harris, Gleason L. Archer, Jr.,** and **Bruce K. Waltke,** *The Theological Wordbook of the Old Testament* (CD-ROM; Chicago: Moody, 1980), in *Bible Works* (CD-ROM; Norfolk: BibleWorks LLC, 1992–2003).

2 **James P. Boyce,** "A Doctrinal Study: The Decrees of God," in *Founders Journal*, Fall 2001, 25–28.

3 Ibid.

4 **Arthur W. Pink,** *The Attributes of God* (Grand Rapids: Baker, 1975), 11.

5 *Westminster Shorter Catechism,* Q. 7: "What are the decrees of God?"

6 **Robert Lewis Dabney,** "The Decrees of God," in *Systematic Theology* ([n.p.]: Providence Baptist Ministries, 2002), 285. Available at: davidcox.com.mx/library/D/Dabney,%20Robert %20-%20Systematic%20Theology.pdf. Accessed November 2010.

7 Ibid.

8 **Pink,** *Attributes of God*, 13. Even the brilliant A. W. Pink occasionally erred by calling the single decree of God "decrees" and "determinations," but he certainly did not blunder by declaring the freedom of God's decree here.

9 "Of God's Decree," The Baptist Confession of Faith of 1689; available from 1689.com/confession.html. Accessed January 2011.

10 **Pink,** *Attributes of God,* 31.

11 Bruce Reichenbach, "God Limits His Power," in **John S. Feinberg** and **David Basinger,** *Predestination and Free Will: Four Views of Divine Sovereignty and Human Freedom* (Downer's Grove, IL: InterVarsity Press, 1986), 111.

12 James P. Boyce, *Abstract of Systematic Theology* (1887); adapted and cited in "A Doctrinal Study: The Decrees of God," 25.

13 A. W. Tozer, *The Knowledge of the Holy* (San Francisco: Harper and Row, 1961), 66.

14 J. I. Packer, *Knowing God* (Downers Grove, IL: InterVarsity Press, 1973), 80.

15 Wayne Grudem, *Systematic Theology: An Introduction to Biblical Doctrine* (Grand Rapids: Zondervan, 1994), 193.

16 Dabney, *Systematic Theology.*

17 William Hendricksen, *Galatians, Ephesians, Philippians, Colossians, and Philemon* (Grand Rapids: Baker, 2002), 55.

18 Pink, *Attributes of God,* 14.

19 Harold Kushner, quoted in **Jerry Bridges,** *Trusting God: Even When Life Hurts* (Colorado Springs: NavPress, 1988), 23.

20 Dabney, *Systematic Theology.*

21 Boyce, "A Doctrinal Study: The Decrees of God."

22 Peter T. O'Brien, *The Letter to the Ephesians* (Pillar New Testament Commentary; Grand Rapids: Eerdmans, 1990), 248.

23 Pink, *Attributes of God,* 12.

24 Curt Daniel, *The History and Theology of Calvinism* (Springfield, IL: Reformed Bible Church, 2003), 243.

25 Richard Muller, cited in **Daniel,** *History and Theology of Calvinism,* 243.

26 Clark Pinnock, cited in **Daniel,** *History and Theology of Calvinism,* 249.

27 Mona A. Fetter, cited under "The Decrees of God" (July 14, 2002), by Friendship Baptist Church at: friendship-baptistchurch.com/sermons/ewlucasnotes/THE_DECREES_OF_GOD.htm. Accessed November 2010.

28 Robert Cowley (ed.), *What If? The World's Foremost Military Historians Imagine What Might Have Been* (New York: American Historical Publications/G. P. Putnam's Sons, 1999), 3.

To What Degree Is God "King"? The Extent of God's Rule

Human kings always have borders and limits to their kingdoms. These come in both external and internal forms. Externally, they can be restricted by geographical terrain, military prowess, time, or oceans. Internally, every human king is limited by health, intelligence, willpower, and knowledge. But nothing can compare to the utter God-ness of the King of kings, because He has no restrictions or limitations. When we think on this further, we realize that human kings are not truly kings over even their own bodies, mortality, and speech. They are dominated by the indwelling slavery of sin, Satan, and ultimately God Himself.

The Chinese developed a term for something that seems strong but is, in fact, a less-than-advertised puppet: "a paper tiger." Man's best rule is more like that of a paper tiger than that of an actual sovereign, because it can be hampered and curtailed. Like the sands of the shore that curb the extent of the oceans, so external and internal factors impinge upon the extent of earthly monarchies, saying, "This far you may come, but no farther, and here your proud waves must stop!" (Job 38:11, NKJV).

Can those words addressed to the ocean be said of God the King? Are there any encroachments upon God's sovereign, absolute rule? Are there any new places for God to conquer? Is God like Alexander the Great, who allegedly became downcast because he had no more places to conquer? Is there any bit or scrap of the universe that is not under God's dominion and rule? Even just a smidgen? As mentioned earlier, Abraham Kuyper's inaugural address at Free University in Amsterdam rightly excluded any notion of God that does not include His reign. He boldly asserted, "There is not a square inch in the whole domain of human existence over which Christ, who is sovereign over all, does not cry, 'Mine!'"[1]

The economy of the triune God leaves no room for majorities, oligarchies, republics, or democracies. God created the universe and it is

His to govern. Thankfully, the Lord of lords is benevolent and gracious in the bestowal of His totalitarian reign. I quoted these words of Curt Daniel earlier: "He both reigns and rules. He rules over all, for He created all and governs all. Some kings have men as slaves, but God is a King who has kings as slaves."[2] Wow! What sheer "otherness" and "aboveness"!

The goal of this chapter is to examine the extent of God's sovereignty as King. There is a biblical pervasiveness to this subject. God's rule and reign permeate every nook and cranny of Scripture. A cursory reading of Scripture rapidly reveals that God shares His authority with no one, and that His dominion is total and exclusive.

Troubled Times

We live in a culture that restricts God's attributes. To most people today, God is holy, but not immutably holy. God is righteous, but not perfectly righteous. God is just, but not always and forever just. The unbeliever fashions a god that is tamer than the biblical God. The culture's god is like a benign grandfather who always loves everyone unconditionally. Natural men and women do not love a downright Sovereign. Why? Because they want to be sovereign themselves. The only time people want God to be sovereign is when they are in a bind and they need Him to be powerful. C. H. Spurgeon's oft-quoted words on this subject are timeless:

There is no doctrine more hated by worldlings, no truth of which they have made such a football, as the great, stupendous, but yet most certain doctrine of the Sovereignty of the infinite Jehovah. Men will allow God to be everywhere except on His throne. They will allow Him to be in His workshop to fashion worlds and make stars. They will allow Him to be in His almonry to dispense His alms and bestow His bounties. They will allow Him to sustain the earth and bear up the pillars thereof, or light the lamps of heaven, or rule the waves of the ever-moving ocean; but when God ascends His throne, His creatures then gnash their teeth, and we proclaim an enthroned God, and His right to do as He wills with His own, to dispose of His creatures as He thinks well, without consulting them in the matter; then it is that we are hissed [at] and execrated, and then it is that men turn a deaf ear to us, for God on His throne is not the God they love.[3]

People are angry because God does not rule with them or under them, and because He does not need created beings as co-regents. The blasphemous "God is my co-pilot" bumper sticker sums up the theology of the majority. Pride doesn't like the outskirts and the periphery; it demands the center. Pride must not have anything or anyone over it.

Pouring gasoline on the fire, the Hollywood machine systematically barrages film audiences with portraits of God that represent the Almighty as a less-than-omniscient ruler. Directors and producers are more than content to depict God as George-Burns-like, all-tolerant and not angry with sin (or sinners). This figment-of-the-imagination god is more like a genie in a bottle who is ever ready and willing to fulfill actors' selfish whims and desires. Expecting precise theology from movies is naïve, but the church must consistently teach about the Lord as He has revealed Himself to her—that is, from the Scriptures.

Society, advertising, and the media have not helped the cause either (not that we should expect that they would). For an example of the culture of me-ism (which means "I am sovereign"), one need look no further than the evolution of the U.S. Army's recruiting slogans and practices. You may not remember "Duty, honor, country," but you will probably recall "Be all that you can be." That is self-centered enough, but apparently young Americans did not like even that approach (Army recruits were down), so the U.S. Army switched to "An Army of one." In one U.S. Army advertisement, Corporal Richard P. Lovett says, "Even though there are 1,045,690 soldiers just like me, I am my own force. With technology, with training, with support, who I am has become better than who I was."[4] It does not take a theological rocket scientist to comprehend why the Army decided to run these ads during television shows like *Friends*, *The Simpsons*, and *Buffy the Vampire Slayer*. The "me-generation" systematically assaults the God of the Bible because God impugns their self-actualization. The U.S. Navy has even used the recruitment slogan "Accelerate your life" to draw the autonomous self, when it should be promoting sacrifice and leadership. Spurgeon was spot on with his analysis: "Now, most men quarrel with this [the sovereignty of God]. But mark, the thing that you complain of in God is the very thing that you love in yourselves. Every man likes to feel that he has a right to do with his own as he pleases. We all like to be little sovereigns."[5]

Assaults on the character of God remind me of the Shooting Star BB gun games common at carnivals and fairs. The player has to completely obliterate the star-shaped target to win the Kewpie doll or stuffed animal. The gun (called a Feltman, named after the Coney Island inventor) rapidly shoots 100–150 lead balls via pneumatic pressure. To remain safe, the game attendant retrieves the target by means of a wheel and string cable. If one tiny bit of black star remains, the contestant does not win the prize. Like these contestants, who are seeking total annihilation of the star, sinful men and women today will not rest until every remnant of the God of the Bible is obliterated from culture, society, politics, and common parlance. Society has a hard time sleeping knowing that the Creator is King and that He rules over all.

Theological *Hari Kiri*

To mentally manufacture a God who is devoid of absolute rule is reminiscent of samurai who committed an ancient form of suicide. Disgraced samurai would disembowel themselves by *hari kiri*[6] (literally "stomach cut"), wielding a short sword (a *wakizashi*). As they committed suicide, the samurai were supposed to remain silent, thereby gaining more honor. The bloody deed was completed when a friend or associate cut the samurai's head off with another, larger, sword (known as a *katana*). Likewise, many people today perform spiritual suicide because they worship the wrong god, not the God revealed in the Word. To tweak God to suit man and his desire for autonomy is more disgraceful than any ritual suicide. The figurative disembowelment of the God of the Scriptures, of His sovereign reign, by created humans is infinitely worse than an actual suicide. It is deicide and aggressively bellows, "We will not have this King rule over us!"

Buckle your seat belt! For when we peruse God's sovereignty we need to brace ourselves to concur with *every* implication this truth uncovers, specifically this: that since God is sovereign, we are not. The pride of man regularly rears its ugly head and heart, shouting and screaming, "But what about free will?" and adding impudent ramblings about man being a puppet or robot. So be ready for a concomitant and fascinating truth: that what hurts the most (that we are not sovereign) is also that which is most beneficial and most wonderful (that God sovereignly controls every thing and every person in the universe). In the midst of slogans and catchphrases such as "freedom," "individualism is king," "my rights," and even that of the American War of Independence, "we serve no sovereign here," be ready for a complete and total annihilation of the false god of self. Let's once and for all clear the fog and haze of self, self-rule, and self-determination, and experience the freedom *from* the will (not freedom *of* the will)!

The Importance of This Study

Could there be a more crucial subject? Certainly the character and nature of God are at the apex of all man's contemplations and thoughts. Calvin believed, "Ignorance of Sovereignty is the ultimate of all miseries; the highest blessedness lies in the knowledge of it."[7] This blessedness entails the ultimate thrill ride for the soul, because it gives us a view of the most exalted Being in the universe. While Six Flags and other amusement parks might offer adventure rides, nothing can compare to the ecstasy and pleasure that knowledge of the Godhead brings. Fasten the safety harness around the lap of your mind and get ready for a ride that is out of this world—with the transcendent God and His attribute of sovereignty.

Where can we find out about the extent of God's rule as absolute Monarch? One question will suffice: What do the Scriptures say or reveal about God? Simply put, the Bible teaches that God is pleased to call Himself King, and this is not a vacant title or a name lacking significance; God is King by name, person, and deed. Holy Writ will not allow Christians to confine their thoughts of God to Savior, Comforter, and Friend; rather it drives home every attribute of God.

God is a King in ways we cannot imagine or concoct from our current culture. Kings in the Western world today reign constitutionally, but they do not rule totally. They boast royal names and titles, but they hardly approximate to kings of Bible times. In those days, kings had absolute authority and all the power their militaries furnished. It is not wise to think of a human king and then multiply his greatness in order to begin to approach the meaning of "God as King," so let us examine the Bible and its sweepingly clear statements about the extent of God's sovereignty.

The LORD has established His throne in the heavens,
And His sovereignty rules over all. (Ps. 103:19)

But our God is in the heavens;
He does whatever He pleases. (Ps. 115:3)

The Bible teaches that God's sovereign rule knows no boundaries or limits. His authority is full, complete, and binding. Charles Hodge said that God's sovereignty "can neither be ignored nor rejected. It binds all creatures, as inexorably as physical laws bind the material universe."[8] "Control freak" is a common, and usually negative, moniker for those who want to sinfully manage and manipulate the affairs of others. But God's sovereignty is holy, good, and righteous. His control is what we would describe as micromanaging or hands-on; that is, God is involved, not just generally, but also intimately—in all the details.

In the rest of this chapter, we will look at six areas that vividly demonstrate the heights and depths of God's rule. We will see that luck, randomness, fate, fortune, happenstance, accidents, and raw chance are nouns not to be used in the realm of the King of kings. These words are best relegated to the reigns of false gods like Dagon, Molech, and Baal; they do not belong in the same sentence with "Creator" and "sustaining King."

Six Realms of God's Sovereignty which Stress that God Is King

Before we analyze each realm, let us highlight a few standard definitions of God's sovereignty.

God's sovereign rule, summarized by the *Westminster Shorter Catechism*, is "His eternal purpose, according to the counsel of His will, whereby, for His own glory, He hath foreordained whatsoever comes to pass."[9]

Being infinitely elevated above the highest creature, He is the Most High, Lord of heaven and earth. Subject to none, influenced by none, absolutely independent, God does as He pleases, only as He pleases, and always as He pleases. "My counsel shall stand, and I will do all My pleasure" (Isa. 46:10). Divine sovereignty means that God is

God in fact as well as in name, and that He is on the Throne of the universe, directing all things, working all things "after the counsel of His own will" (Eph. 1:11).[10]

With reference to God, it means that God is the supreme ruler and authority, that He ordains whatever comes to pass, and that His divine purpose is always accomplished.[11]

God's sovereignty requires that He be absolutely free, which means simply that He must be free to do whatever He wills to do anywhere at any time to carry out His eternal purpose in every detail without interference. Where He is less than free, He must be less than Sovereign.[12]

Even the vocabulary of sovereign rule bellows forth the rule of God. When we see the following biblical words, the idea of total control should rush into our minds: Lord, LORD, Lord of Hosts, Most High, King, Sovereign, Almighty, throne, appointed, established, reign, dominion, rule, decree, ordain, command, predestine, foreordain, authority, and control. Words like these offer no middle ground, no "God is sovereign, *but* ..." Biblical descriptions of God's rule point to all-or-nothing control.

What would the alternative be? Instead of having a controlled world, we would have an uncontrolled world, on its own, spiraling around with no order and no guidance. Freakish as the bearded woman at the carnival show may be, that is nothing compared with the weirdness of a god who did not reign and rule over the universe. The essence of God-ness is rule! The name "God" implies total dominion. Picture a teacher who takes out three double-sided flash cards, with the front sides showing the words "Lord," "throne," and "established." The back of each card would say "sovereignty."

Arguably, the best verses that summarize God's ultimate rule come from one who was a king himself:

But at the end of that period, I, Nebuchadnezzar, raised my eyes toward heaven and my reason returned to me, and I blessed the Most High and praised and honored Him who lives forever;

For His dominion is an everlasting dominion,
And His kingdom endures from generation to generation.
All the inhabitants of the earth are accounted as nothing,
But He does according to His will in the host of heaven
And among the inhabitants of earth;
And no one can ward off His hand
Or say to Him, "What have You done?"   (Dan. 4:34–35)

If the positive aspect of God's sovereignty is His rule, the flip side is that God's plans and counsels cannot be frustrated by anyone or anything. Isaiah said, "This is the plan devised against the whole earth; and this is the hand that is stretched out against all the nations. For the LORD of hosts has planned, and who can frustrate it? And as for His stretched-out hand, who can turn it back?" (Isa. 14:26–27).

Now that we've clearly defined God's sovereignty, we can examine the six realms which emphasize that God is King.

GOD IS KING OVER ALL OF HIS CREATION
God Himself has decided, by His own good pleasure, to make the earth the way it is. From expansive waterfalls to arid deserts, from polar caps to dense jungles, planet earth is the handiwork of a meticulous, all-wise, and sovereign God. The world could just as easily have been two-thirds land instead of two-thirds water; it could have had no Mt. Everest or thousands of them. Creation follows the decree of the King:

Whatever the LORD pleases, He does,
In heaven and in earth, in the seas and in all deeps.
He causes the vapors to ascend from the ends of the earth;
Who makes lightnings for the rain,
Who brings forth the wind from His treasuries.   (Ps. 135:6–7)

Your faithfulness continues throughout all generations;
You established the earth, and it stands.
They stand this day according to Your ordinances,
For all things are Your servants.   (Ps. 119:90–91)

Imagine the moon, stars, and sun as God's servants. "Stay there." "Come here." "Do as you're told." With fascinating obedience, the galaxies instantly respond to the precise commands of God.

The same is true regarding the weather. Weather does not just happen; rather, it occurs by God's explicit purpose and control. Climate is the exact result of God's direct intervention in the universe.

Do you ever wonder why people are fond of saying, "It's raining outside," somehow implying that rain randomly occurs? It is as if somehow, in some way, because of a random state of affairs, rain pellets begin to serendipitously form and drop from the heavens.

Chance of rain? Dictionaries tend to define "chance" as the abstract nature or quality shared by unexpected, random, or unpredictable events; the likelihood of occurrence of an event. Chance suggests total absence of design or predictability. Do you think rain is more than moisture condensing in the sky and then precipitating? Did you know that the Bible regularly speaks of rain very differently from the way we do? Notice the binding refrain that rain is passive in these verses:

Now no shrub of the field was yet in the earth, and no plant of the field had yet sprouted, for the LORD God had not sent rain upon the earth, and there was no man to cultivate the ground.   (Gen. 2:5)

I shall give you rains in their season, so that the land will yield its produce and the trees of the field will bear their fruit.   (Lev. 26:4)

He will give the rain for your land in its season, the early and late rain, that you may gather in your grain and your new wine and your oil.   (Deut. 11:14)

The LORD will open for you His good storehouse, the heavens, to give rain to your land in its season and to bless all the work of your hand; and you shall lend to many nations, but you shall not borrow.   (Deut. 28:12)

Now it happened after many days that the word of the LORD came to Elijah in the third year, saying, "Go, show yourself to Ahab, and I will send rain on the face of the earth."
                                                                                                        (1 Kings 18:1)

In the hydrologic cycle, theologically speaking, rain is passive and God is active! Every drop falls exactly where God planned it to land. Calvin echoed Scripture when he penned, "It is certain that not one drop of rain falls without God's sure command."[13] Do you complain about God's weather? Fault-finding and carping about the weather indict God, the King of the weather. It is better to praise the King for the weather, whatever it may be.

Similarly, Scripture speaks of God controlling the humanly uncontrollable wind, unpredictable sea, and untetherable sun:

For He spoke and raised up a stormy wind,
Which lifted up the waves of the sea.   (Ps. 107:25)

He caused the storm to be still,
So that the waves of the sea were hushed.   (Ps. 107:29)

So the sun stood still, and the moon stopped,
Until the nation avenged themselves of their enemies.
Is it not written in the book of Jashar? And the sun stopped in the middle of the sky and did not hasten to go down for about a whole day.   (Josh. 10:13)

What kind of entity could accomplish these incredible acts? Only a sovereign and omnipotent God would have enough raw power to rule the humanly un-ruleable.

Do not succumb to anything less than Bible truth when it comes to the King's rule over creation. Rabbi Kushner is one proponent of a less-than-sovereign God over creation. His bestselling book *When Bad Things Happen to Good People* declares that insurance companies should not regard fires, earthquakes, and tornadoes as "acts of God" because that would be "a case of using God's name in vain."[14] Instead of following Kushner's faulty theology, acknowledge that these are indeed acts of God, and praise Him who presides over the sun, moon, rain, sleet, hail, snow, clouds, wind, storm, thunder, lightning, earthquakes, fire, ice, floods, famines, tsunamis, forests, and the seas.

As well as being sovereign over the weather, the King is sovereign over all people. God decides who is born, to whom children are born, who will be able to bear children, and who will not. Jacob's response to Rachel reveals his understanding of God's rule. Genesis 30:2 says, "Then Jacob's anger burned against Rachel, and he said, 'Am I in the place of God, who has withheld from you the fruit of the womb?'"

God was sovereign in creating you! Deep down, in the crevasses of your being, you know this fact! Boettner states what every person knows to be true:

Every thinking person readily sees that some sovereignty rules his life. He was not asked whether or not he would have existence, when or what or where he would be born, whether in the twentieth century or before the Flood; whether male or female, whether white or black, whether in the United States, or China, or Africa ... It has been recognized by Christians in all ages that God is the Creator and Ruler of the world.[15]

I am the thankful recipient of four children, and it was always fun to make a proclamation when my babies were birthed. No, I did not say, "I'm a dad!" or "It's a girl!" Rather, I loudly and sarcastically (complete with Cheshire-Cat grin) exclaimed, "Ain't evolution grand!" The looks on the nurses' and doctors' faces were always priceless. The hospital staff never seemed to appreciate my remarks, but I hope they were reminded that God alone grants life.

Created man's response to such a sovereign God should mimic that of the twenty-four elders who "fall down before Him who sits on the throne ... saying, 'Worthy are You, our Lord and our God, to receive glory and honor and power; for You created all things, and because of Your will they existed, and were created'" (Rev. 4:10–11).

GOD IS KING OVER ALL OF HISTORY

God the King rules everything in time and place. From the creation of a speck of dust to the election of world rulers, God sits on His throne. Even the timing of inventions and important discoveries has been irrevocably fixed in the annals of history by an outside Being: God the triune King. Let us learn from Daniel and Paul:

Daniel said,
"Let the name of God be blessed forever and ever,
For wisdom and power belong to Him.
It is He who changes the times and the epochs;
He removes kings and establishes kings;
He gives wisdom to wise men,
And knowledge to men of understanding."

(Dan. 2:20–21)

He made from one man every nation of mankind to live on all the face of the earth, having determined their appointed times and the boundaries of their habitation.

(Paul preaching in Acts 17:26)

Every person is to be in subjection to the governing authorities. For there is no authority except from God, and those which exist are established by God. (Rom. 13:1)

Knowledge of this fact is not only the grounds for our trusting in God's future prophecies, but it is also the basis for our complete confidence and dependence upon God—for today and for the future. Jerry Bridges concurs:

Confidence in the sovereignty of God in all that affects us is crucial to our trusting Him. If there is a single event in all of the universe that can occur outside of God's sovereign control then we cannot trust Him. His love may be infinite, but if His power is limited and His purpose can be thwarted, we cannot trust Him. You may entrust to me your most valuable possessions. I may love you and my aim to honor your trust may be sincere, but if I do not have the power or ability to guard your valuables, you cannot truly entrust them to me.[16]

Political parties, governmental legislation, and everything in between are guided by and determined by God—not the other way around. In God's universe, "what ifs" and "if onlys" are actually "not reallys" and "never a doubts." Trusting the King in unsettling times is much better than trusting in horses, chariots, and governments.

Job properly identified God's hand behind his circumstances, and it gave him comfort and the resolve to submit respectfully:

He said,
"Naked I came from my mother's womb,
And naked I shall return there.
The LORD gave and the LORD has taken away.
Blessed be the name of the LORD."
Through all this Job did not sin nor did he blame God.   (Job 1:21–22)

But he [Job] said to her [his wife], "You speak as one of the foolish women speaks.
Shall we indeed accept good from God and not accept adversity?" In all this Job did not
sin with his lips.   (Job 2:10)

GOD IS KING OVER THE SPECIFIC DETAILS IN LIFE

The Bible gives many examples of seemingly small details that God
oversees, sustains, and ordains. From the seemingly fortuitous to the
overtly calamitous, God is King over everything.

Retractors might argue that God controls the big events and
circumstances but allows the small things to take their own course. They
imply that there are trifling atoms and frivolous molecules that go their
own way. But God's Word plainly states the opposite:

The lot is cast into the lap,
But its every decision is from the LORD.   (Prov. 16:33)

Each man said to his mate, "Come, let us cast lots so we may learn on whose account
this calamity has struck us." So they cast lots and the lot fell on Jonah.   (Jonah 1:7)

Luck, fortune, and random chance simply don't exist, except in the
vocabulary of uneducated pagans. "Odds" in Las Vegas are 100-percent
certainties in the plan of God the King. The Bible states that "random"
events are anything but accident or coincidence. Instead, they are destined
to occur because God is *making* them happen. B. B. Warfield says,

In the infinite wisdom of the Lord of all the earth, each event falls with exact precision
into its proper place in this unfolding of His eternal plan; nothing, however small,
however strange, occurs without His ordering, or without its peculiar fitness for its

place in the working out of His purposes; and the end of all shall be the manifestation of His glory, and accumulation of His praise. This is the Old Testament (as well as the New Testament) philosophy of the universe's world-view which attains concrete unity in an absolute decree, or purpose, or plan of which all that comes to pass is the development in time.[17]

Find the most minute, insignificant, minuscule, microscopic, infinitesimal, or diminutive event or activity in the history of the world, and behind it will be God's sovereign rule, making it happen exactly the way God intended. God's rule as King is exhaustive and thorough. Jesus said, "Are not two sparrows sold for a cent? And yet not one of them will fall to the ground apart from your Father. But the very hairs of your head are all numbered" (Matt. 10:29–30). Which is more reassuring in a world that is full of tragedy, trouble, and crime: randomness or God at the helm?

But you might ask, "What about calamities and other tragic events?" Here is a question in response: What would it do to your perception of God if He were sovereign only over good and not over evil or trouble? The Christian's hope is that God is triumphantly sovereign over everything. The following "stomach-punch" verses should take our breath away:

In the day of prosperity be happy,
But in the day of adversity consider—
God has made the one as well as the other
So that man will not discover anything that will be after him.   (Eccles. 7:14)

Who is there who speaks and it comes to pass,
Unless the Lord has commanded it?
Is it not from the mouth of the Most High
That both good and ill go forth?   (Lam. 3:37–38)

Does a bird fall into a trap on the ground when there is no bait in it?
Does a trap spring up from the earth when it captures nothing at all?
If a trumpet is blown in a city will not the people tremble?
If a calamity occurs in a city has not the LORD done it?   (Amos 3:5–6)

The One forming light and creating darkness,
Causing well-being and creating calamity;
I am the LORD who does all these. (Isa. 45:7)

Our response should be, "How can this be?" In light of these verses, Romans 8:28 can truly be appreciated, because God can use sin, Satan, trouble, joys, and everything else to accomplish His eternal purpose: "And we know that God causes all things to work together for good to those who love God, to those who are called according to His purpose."

Where are the pastors who teach these things? Are they afraid, embarrassed, or ashamed of or for God the King? God is sovereign over all the good and bad that has ever happened to you and will ever happen to you in the future! The proper response to this black-and-white fact is to depend totally upon the Lord who controls the future. James said it this way:

Come now, you who say, "Today or tomorrow we will go to such and such a city, and spend a year there and engage in business and make a profit." Yet you do not know what your life will be like tomorrow. You are just a vapor that appears for a little while and then vanishes away. Instead, you ought to say, "If the Lord wills, we will live and also do this or that." (James 4:13–15)

GOD IS KING OVER YOUR BIRTHDAY AND YOUR FUNERAL

The King of the universe could have decided that you were never to be born, or that you would be born in another country, at another time, and to other parents. He chose your exact parents, the very strands of your DNA, the day of your birth, the color of your eyes, hair, and skin, your sex, and everything else about you. He has even planned the day and cause of your death. There is nothing about you that was not sovereignly decided upon by the triune God. Nothing. Revel in that fact as you read these verses:

Since his days are determined,
The number of his months is with You;
And his limits You have set so that he cannot pass. (Job 14:5)

My times are in Your hand;
Deliver me from the hand of my enemies and from those who persecute me. (Ps. 31:15)

Your eyes have seen my unformed substance;
And in Your book were all written
The days that were ordained for me,
When as yet there was not one of them.   (Ps. 139:16)

While I encourage exercise for health, stress release, and other factors, no amount of exercise, surgery, vitamins, or anything else will prevent you from dying on the precise day you are supposed to die. Physical exercise does profit a little (1 Tim. 4:8), but zinc, echinacea, and vitamin C will not decelerate the approach of your funeral. Remember what Jesus said to John, speaking of Peter's ordained death:

"Truly, truly, I say to you, when you were younger, you used to gird yourself and walk wherever you wished; but when you grow old, you will stretch out your hands and someone else will gird you, and bring you where you do not wish to go." Now this He said, signifying by what kind of death he would glorify God. And when He had spoken this, He said to him, "Follow Me!"   (John 21:18–19)

Because God ordains your life and your death, you should have peace that you cannot die, even if 10,000 gang members are pursuing you, unless it is God's will. Likewise, you cannot be delivered, even if 10,000 SWAT team members are trying to protect you, unless the King ordains it. God wants His people to derive comfort and fear from this truth! A. W. Pink and C. H. Spurgeon both knew this, declaring,

To *deny* the Divine decrees would be to predicate a world and all its concerns regulated by *un*designed chance or blind fate. Then what peace, what assurance, what comfort would there be for our poor hearts and minds? What refuge would there be to fly to in the hour of need and trial? None at all. There would be nothing better than the black darkness and abject horror of atheism … How thankful should we be that everything is determined by infinite wisdom and goodness! What praise and gratitude are due unto God for His Divine decrees [emphasis in original].[18]

There is no attribute of God more comforting to his children than the doctrine of Divine Sovereignty. Under the most adverse circumstances, in the most severe troubles, they believe that Sovereignty hath ordained their afflictions, that Sovereignty overrules them, and that Sovereignty will sanctify them all.[19]

Do you know this truth?

GOD IS KING OVER EVERY ACT COMMITTED BY MAN

Our good acts have God's sovereignty stamped upon them, "for we are His workmanship, created in Christ Jesus for good works, which God prepared beforehand so that we would walk in them" (Eph. 2:10).

Did you know that Isaiah, under inspiration from the Holy Spirit, named Cyrus as both "My [God's] shepherd" and "His anointed"? Cyrus assisted the Hebrews in reoccupying and rebuilding Jerusalem:

It is I who says of Cyrus, "He is My shepherd!
And he will perform all My desire." (Isa. 44:28)

Thus says the LORD to Cyrus His anointed,
Whom I have taken by the right hand,
To subdue nations before him,
And to loose the loins of kings;
To open doors before him so that gates will not be shut:
"I will go before you and make the rough places smooth;
I will shatter the doors of bronze and cut through their iron bars.
I will give you the treasures of darkness,
And hidden wealth of secret places,
So that you may know that it is I,
The LORD, the God of Israel, who calls you by your name.
For the sake of Jacob My servant,
And Israel My chosen one,
I have also called you by your name;
I have given you a title of honor
Though you have not known Me.
I am the LORD, and there is no other;

Besides Me there is no God.
I will gird you, though you have not known Me;
That men may know from the rising to the setting of the sun
That there is no one besides Me.
I am the LORD, and there is no other,
The One forming light and creating darkness,
Causing well-being and creating calamity;
I am the LORD who does all these." (Isa. 45:1–7)

Few would argue that God is King over the righteous behavior of men and women. From a philosophical point of view, that is very easy to digest, a bit like saltines and ginger ale for the sick stomach. But when some people are confronted by the Bible truth that even the sinful and unrighteous deeds of humans are under God's sovereign control, they shudder and squirm like frightened five-year-olds on their first day of school. Why is this the case? Could it possibly be that these people have not bowed their minds to the clear teaching of Scripture? Perhaps some of them have not read through the Bible. Could it be that Bible teachers place a false theology over these verses to blunt the trauma that they perceive these jack-hammer verses will cause?

Evil and evil people are not outside of the sovereign umbrella of the King. Joseph understood the sovereign rule of Yahweh in the midst of his sinful brothers' actions:

Now, therefore, it was not you who sent me here, but God; and He has made me a father to Pharaoh and lord of all his household and ruler over all the land of Egypt.

(Gen. 45:8)

As for you, you meant evil against me, but God meant it for good in order to bring about this present result, to preserve many people alive. (Gen. 50:20)

Even Absalom's heinous sin happened under the sovereign rule of God. We read in 2 Samuel 16:22 that "they pitched a tent for Absalom on the roof, and Absalom went in to his father's concubines in the sight of all Israel." How horrible! How preposterous! How sinful! Surely this must fall outside the pale of God's rule? If any behavior known to man would be called aberrant and immoral, this was it. Acts like this are sickening and would make even Jerry Springer blush, yet God's Word says, shockingly, that it was all in God's plan: "Thus says the LORD, 'Behold, I will raise up evil against you from your own household; I will even take your wives before your eyes and give them to your companion, and he will lie with your wives in broad daylight. Indeed you did it secretly, but I will do this thing before all Israel, and under the sun'" (2 Sam. 12:11–12).

Make no theological mistake: the human agents were responsible and had a complete duty to obey God—yet God's sovereign rule is seen alongside human responsibility.

Did you know that God ordained Ahab's deception through Satan himself?

The LORD said, "Who will entice Ahab to go up and fall at Ramoth-gilead?" And one said this while another said that. Then a spirit came forward and stood before the LORD and said, "I will entice him." The LORD said to him, "How?" And he said, "I will go out and be a deceiving spirit in the mouth of all his prophets." Then He said, "You are to entice him and also prevail. Go and do so." (1 Kings 22:20–22)

In Jeremiah 25:9–11, Nebuchadnezzar is heralded as God's servant; in Jeremiah 1:15 and 50:25 we read that the Chaldeans' actions toward the cities of Judah were orchestrated by God; and Exodus 9:12 and Psalm 105:24–25 clearly state that the Lord tampered with the hearts of both Pharaoh and the Egyptians.

Can anything be done in the world without God's will and divine pleasure? If you remain unconvinced, I have one more question for you: What was the worst sin ever committed by mankind? The answer must be the crucifixion of the innocent Man, Jesus Christ. No one deserved execution less than the Messiah, yet note carefully these words of Scripture:

When they [Peter and John] had been released, they went to their own companions and reported all that the chief priests and the elders had said to them. And when they heard this, they lifted their voices to God with one accord and said, "O Lord, it is You who made the heaven and the earth and the sea, and all that is in them, who by the Holy Spirit, through the mouth of our father David Your servant, said,

'Why did the Gentiles rage,

And the peoples devise futile things?

The kings of the earth took their stand,

And the rulers were gathered together

Against the Lord and against his Christ.'

For truly in this city there were gathered together against Your holy servant Jesus, whom You anointed, both Herod and Pontius Pilate, along with the Gentiles and the peoples of Israel, to do whatever Your hand and Your purpose predestined to occur."

(Acts 4:23–28)

The death of Christ Jesus at Golgotha was sovereignly planned by God, even though sinful men will have to give an account for their sinful actions. Both must be true! On these verses Derek Thomas comments, "God reigns through the stumbling, hobbling service of his people and the rage and malice of his foes to establish his eternal purpose for this world."[20] The alternatives are frightening. Aren't you glad that you serve a God with such power and wisdom—and rule?

GOD IS KING OVER THE ETERNAL DESTINY OF EVERY PERSON

The stumbling block of all stumbling blocks is God's control over who goes to heaven and who goes to hell. Have you ever stubbed your big toe on a rock? That God alone chooses the destiny of every human being is very offensive to the natural man, and the effect this truth has on us is like the feeling the toe's nerves send to the brain after it is split wide open. But if you feel this way, you are not alone. The great American theologian Jonathan Edwards experienced similar chagrin:

From my childhood up, my mind had been wont to be full of objections against the doctrine of God's sovereignty, in choosing whom he would to eternal life, and rejecting whom he pleased; leaving them eternally to perish, and be everlastingly tormented in hell. It used to appear like a horrible doctrine to me. But I remember the time very well when I seemed to be convinced and fully satisfied as to this sovereignty of God, and his justice in thus eternally disposing of [dealing with] men, according to his sovereign pleasure. But [I] never could give an account, how, or by what means, I was thus convinced; not in the least imagining, in the time of it, nor a long time after, that there was any extraordinary influence of God's Spirit in it; but only that now I saw further, and my reason apprehended the justice and reasonableness of it. However my mind rested in it, and it put an end to all those cavils and objections that had till then abode with me all the preceding part of my life. And there has been a wonderful alteration in my mind, with respect to the doctrine of God's sovereignty, from that day to this, so that I scarce ever have found so much as the rising of an objection against God's sovereignty in the most absolute sense, in showing mercy to whom he will show mercy, and hardening and damning whom he will. God's absolute sovereignty and justice, with respect to salvation and damnation, is what my mind seems to rest assured of, as much as of any thing that I see with my eyes; at least it is so at times.[21]

The doctrine has very often appeared exceeding pleasant, bright, and sweet. Absolute sovereignty is what I love to ascribe to God.[22]

Never forget that all men and women are born rebels, deserving death and eternal judgment. Somehow, in today's evangelical culture, many have imbibed too deeply the lie that grace is contingent upon work or merit. Yet no one, left in his or her sinfully fallen state, could ever approach, let alone dwell with, a thrice-holy God.

In addition, God must be sovereign over who enters heaven since salvation is something that is given to people by God. In other words, in salvation, God is the one who acts, and the person who is saved is passive. Theologians call this the "passivity of regeneration." If we were sovereign over our own salvation, no one would ever be born again, because that would be an utter impossibility. Thomas Arnold echoes this truth: "The distinction between Christianity and all other systems of religion consists largely in this, that in these others men are found seeking after God, while Christianity is God seeking after men."[23]

We are not saved by *anything* that we can or will do; we are saved only by the King's good pleasure:

So then it does not depend on the man who wills or the man who runs, but on God who has mercy. (Rom. 9:16)

But as many as received Him, to them He gave the right to become children of God, even to those who believe in His name, who were born, not of blood nor of the will of the flesh nor of the will of man, but of God.   (John 1:12–13)

Every good thing given and every perfect gift is from above, coming down from the Father of lights, with whom there is no variation or shifting shadow. In the exercise of His will He brought us forth by the word of truth, so that we would be a kind of first fruits among His creatures.   (James 1:17–18)

Salvation is the sovereign choice of the King. Just as King Ahasuerus "delighted" in Esther and "summoned" her by name (Esth. 2:14), so God the King beckons people. The only difference is that God's pleasure is in spite of the person, while Ahasuerus was delighted "because of" Esther's beauty.

This doctrine should come as no surprise to any Bible student, since God's sovereign choice is regularly seen throughout the entire corpus of Scripture. God chose which angels would remain holy and which ones would fall; He selected only Israel for Himself; Jesus healed many but left others in their sickness; and God chose the bride for His Son.

You might say, "But it was I who believed!" Of course it was, but surely you don't mean to imply that your belief is the *cause* of your salvation? Believing is the result or consequence of salvation, not the origin of it. Acts 13:48 could not be clearer: "When the Gentiles heard this, they began rejoicing and glorifying the word of the Lord; and as many as had been appointed to eternal life believed." Spurgeon commented on this verse,

Attempts have been made to prove that these words do not teach predestination, but these attempts so clearly do violence to language that I will not waste time in answering them. I shall not twist that text but shall glorify the grace of God by ascribing to it every man's faith. Is it not God who gives the disposition to believe? Is it wrong for God to give grace? If it be right for Him to give it, is it wrong for Him to purpose to give it? Would you have Him give it by accident?[24]

Ephesians 2:4 states the motivation for God saving sinners: "because of His great love," not because of our faith. It is, according to Ephesians 2:8, "through faith" that we are saved, not "according to" or "because of" faith. The difference is fundamental—fundamental enough to turn grace into works and to lay a foundation of a merit-based righteousness that would rob God of the glory due His name.

You might say, "I thought that God looked down the annals of time and then foresaw who would believe." This is wrong on many levels (for example, concerning the doctrine of the depravity and inability of a fallen sinner), but in particular it ignores the fact that God Himself is the One who grants faith. It is like saying, "God cannot foresee the faith that He will one day grant." Second Thessalonians 2:13 declares, "But we should always give thanks to God for you, brethren beloved by the Lord, because God has chosen you from the beginning for salvation through sanctification by the Spirit and faith in the truth." What thanks to God would be given if this choice were based on man and his contribution? B. B. Warfield knew that faith was a divine gift, stating,

It is never on account of its formal nature as a psychic act that faith is conceived in Scripture to be saving ... It is not, strictly speaking, even faith in Christ that saves, but Christ that saves through faith. The saving power resides exclusively, not in the act of faith or the attitude of faith or nature of faith, but in the object of faith.[25]

The next obvious question is: What happens to those who are not granted saving faith? Theology supplies the answer (they are judged for their sins), but this sticky-wicket ban can be solved exegetically as well. Listen to the words of God:

They stumble because they are disobedient to the word, and to this doom they were also appointed.   (1 Peter 2:8)

The LORD has made everything for its own purpose,
Even the wicked for the day of evil.   (Prov. 16:4)

What if God, although willing to demonstrate His wrath and to make His power known, endured with much patience vessels of wrath prepared for destruction?

(Rom. 9:22)

Luther said,

Mere human reason can never comprehend how God is good and merciful; and therefore you make to yourself a god of your own fancy, who hardens nobody, condemns nobody, pities everybody. You cannot comprehend how a just God can condemn those who are born into sin, and cannot help themselves, but must, by a necessity of their natural constitution, continue in, and remain children of wrath. The answer is, God is incomprehensible throughout, and therefore His justice, as well as His other attributes, must be incomprehensible. It is on this very ground that St. Paul exclaims, "O the depth of the riches of the knowledge of God! How unsearchable are His judgments, and His ways past finding out!"[26]

Summary
My prayer is that you would more fully know the extent of God's rule. May the following five exhortations increase your understanding and worship of our King.

SAY WITH DAVID ...
Many, O LORD my God, are the wonders which You have done,
And Your thoughts toward us;
There is none to compare with You.
If I would declare and speak of them,
They would be too numerous to count. (Ps. 40:5)

REMEMBER THAT ...
... God hates sin, humans are completely obligated to obey God, and that whatever God does is right and good.

REST IN THE KING'S GREAT RULE
While providence supports,
Let saints securely dwell;
That hand, which bears all nature up,
Shall guide his children well.
(Philip Doddridge, "How Gentle God's Commands," 1755)

Spurgeon said,

I believe that every particle of dust that dances in the sunbeam does not move an atom more or less than God wishes—that every particle of spray that dashes against the steamboat has its orbit as well as the sun in the heavens—that the chaff from the hand of the winnower is steered as the stars in their courses. The creeping of an aphis over the rosebud is as much fixed as the march of the devastating pestilence—the fall of sere leaves from a poplar is as fully ordained as the tumbling of an avalanche. He that believes in a God must believe this truth. There is no standing-point between this and atheism. There is no half way between a mighty God that worketh all things by the sovereign counsel of his will and no God at all.[27]

WALK BY FAITH IN A SIN-CURSED WORLD THAT IS ULTIMATELY RULED BY THE KING

Martin Luther understood walking by faith: "Our Lord God doeth work like a printer, who setteth the letters backwards; we see and feel well his setting, but we shall see the print yonder—in the life to come."[28]

John Flavel, knowing the same Bible Luther knew, echoed him: "Sometimes providences, like Hebrew letters, must be read backwards."[29]

LOOK UP EACH OF THESE VERSES AND READ THEM IN THEIR CONTEXT

Blessed be the LORD, the God of our fathers, who has put such a thing as this in the king's heart, to adorn the house of the LORD which is in Jerusalem, and has extended lovingkindness to me before the king and his counselors and before all the king's mighty princes. Thus I was strengthened according to the hand of the LORD my God upon me, and I gathered leading men from Israel to go up with me.   (Ezra 7:27–28)

Then the LORD raised up an adversary to Solomon, Hadad the Edomite; he was of the royal line in Edom.   (1 Kings 11:14)

God also raised up another adversary to him, Rezon the son of Eliada, who had fled from his lord Hadadezer king of Zobah.   (1 Kings 11:23)

So the king did not listen to the people; for it was a turn of events from the LORD, that

Chapter 3

He might establish His word, which the LORD spoke through Ahijah the Shilonite to Jeroboam the son of Nebat. (1 Kings 12:15)

Now the destruction of Ahaziah was from God, in that he went to Joram. For when he came, he went out with Jehoram against Jehu the son of Nimshi, whom the LORD had anointed to cut off the house of Ahab. (2 Chr. 22:7)

Hymn

Jehovah reigns on high
In peerless majesty;
Boundless power his royal robe,
Purest light his garment is;
Rules his word the spacious globe,
Stablished it in floating seas.

Ancient of days! Thy name
And essence is I AM;
Thou, O Lord, and thou alone,
Gav'st whatever is to be;
Stood thine everlasting throne,
Stands to all eternity.

The floods, with angry noise,
Have lifted up their voice,
Lifted up their voice on high;
Fiends and men exclaim aloud;
Rage the waves and dash the sky,
Hell assails the throne of God.

Their fury cannot move
The Lord who reigns above;
Him the mighty waves obey,
Sinking at his awful will,
Ocean owns his sovereign sway;
Hell at his command is still.

Thy statutes, Lord, are sure,
And as thyself endure;
Thine eternal house above
Holy souls alone can see,
Fitted here by perfect love,
There to reign enthroned with thee.

(Charles Wesley, Hymn 601 in *Methodist Hymnal*, 1889[30])

Notes

1 The address was given on October 20, 1880. For the whole address, see "Sphere Sovereignty," in **James D. Bratt** (ed.), *Abraham Kuyper: A Centennial Reader* (Grand Rapids: Eerdmans, 1998), 463–490. The quotation itself comes near the end of the address; see p. 488.

2 **Curt Daniel,** *The History and Theology of Calvinism* (Springfield, IL: Reformed Bible Church, 2003), 229.

3 **Charles Spurgeon,** "Divine Sovereignty," sermon on Matthew 20:15, May 4, 1856, in *The Spurgeon Collection* (CD-ROM; Ages Software, 1998).

4 **James Dao,** "Ads Now Seek Recruits for 'An Army of One,'" January 10, 2001, at: nytimes.com.

5 **Charles Spurgeon,** "The Two Talents," sermon, January 31, 1858; cited at: apibs.org/chs/0175.htm.

6 The actual words are "hari kiri," but they are most often misspelled and mispronounced as "hari kari."

7 **John Calvin,** *Institutes of the Christian Religion*, book 1, tr. by John Allen (Philadelphia: Presbyterian Board of Publication and Sabbath School Work, 1921), 1:17:11.

8 **Charles Hodge,** *Systematic Theology*, vol. 1 (New York: Scribner, Armstrong, and Co., 1873), 440.

9 *Westminster Shorter Catechism,* Q. 7: "What Are the Decrees of God?"

10 **Arthur W. Pink,** *The Attributes of God* (Grand Rapids: Baker, 1975), 27.

11 **Paul Enns,** *Moody Handbook of Theology* (Chicago: Moody, 1996), 647.

12 **A. W. Tozer,** *The Knowledge of the Holy* (San Francisco: Harper & Row, 1961), 115.

13 **Calvin,** *Institutes*, 1:188.

14 **Harold S. Kushner,** *When Bad Things Happen to Good People* (New York: Avon, 1983), 58.

15 Loraine Boettner, "The Sovereignty of God," in *The Reformed Faith*, cited at Center for Reformed Theology and Apologetics, at: reformed.org/calvinism/trf/index.html?mainframe= /calvinism/trf/part_1.html. Accessed November 2010.

16 Jerry Bridges, *Trusting God: Even When Life Hurts* (Colorado Springs: NavPress, 1988), 37.

17 B. B. Warfield, *Biblical Doctrines*, 13, 22; quoted by **Lorraine Boettner,** "God Has a Plan" and cited at Sola Scriptura!, at: mbrem123.com.

18 A. W. Pink, *The Sovereignty of God*, quoted at: pbministries.org/books/pink/Attributes/ attrib_02.htm.

19 Charles Spurgeon, "Divine Sovereignty," sermon no. 77 in *The New Park Street Pulpit*, delivered on May 4, 1856; at: spurgeon.org/mainpage.htm. Accessed January 2011.

20 Derek W. H. Thomas, *What Is Providence?* (Phillipsburg: P & R, 2008), 9.

21 Jonathan Edwards, "A Sketch of the Life of President Edwards," in *A Treatise concerning the Religious Affections in Three Parts* (Philadelphia: James Crissy, 1821), xxiv; available at: books.google.com.

22 Jonathan Edwards, *Selections* (New York: Hill and Wang, 1962), 58–59.

23 Thomas Arnold, quoted in **Josiah Hotchkiss Gilbert,** *Dictionary of Burning Words of Brilliant Writers: A Cyclopaedia of Quotations from the Literature of All Ages* (New York: W. B. Ketcham, 1895), 133.

24 Charles Spurgeon, quoted in **George Sayles Bishop,** *The Doctrines of Grace* (Grand Rapids: Baker, 1954), 171.

25 B. B. Warfield, "Faith," in **James Hastings, Samuel Rolles Driver,** and **Henry Barclay Swete** (eds.), *A Dictionary of the Bible*, vol. 1 (New York: Charles Scribner's Sons, 1908), 837.

26 Cited in **Robert Haldane,** *Exposition of the Epistle to the Romans* (MacDill, FL: MacDonald, 1839), 492.

27 Charles Spurgeon, "God's Providence," sermon no. 3114, cited at The Spurgeon Archive, at: spurgeon.org.

28 Martin Luther, quoted in **Tryon Edwards,** *A Dictionary of Thoughts: Being a Cyclopedia of Laconic Quotations From the Best Authors of the World, Both Ancient and Modern* (Detroit: F. B. Dickerson, 1908), 454.

29 John Flavel, quoted in **Herbert Lockyer,** *Psalms: A Devotional Commentary* (Grand Rapids: Kregel, 1993), 257.

30 Reproduced with permission. Copyright 1998, 2001 by the Wesley Center for Applied Theology of Northwest Nazarene University, Nampa, Idaho 83686.

Prophet, Priest, and King

If you ask the average Christian today "To what threefold office was Christ anointed?" you would most certainly *not* hear the response from Luther's *The Small Catechism*: "Christ was anointed to be our Prophet, Priest, and King."[1] Many would say, "I didn't know Jesus ever held public office," or something to that effect. Likewise, if you asked the average church member to state three words or phrases to describe Jesus Christ and who He is, you would probably get responses like "Lover of my soul," "trusted Friend," and "close Comforter." Prophet, Priest, or King? Hardly.

What is the reason for this ignorance? It is not because the people polled do not live in Germany or because Luther wrote his *Catechism* over 400 years ago. While these factors may contribute to the theological unawareness, the real reason is that most evangelicals are rarely exposed to the doctrines that support these truths. They do not hear these biblical verities from the pulpits, and they do not read about these critical offices of Christ in popular Christian books.

Losing the concept of Jesus being simultaneously Prophet, Priest, and King is nothing less than a travesty. Those words should be common in every church today. The good news is that these classic monikers are easy to remember, full of praise-inspiring truth, and thoroughly biblical. Everyone would agree that people are in dire need of seeing the greatness of who Jesus is and how He is the fulfillment of the Old Testament prophecies of the Anointed One. Seeing Jesus as Prophet, Priest, and King is the right remedy for the church's lethargy and the perfect antidote for personal spiritual doldrums.

The function of this chapter is to provide instruction, through a quick overview, about these well-known historical designations for Jesus: Prophet, Priest, and King. As Messiah (the Anointed One), Jesus had to be and fulfill each of these offices/titles. It is a great comfort to us to know how Jesus, as Prophet, Priest, and King, is specifically able to help, protect, comfort, and guide His people! Calvin vehemently declared, "Among heretics and false Christians, Christ is found in name only; but by those who are truly and effectually called of God, he is acknowledged as a Prophet, King, and Priest."[2] Do you acknowledge Jesus as the Prophet? The Priest? The King? This chapter will confirm each of these offices, leaving you to affirm Jesus as Prophet, Priest, and King in your heart and mind. While this book is about God as King, the threefold designation of Prophet, Priest, and King is so rarely to be found in most Christian books that I will fully develop all three offices by providing some historical background.

Old Testament

The Bible reveals many prophets (such as Isaiah, Daniel, Amos, Nathan, Jonah, and Elijah), priests (Aaron, Nadab, Abihu, Eli, Zadok, and Abiathar), and kings (Saul, Solomon, Jeroboam, Asa, Ahab, Rehoboam, and Abijam). God ordained these three major offices for the nation of Israel. Usually, one man was the holder of one office. The prophets proclaimed God's Word, the priests stood between God and man, offering sacrifices and intercessions, and the kings ruled and protected the people. The list of those holding two of the offices simultaneously is much shorter. There are a few exceptions, but they are extremely rare. Moses, for example, was a priest and a prophet, Samuel was a priest and a prophet, and David was a king and a prophet. Where is the person who could fill all three offices at the same time?

Church History

Though the theological concept of Jesus as Prophet, Priest, and King is not new, there has been some debate about when this threefold designation became popular. Mueller says,

From the earliest times Jesus has been recognized as the representative of a twofold and yet unitary theocratic function, as king and priest. The spiritual kingdom of the Messiah has its foundation in the sacrifice of his life (Matt. xvi. 16–25, xx. 25–28). This thought may be traced from the second century to the time of the Reformation. But as early as Eusebius a threefold office is ascribed to Christ, that of prophet, priest, and king, and this is traceable to Jewish sources. The view of a threefold office, however, did not suppress the tradition of a twofold office, although the three designations of

Christ were always used separately. Among the medieval theologians, Thomas Aquinas approaches closely the conception of Eusebius since he speaks of *legislator*, *sacerdos*, and *rex*, but with him this is merely a mechanical division, and Thomas makes no further use of the threefold scheme.[3]

Wayne Grudem says, "John Calvin (1509–64) was the first major theologian to apply these three categories to the work of Christ (see his *Institutes of the Christian Religion* Book 2, Chapter 15). The categories have been adapted by many subsequent theologians as a helpful way of understanding various aspects of Christ's work."[4] Instead of playing Eusebius against Calvin, the best approach is to see both views as correct. Eusebius was the first "Father of Church History" and Calvin the first "major theologian" to see Christ's work designated as "Prophet, Priest, and King." Either way, this concept is not new or just recently fashionable.

New Testament
Wonderfully and singularly, Jesus of Nazareth held (on earth, and now holds in heaven) each office—Prophet, Priest, and King—at the same time. *The Heidelberg Catechism* gives a brilliant overview:

Question 31: Why is he called "Christ," that is anointed?
Answer: Because he is ordained of God the Father, and anointed with the Holy Ghost, to be our chief Prophet and Teacher, who has fully revealed to us the secret counsel and will of God concerning our redemption; and to be our only High Priest, who by the one sacrifice of his body, has redeemed us, and makes continual intercession with the Father for us; and also to be our eternal King, who governs us by his word and Spirit, and who defends and preserves us in that salvation, he has purchased for us.[5]

Now let's establish the truths in that catechism through the Bible.

Jesus As Prophet
As Prophet, Jesus preached on earth and revealed the mind of God. He proclaimed the mind of God. Since He, the Son of Man, was God incarnate, He, unlike all other prophets, was the innate source of truth. Grudem says, "Jesus was not merely a messenger of revelation from God

(like all the other prophets), but was himself the *source* of revelation from God. Rather than saying, as all the Old Testament prophets did, 'Thus says the Lord,' Jesus could begin divinely authoritative teaching with the amazing statement, 'But I say unto you' (Matthew 5:22 et al.)."[6] As both the messenger and source of God's truth, Jesus was the Prophet of prophets. Jesus excelled all other prophets, even Moses.

Jesus regularly stated that He, like prophets of old, spoke revelation directly from the Father:

"I have many things to speak and to judge concerning you, but He who sent Me is true; and the things which I heard from Him, these I speak to the world." They did not realize that He had been speaking to them about the Father. So Jesus said, "When you lift up the Son of Man, then you will know that I am He, and I do nothing on My own initiative, but I speak these things as the Father taught Me." (John 8:26–28)

For I did not speak on My own initiative, but the Father Himself who sent Me has given Me a commandment as to what to say and what to speak. I know that His commandment is eternal life; therefore the things I speak, I speak just as the Father has told Me. (John 12:49–50)

Do you not believe that I am in the Father, and the Father is in Me? The words that I say to you I do not speak on My own initiative, but the Father abiding in Me does His works. (John 14:10)

Jesus also directly said that He was a Prophet:

Nevertheless I must journey on today and tomorrow and the next day; for it cannot be that a prophet would perish outside of Jerusalem. (Luke 13:33)

Speaking of Jesus, Moses foretold of *the* prophet God would send. In Acts 3, Peter declared that Jesus was the fulfillment of Moses' words in Deuteronomy 18:15–18:

Moses said, "The Lord God will raise up for you a prophet like me from your brethren; to Him you shall give heed to everything He says to you. And it will be that every soul that does not heed that prophet shall be utterly destroyed from among the people." And likewise, all the prophets who have spoken, from Samuel and his successors onward, also announced these days. It is you who are the sons of the prophets and of the covenant which God made with your fathers, saying to Abraham, "And in your seed all the families of the earth shall be blessed." For you first, God raised up His Servant and sent Him to bless you by turning every one of you from your wicked ways." (Acts 3:22–26)

Lastly, others recognized Jesus as a Prophet, even when He was in His glorified body:

And He said to them, "What things?" And they said to Him, "The things about Jesus the Nazarene, who was a prophet mighty in deed and word in the sight of God and all the people, and how the chief priests and our rulers delivered Him to the sentence of death, and crucified Him." (Luke 24:19–20)

Jesus As Priest

With what does a priest primarily concern himself? Two words give an overarching answer to that question: sacrifice and intercession. The Old Testament priest was to constantly sacrifice offerings to the Lord for the sins of the people of Israel, and he was to plead with God on behalf of these same people.

Prophets, representing God, stood before men and declared God's will to them. Priests did the opposite: they represented man as they stood before God. Wayne Grudem is accurate in his summary: "In the Old Testament, the priests were appointed by God to offer sacrifices. They also offered prayers and praise to God on behalf of the people."[7] Similarly, Jesus' work as Priest is summarized as sacrifice and intercession. While the Levitical priests offered up a variety of animals for the sins of Israel, Jesus offered Himself (His own body) as the once-and-for-all sacrifice.

If we were to open the New Testament book of Hebrews at any page, we would likely find Jesus Christ described as "Priest" on that page. Hebrews is the most important New Testament book to exhaustively teach about Christ's work of mediation, and the treatment is extensive. Jesus is shown as superior to every person, sacrifice, or religious system. The best way to prove this is to simply list a number of verses directly from Hebrews. As you read these verses, note the common thread: Jesus is the High Priest. Jesus must be seen as the ultimate fulfillment of the promises found in the Old Testament concerning the Great High Priest.

First note those verses that describe Christ in His humiliation as Priest. Jesus offered Himself as the final sacrifice for sins. Every other sacrifice pointed to Christ's sufficient, once-for-all sacrifice.

Therefore, He had to be made like His brethren in all things, so that He might become a merciful and *faithful high priest* in things pertaining to God, to make propitiation for the sins of the people. For since He Himself was tempted in that which He has suffered, He is able to come to the aid of those who are tempted.   (2:17–18)

Therefore, holy brethren, partakers of a heavenly calling, consider Jesus, the Apostle and *High Priest* of our confession.   (3:1)

Therefore, since we have a *great high priest* who has passed through the heavens, Jesus the Son of God, let us hold fast our confession.   (4:14)

He says also in another passage,
"You are a priest forever
According to the order of Melchizedek."
In the days of His flesh, He offered up both prayers and supplications with loud crying and tears to the One able to save Him from death, and He was heard because of His piety. Although He was a Son, He learned obedience from the things which He suffered. And having been made perfect, He became to all those who obey Him the source of eternal salvation, being designated by God as a *high priest* according to the order of Melchizedek.   (5:6–10)

This hope we have as an anchor of the soul, a hope both sure and steadfast and one which enters within the veil, where Jesus has entered as a forerunner for us, having become a *high priest* forever according to the order of Melchizedek.   (6:19–20)

For it was fitting for us to have such a *high priest*, holy, innocent, undefiled, separated from sinners and exalted above the heavens; who does not need daily, like those high priests, to offer up sacrifices, first for His own sins and then for the sins of the people, because this He did once for all when He offered up Himself. For the Law appoints men as high priests who are weak, but the word of the oath, which came after the Law, appoints a Son, made perfect forever. (7:26–28)

Notice in the following verses the writer's determination to clearly and repeatedly state that Jesus was the Sacrifice (this was important for the Hebrew readers, who understood habitual sacrifices for sins).

If the blood of goats and bulls and the ashes of a heifer sprinkling those who have been defiled sanctify for the cleansing of the flesh, how much more will the blood of Christ, who through the eternal Spirit *offered Himself without blemish* to God, cleanse your conscience from dead works to serve the living God? (9:13–14)

For Christ did not enter a holy place made with hands, a mere copy of the true one, but into heaven itself, now to appear in the presence of God for us; nor was it that He would offer Himself often, as the high priest enters the holy place year by year with blood that is not his own. Otherwise, He would have needed to suffer often since the foundation of the world; but now once at the consummation of the ages He has been manifested to put away sin by the sacrifice of Himself. (9:24–26)

After saying ... "Sacrifices and offerings and whole burnt offerings and sacrifices for sin you have not desired, nor have you taken pleasure in them" (which are offered according to the Law), then He said, "Behold, I have come to do your will." He takes away the first in order to establish the second. By this will we have been sanctified through *the offering of the body of Jesus Christ* once for all. (10:8–10)

Therefore, brethren, since we have confidence to enter the holy place by the blood of Jesus, by a new and living way which He inaugurated for us through the veil, that is, His flesh, and since we have a *great priest* over the house of God, let us draw near with a sincere heart in full assurance of faith, having our hearts sprinkled clean from an evil conscience and our bodies washed with pure water. (10:19–22)

Additionally, Jesus, as the Exalted One, now intercedes for his people. His priestly work did not terminate at the cross. Just as the Old Testament priests prayed for the people, so too does Jesus mediate for His church.

But Jesus, on the other hand, because He continues forever, holds His priesthood permanently. Therefore He is able also to save forever those who draw near to God through Him, since He always lives to make *intercession* for them.   (7:24–25)

Paul obviously is in concert with the writer of Hebrews. Paul said,

Who will bring a charge against God's elect? God is the one who justifies; who is the one who condemns? Christ Jesus is He who died, yes, rather who was raised, who is at the right hand of God, who also *intercedes* for us.   (Rom. 8:33–34)

For there is one God, and one *mediator* also between God and men, the man Christ Jesus.   (1 Tim. 2:5)

Jesus' intercession is vitally linked to His sacrifice. The death of Christ obtained complete salvation from sins and, as Priest, Jesus' intercession applies every blessing won at Calvary. The resurrection of Jesus Christ proves the Father's satisfaction and pleasure in the substitutionary atonement of the Son. Therefore, the Father is happy to bestow any and all requests of the Son. "My little children, I am writing these things to you so that you may not sin. And if anyone sins, we have an Advocate with the Father, Jesus Christ the righteous; and He Himself is the propitiation for our sins; and not for ours only, but also for those of the whole world" (1 John 2:1–2). What a joy in times of trouble! Berkhof assures the weak and weary Christian,

It is a consoling thought that Christ is praying for us, even when we are negligent in our prayer life; that He is presenting to the Father those spiritual needs which were not present to our minds and which we often neglect to include in our prayers; and that He prays for our protection against the dangers of which we are not even conscious, and against the enemies which threaten us, though we do not notice it. He is praying that our faith may not cease, and that we may come out victoriously in the end.[8]

A reading of John chapter 17 causes us to marvel at the close relationship between the Father and the Son. The intimate, triune relationship ensures that the Father will hear the mediation of His Son, the High Priest, and answer Him, no matter how weak and sinful Christ's chosen ones are. Our weakness should drive us to the prayers of the Strong One, Jesus the Son, who is "face to face" with God the Father (see John 1:1).

The High Priest, Jesus Christ, bore sins, was Himself the perfect sacrifice, and made both expiation (cancellation of sin debt) and propitiation (atonement for God's wrath); He now stands before the throne for His people as the perfect Intercessor. If you remember the phrase "on our behalf," you can encapsulate the work of Jesus as Priest.

Jesus As King

Zechariah 6:13 describes the Messiah to come as "a priest on His throne." Jesus Christ is Prophet and Priest, yet He is also King. Jesus, as King, protects us, equips us for eternal life, and guards us against each and every enemy. Thomas Boston said that Jesus was "not a King in name only, or an inactive monarch, but exercising acts of jurisdiction and government."9 Unlike all other kings, Jesus was anointed by the Holy Spirit, not by oil (like Saul, for example). Speaking on Isaiah 11:2, John Calvin discussed Christ as King: "Accordingly, his royal unction is not set before us as composed of oil or aromatic perfumes; but he is called the Christ of God, because 'the Spirit of the Lord' rested upon him; 'the Spirit of wisdom and understanding, the Spirit of counsel and might, the Spirit of knowledge and of the fear of the Lord.'"10

While Psalms 2, 45, 72, and 110 were all given to show the Messiah as King, we will focus on Daniel 7:13–14:

I kept looking in the night visions,
And behold, with the clouds of heaven
One like a Son of Man was coming,
And He came up to the Ancient of Days
And was presented before Him.
And to Him was given dominion,
Glory and a kingdom,
That all the peoples, nations and men of every language
Might serve Him.
His dominion is an everlasting dominion

Which will not pass away;
And His kingdom is one
Which will not be destroyed.

The Messiah, here called "the Son of Man," is, as King, given dominion and a kingdom by the Father. On earth, Jesus regularly called himself the Son of Man, a title which comes directly from this passage in Daniel. Jesus was the Son of David, but He was more than that.

Do you remember when Jesus stood on trial before the Sanhedrin and the high priest?

The high priest stood up and said to Him, "Do You not answer? What is it that these men are testifying against You?" But Jesus kept silent. And the high priest said to Him, "I adjure You by the living God, that You tell us whether You are the Christ, the Son of God." Jesus said to him, "You have said it yourself; nevertheless I tell you, hereafter you will see the Son of Man sitting at the right hand of power, and coming on the clouds of heaven." Then the high priest [Caiaphas] tore his robes and said, "He has blasphemed! What further need do we have of witnesses? Behold, you have now heard the blasphemy; what do you think?" They answered, "He deserves death!" Then they spat in His face and beat Him with their fists; and others slapped Him.   (Matt. 26:62–67)

Everyone within earshot knew that Jesus was quoting the Messianic text from Daniel 7:13–14. In contrast to popular opinion, Jesus proclaimed that Daniel's message did not apply to those who would be granted access to the kingdom, but, instead, it was a stinging rebuke to His listeners. Jesus was saying that He was the Son of Man and that He would judge them upon His return. What a slap in the face for some! No wonder they shrieked, "Blasphemy!", likely with saliva-drenched beards, and called for His immediate death.

In the New Testament, then, Christ is displayed as a King, in perfect agreement with the prophecies found in the Old Testament. Meditate on the following proclamations of Jesus' Kingship by well-known preachers:

And behold, you will conceive in your womb and bear a son, and you shall name Him Jesus. He will be great and will be called the Son of the Most High; and the Lord God will give Him the throne of His father David; and He will reign over the house of Jacob forever, and His kingdom will have no end.   (Gabriel, Luke 1:31–33)

"Repent, for the kingdom of heaven is at hand." For this is the one referred to by Isaiah the prophet when he said,
"The voice of one crying in the wilderness,
'Make ready the way of the Lord,
Make his paths straight!'"   (John the Baptist, Matt. 3:2–3)

Now to the King eternal, immortal, invisible, the only God, be honor and glory forever and ever. Amen.   (The apostle Paul, 1 Tim. 1:17)

Jesus Christ, born a King (Matt. 2:2), entered Jerusalem as King (see Matt. 21:5), accepted Pilate's description of Him as King (Matt. 27:11), and now sits at the right hand of the throne of heaven as King (Heb. 8:1).

Implications

An understanding of Christ's threefold office ought to give us encouragement and strength to hold fast our confession and draw near with confidence to God. It is glorious and very comforting to know that He rules the world for the sake of the church: "And He put all things in subjection under His feet, and gave Him as head over all things to the church" (Eph. 1:22).

I ask with Thomas Boston, "Are we not always needing protection against our enemies? How then should we break through the armies of hell, if our King were not on our head, to subdue them under us?"[11] The King is for us!

But heed these words of Boston as he warns those who have not bowed their knee to the King of kings:

Ye cannot take Christ, as a Redeemer, if ye take him not in all his offices. He offers himself to sinners no other way. And what God has joined together let no man put asunder. Many pretend to take Christ as a Saviour to save them from hell and wrath, who do not hearken to him as a Prophet to teach them the saving knowledge of God, nor submit to his laws and commandments … O the madness of those who contemn Christ as a King, refusing to submit to his royal authority, and who spurn at his laws and government! And how foolish are the princes of the earth that will not suffer Christ to reign freely in their dominions, but encroach on his authority, and make laws opposite to and inconsistent with his![12]

Summary

Louis Berkhof concisely summarizes Jesus' role in His three offices: "As Prophet He represents God with man; as Priest He represents man in the presence of God; and as King He exercises dominion and restores the original dominion of man."[13]

When we think of Jesus Christ, we must consider that He is Prophet, Priest, and King. Do you?

Hymn

O worship the King, all glorious above,
O gratefully sing His power and His love;
Our Shield and Defender, the Ancient of Days,
Pavilioned in splendor, and girded with praise.

O tell of His might, O sing of His grace,
Whose robe is the light, whose canopy space,
His chariots of wrath the deep thunderclouds form,
And dark is His path on the wings of the storm.

The earth with its store of wonders untold,
Almighty, Thy power hath founded of old;
Established it fast by a changeless decree,
And round it hath cast, like a mantle, the sea.

Thy bountiful care, what tongue can recite?
It breathes in the air, it shines in the light;
It streams from the hills, it descends to the plain,
And sweetly distills in the dew and the rain.

Frail children of dust, and feeble as frail,
In Thee do we trust, nor find Thee to fail;

Thy mercies how tender, how firm to the end,
Our Maker, Defender, Redeemer, and Friend.

O measureless might! Ineffable love!
While angels delight to worship Thee above,
The humbler creation, though feeble their lays,
With true adoration shall all sing Thy praise.

(Robert Grant, 1833)

Notes

1 "The Office of Christ," from **Luther's** *Small Catechism*; cited at Issues, Etc., at: mtio.com.
2 **John Calvin,** *The Institutes of the Christian Religion*, tr. by Henry Beveridge, vol. 2 (Edinburgh: Calvin Translation Society, 1845), 35.
3 **E. F. Karl Mueller** in **Samuel Macauley Jackson** (ed.), *The New Schaff-Herzog Encyclopedia of Religious Knowledge*, vol. 6 (Grand Rapids: Baker, 1953); cited at Christian Classics Ethereal Library, at: ccel.org/s/schaff/encyc/encyc06/htm/iii.lvii.v.htm. Accessed November 2010.
4 **Wayne Grudem,** *Systematic Theology: An Introduction to Biblical Doctrine* (Grand Rapids: Zondervan, 1995), 624.
5 *The Heidelberg Catechism*, cited at Center for Reformed Theology and Apologetics, at: reformed.org. Accessed November 2010.
6 **Grudem,** *Systematic Theology*, 625–626.
7 Ibid. 626.
8 **Louis Berkhof,** *Systematic Theology* (Grand Rapids: Eerdmans, 1996), 403.
9 **Thomas Boston,** "Of Christ's Offices in General," cited at A Puritan's Mind, at: apuritansmind.com/ChristianWalk/BostonThomasOfChristsOfficesInGeneral.htm. Accessed November 2010.
10 **Calvin,** *Institutes of the Christian Religion*, 41.
11 **Thomas Boston,** "Of Christ's Offices in General," in *The Complete Works of Thomas Boston*, vol. 1; under "The Christian Walk" at A Puritan's Mind: apuritansmind.com. Accessed January 2011.
12 Ibid.
13 **Berkhof,** *Systematic Theology*, 357.

The Coronation of the King

"Coronation" is another word associated with kings. It is used for the ceremony of the crowning of a monarch. During the coronation, the crown is literally laid upon the new king's head as a visual reminder of the significance of the event. Ceremonies of this magnitude often combine both civil and religious aspects, replete with all the pomp and circumstance that the state, country, or church can muster and afford.

My objective for Part 2 is for you to figuratively "crown" God as King by actively living in the light of the truth that God is the King. Does that sound odd? The whole Christian life is a process of becoming more the people that we actually are. Christians, because of Christ's active and passive obedience, are positionally holy and righteous. By the Holy Spirit's enabling power, we should then strive to live up to that position on a day-by-day basis. This is called sanctification.

To put it another way, Part 2 is the practical application and outworking of the theology found in Part 1 (that the Scriptures speak of God as King). Part 1 proves that God is King, and Part 2 gives the answer to the "So what?" response to the established truth of Part 1. This concept, that "theology determines methodology," is common in Scripture. For example, the hinge verse of Ephesians (the hinge between the doctrine in chapters 1 through 3 and the practical outworking of that doctrine in chapters 4 through 6) says, "Therefore I, the prisoner of the Lord, implore you to walk in a manner worthy of the calling with which you have been called" (Eph. 4:1).

To "walk in a manner worthy of the calling" is Paul's illustrative method of calling the church to act like people who have been actually affected and infected by Ephesians 1 through 3. To use military language, Paul is exhorting his readers to "conduct themselves with actions befitting officers." In the Old Testament, the common standard to Israel was, "If you obey, you will be blessed; and if you disobey, you will be cursed." Here Paul declares, "Since you have been blessed by all the wondrous demonstrations of grace I've described in chapters 1 through 3, obey." The proper response to God's love, found in Christ Jesus, is obedience. The real incentive to holy living is who God is and what He has done for the believer. The apostle never considered doctrine as something abstract and irrelevant.

Doctrine is absolutely necessary for the Christian. But never forget that it is not the terminal point of a person's life. The daily conduct of a saved person (commonly signified in the Bible through the verb "walk") is just as important as the creed of the Christian. Paul is very clear in Ephesians 4:1 when he writes, "Walk in a manner *worthy* of the calling." The word translated "worthy" literally means "bringing up the other beam of the scales," and therefore indicates equivalence."[1] Paul wants his readers to give equal weight and importance to their calling and to their conduct. How? By learning doctrine and, through the Holy Spirit's power, living out what they know to be true about God and His church. For the same reasons (as an incentive for holy living), Paul uses the word "Lord" twenty-six times in Ephesians, with twenty occurrences found in chapters 4 through 6. Lordship implies obedience on the part of Christians to what has been taught and is commonly believed. Scholar Snodgrass declares this is to be in "keeping with Paul's tendency to use 'Christ' in texts about salvation and 'Lord' in texts about ethics."[2]

Lloyd-Jones brilliantly emphasizes this verity:

The Apostle ... is beseeching them and exhorting them always to give equal weight in their lives to doctrine and practice. They must not put all the weight on doctrine and none on practice; not all the weight on practice and just a little, if any at all, on doctrine. To do so produces imbalance and lopsidedness. The Ephesians must take great pains to see that the scales are perfectly balanced.[3]

In summary, in Part 2 I hope to propel you to obey God the King, to live in light of the truth that God is King. If you do this, you will be figuratively placing a crown on God's head.

"Zadok the priest then took the horn of oil from the tent and anointed Solomon. Then they blew the trumpet, and all the people said, 'Long live King Solomon!' All the people went up after him, and the people were playing on flutes and rejoicing with great joy, so that the earth shook at their noise" (1 Kings 1:39–40). Imagine your theologically informed conduct shouting out to the Lord God, "Long live King Jesus!" Now imagine the heavenly Father's response.

Notes

1 **Gerhard Kittel, Gerhard Friedrich,** and **Geoffrey W. Bromiley** (eds.), *Theological Dictionary of the New Testament* (TDNT), vol. 1 (Grand Rapids: Eerdmans, 1964), 379.

2 **Klyne Snodgrass,** *Ephesians* (NIV Application Commentary Series; Grand Rapids: Zondervan, 1996), 196.

3 **David Martyn Lloyd-Jones,** *Christian Unity: An Exposition of Ephesians 4:1–16* (Grand Rapids: Baker, 1981), 24.

"Kingship Salvation"

Consider the following scenarios and ask yourself this question: If God is King, can I still live just as I did before I was in His kingdom?

Scenario 1

A rich and powerful king is about to address the assembled people in his realm. With full pomp and circumstance, the king makes a grand and elegant entrance. When he steps up to the speaking platform, a hush moves over the crowd. Then he begins to speak:

"Since I became your king, you are now safe from all your old enemies, you have been given wives from foreign lands that I have conquered, and you have stockpiles of food that I have richly given you from my storehouses. Now, even though I have not had to raise taxes for the past six years, I must raise taxes for the good of the kingdom."

What would be the response of the people? How would they receive such an edict from their good and beneficent monarch? It would be treasonous for the people in the kingdom to respond, "We will not have you rule over us. We will not obey you. We will take you as provider of everything that we need, from wives to food, but we will not take you as a king we have to obey! Let's begin to riot!"

Scenario 2

A king approaches a group of renegades from another land. He tells them, "My requirements for you to enter my kingdom are simple: completely renounce your old king and be willing to submit to my rule and reign. There are no negotiations, and this is my first and final offer for clemency."

Never would we expect to hear a person respond, "My daughter wants to have you be a king when she needs you, but, besides that, she wants to act as if she is your king while she lives in your kingdom. She will give you the title of 'King,' but it is a vacuous title, void of meaning, because she will still do what she wants, as often as she wants, and to whom she wants."

Scenario 3

In the same situation as in Scenario 2, a man with a large family initially says, "Yes, King, we will give you total allegiance if you allow us the privilege of becoming members of your kingdom."

The king allows this family entrance. As the months turn into years, however, the man's family begins to waver in its allegiance to the good king. Only two options seem available to the man. The first option is to keep his word: he entered on the king's terms, and his family must do what the king says. The second option is less objective, but it helps soothe the inner recesses of the man's conscience. With reluctance, the man mentally "lowers the bar" of standards that the king originally set for all kingdom citizens. Nothing has actually changed, but the man feels much better about his wife and children although they no longer, in their hearts, actually bow to the king and his standards. Their homage is false and fake, but the man is so grief-stricken that he either "misremembers" the king's initial demands, or he purposely dilutes them.

These three scenarios perfectly describe what the "anti-lordship" people, and some "non-lordship" people, do. In essence, they theologically attempt to "take Jesus as Savior" but they do not submit to him as "Lord." Many more scenarios abound, but these three make the point. Sadly, however, we are not talking about any old human king, but the King of kings, the Lord Jesus Christ. God is the Monarch, and He will not stoop to anything less than full loyalty.

Understanding that God is King should immediately assist the thinking Christian to see through the thin shellac of a bifurcated, unbiblical God who is Savior but not Lord. It is untenable to perceive God this way. The intention of this chapter is to briefly study what is termed "kingship salvation." This is equivalent to "lordship salvation," but it desires to milk out the nuances of God as King. My goal is not to revisit the whole debate on lordship salvation; there are more comprehensive books on that subject.[1] Since MacArthur does not like the name "lordship salvation," he might prefer the term "kingship salvation." He writes, "I don't like the term lordship salvation. I reject the connotation intended by those who coined the phrase. It insinuates that a submissive heart is extraneous or supplementary to saving faith. Although I have reluctantly used the term to describe my views, it is a concession to popular usage."[2]

You might ask, "Just what is 'lordship salvation'?" Two quotes should aid your understanding of the issues. William Webster is insightful, describing the debate this way:

The controversy is not over the essential nature of Christ, but whether submission to him, as Lord of one's life, is a necessary aspect of saving faith. There are those who claim that lordship is a betrayal of the Reformation in that it undermines the vital reformation principle of "faith alone." And there are those who state that rather than a betrayal, the teaching of lordship is, in fact, an affirmation of both the biblical gospel and the historic Protestant faith.[3]

R. C. Sproul expands Webster's idea:

Advocates of "Lordship salvation" argue that saving faith involves embracing Christ as both Savior and Lord and that true faith inevitably, necessarily, and immediately begins to display the fruit of obedience. That is, the process of sanctification by which we are conformed to the image of Christ begins certainly and immediately upon our justification. This process of sanctification is neither perfect in this life nor is it in any way the ground of our justification. This ground remains exclusively the righteousness of Christ imputed to us by faith alone. But the justified person is manifestly a changed person who is regenerated and indwelt by the Holy Spirit. He acknowledges, embraces, and to some degree submits to Christ as Lord.[4]

Put in language of the monarchy, "kingship salvation" denotes the proper response to God's monergistic[5] regeneration. When God redeems a sinner, the sinner is predisposed to follow God as his or her new Master, Lord, and King. New Christians do not say or believe that, since they now have Jesus as Savior, they will be able to "make Him King" later in life (especially when they are in a tight spot or under extreme circumstances). Christians must always embrace Jesus, the King, as Lord.

A passage in the Bible that is rarely discussed in the lordship-salvation debate is Ephesians 4:20–21, which clearly supports kingship salvation. In this passage we can observe five verities about God's working in His people, and how this can help us stay away from false theories about "carnal Christians."

God the King Never Grants People Citizenship to His Holy Kingdom without their Being "On the Inside"

In Ephesians 4, Paul is fleshing out what it means, practically and ethically, to be "in Christ," which was the overarching theme of the first three chapters. Christians are to conduct themselves in holiness, remembering what they were taught early in their Christian lives: "You did not learn Christ in this way, if indeed you have heard Him and have been taught in Him, just as truth is in Jesus" (Eph. 4:20–21).

Paul, an expert in communicating God's truth, utilizes a figure of speech called "litotes." A litotes (pronounced "lie-toe-tease") communicates emphasis by extreme understatement. The apostle dramatically calls pre-Christian behavior unacceptable. It should be out of the question to live as you used to before God regenerated you. To go from "outside Christ" to "in Christ" and to have no change in your life is, according to Lloyd-Jones, "utterly impossible; it is unthinkable; the thing is ludicrous."[6] You cannot live as you did before. God "made you alive" (Eph. 2:5; Col. 2:13).

The following litotes accent and deliberately highlight this truth:

All that the Father gives Me will come to Me, and the one who comes to Me I will certainly not cast out. (John 6:37)

He who overcomes will thus be clothed in white garments; and I will not erase his name from the book of life. (Rev. 3:5)

For I am not ashamed of the gospel, for it is the power of God for salvation to everyone who believes, to the Jew first and also to the Greek. (Rom. 1:16)

Jesus guarantees the reception of those who come to Him (John 6:37), He promises to keep their names written in the book of life (Rev. 3:5), and Paul boasts in the honor of the gospel (Rom. 1:16). In Ephesians 4:20, Paul says that the Ephesians learned Christ in a manner that was the polar opposite of the way the Gentiles behaved. The pagans lived for themselves;

the blood-bought Ephesians must live for Jesus. Paul taught the church these truths when he was there in person, so they would not have come as a surprise; rather, his readers should take these truths for granted.

To put it positively, the Ephesians had learned Christ in a quite different manner. The manner of life they had been taught by Paul was the extreme opposite of the one practiced by the Gentiles. Gerstner exhorts, "Maybe you did so learn Diana; but you did not so learn Christ. Here was the radical element in Christianity—it tampered with people's lives. Association with Christ had to change his followers."[7]

Why is it so shocking to be told that the Christian must no longer submit to his old king, Satan? The Christian has a new King, and He demands a completely different life, one which He also enables the Christian to live. The Ephesian church should have learned this. You should have learned this truth as well. You cannot believe in Jesus Christ with saving faith and then live the way you used to. Paul does not beg—he does not approach the church emotionally; rather, he goes for the throat of the mind.

With typical Pauline contrast, Paul had just written,

So this I say, and affirm together with the Lord, that you walk no longer just as the Gentiles also walk, in the futility of their mind, being darkened in their understanding, excluded from the life of God because of the ignorance that is in them, because of the hardness of their heart; and they, having become callous, have given themselves over to sensuality for the practice of every kind of impurity with greediness.   (Eph. 4:17–19)

Gentiles, or unbelievers, aim for "futility," and they strike it every time. Their lives are characterized by emptiness, meaninglessness, and purposelessness. Once people reject the knowledge of the living God, all other thoughts about life yield emptiness and futility. Mentally, unbelievers cannot grasp spiritual verity and their understanding of God becomes dulled. Pagans spiral from bad to worse, with nothing to show for their efforts except calloused, hardened hearts which are impervious to God's Word and ways. Lastly, Paul says, excessive sensuality screams out with greedy covetousness. Gentiles have baptized themselves in the impure water of sin. Before coming to Christ, people live with sinful purpose, but, to their eternal regret, they flaunt their sin without shame or embarrassment. Public decorum is stepped on willingly (sinners are not forced to sin lustfully). To put it bluntly, Gentiles love themselves with all their hearts, souls, minds, and strength. Unbelievers drool over sin and the opportunities it presents, void of all guilt. One commentator has said, "Their consciences are so atrophied that sin registers no stab of pain."[8]

Now here is the question: Did you learn Christ this way, replete with a love for sin and unrighteousness? Since you are "in Ephesus," a world laden with sin, should you act like unconverted Ephesians? Should you run pell-mell into a complete preoccupation with vile and filthy sin? Are you to deliberately sin and then wipe your mouth, saying, "I have done no wrong"? Will you abandon yourself to the ravaging excesses of debauchery and sexual sin?

No—may it never be! Why? Because you did not learn Christ this way, did you? Does your life confirm or deny your education?

God the King, by the power of the Holy Spirit, changes people. After you have entered God's kingdom, you have a hard time finding something in your life that is not new. For example:

- You have a new standing with God: you are counted righteous by the work of Jesus Christ.
- You have a new relationship to your sins: you are completely forgiven by Jesus' death for you.
- You are a new creation in Christ Jesus (2 Cor. 5:17).
- You have new friends and a new family: the local church.
- You have new goals: e.g. to glorify God, to evangelize.
- You have a new Master: Jesus, not Satan.
- You have a new eternal destiny: heaven, not hell.
- You have new priorities: the Lord's, not your own.
- You have new longings: spiritual, not earthly and temporal.
- You have a new view of Bible study, worship, and giving: once you hated them, now you love them.
- You have a new love of virtue, godliness, and holiness.

The slogan for the Christian can never be "same old, same old." Change has occurred, and you cannot simply add Jesus to your life and keep living as you used to live. Morris, expounding Ephesians 4:20 and "learning Christ" as being *contra mundum* (against the world), said, "It [the new birth and all that goes with it] does not mean to carry on with the old way with perhaps a few of our worst habits dusted off."[9] At regeneration, God instilled in you a new love for the things you used to hate, and a hate for the things you used to love. "Kingship salvation" recognizes the work of God in the heart of every believer.

God the King Is Not Satisfied with a Mere Intellectual Assent to the Facts of Christianity

When Paul says in Ephesians 4:20 "You did not learn Christ in this way," he is saying something unheard of in the world of biblical literature. "Learning" a person is quite different from "learning" a subject. Language like this is "without parallel ... it appears nowhere else in the Greek Bible."[10] Boice agrees: "The idea of learning a person ... is found nowhere else in the NT."[11] Why the strange language here? Paul is stressing the fact that we did not learn *about* Jesus at conversion, with some kind of increased information or mental knowledge, full of facts, figures, and statistics. Acquiring new information is not the point Paul is hammering home. His emphasis, rather, is on *knowing* the Person and the work of the Messiah Himself, in a real and personal manner, not merely knowing *about* Him.

The root of the Greek word translated "learn" is also the root of the word "mathematics." At salvation, we entered a schoolroom to get personally acquainted with the Savior, not simply to learn our spiritual times tables. Such an acquaintance with the Holy One of God would never allow us to think that we could keep living the way we used to. To continue with the math class illustration: we did not simply learn our multiplication and division formulas; we got to know the teacher.

What I remember most about the time I spent learning New Testament Greek in seminary was not how to parse, translate, understand syntax, and grasp lexical issues. Although extremely important, the language's technical apparatus took a back seat to learning the New Testament through my professor. I learned about Greek, but I also "learned the professor." While the analogy is not a perfect fit, the principle is still valid: I did not simply learn facts about my professor, I also comprehended who he was, and, to a large degree, what motivated him and how he approached the Christian life.

Commentator Wood perfectly captures the meaning in Ephesians 4:20 when he explains, "The expression is 'to learn Christ' (*emathete tou Christou*), which implies more than receiving catechetical instruction, though that is included. It is to learn in such a way as to become a devotee or disciple (*mathetes*)."[12] Far from being a mere factual tutorial, "to learn Christ" is to study the Messiah so closely and intimately that we learn about Him in order to become more like Him. The more we "learn Jesus," the more we are transformed into His likeness. As an analogy, online educational courses impart facts well, but they do not contain the personal aspect of the teacher/student relationship that many students come to appreciate. Getting to personally know teachers seems to give the course material an "incarnational" value. The truth is literally "fleshed out" before the students, which often serves as an example for them to imitate. Paul yearns for the readers to so "learn" Christ that they cannot help but resemble Him.

Evangelicalism today seems content to accept cognitive knowledge as the only prerequisite for calling oneself a Christian. To know a person and to know about a person are radically different concepts. To learn that Jesus is Lord and King and then to say, "Well, that is how I mentally understand Jesus, but it never relates to holy living" is insane and illogical. If you are saved, when God saved you, you were taught the Person of Christ the King.

When people say that they are "pleased to make your acquaintance," no change is necessary in either person; but when we "make Jesus our acquaintance," there are ethical implications galore. Jesus has taught Christians that following Him as King and Lord will force them to turn from and abandon all other competing idols, especially that of self.

Charles Hodge is right when, in discussing a person's conversion, he notes that it is at that point that Jesus is "set ... forth as the object of supreme love and confidence, so 'to learn Christ' does not mean merely, to learn his doctrines, but to attain the knowledge of Christ as the Son of God, God in our nature, the Holy One of God, the Savior from sin, whom to know is holiness and life."[13] Miles apart from Charles Hodge's understanding is that of Zane Hodges (no relationship by family or by theology), who declared, "Thus it is utterly impossible for us to give credence to the gospel message without knowing that we are saved."[14] Zane Hodges is stressing a mere "learning about" not a "learning Christ." Intellectual knowledge is a must, but it is, in all actuality, a stepping-stone for intimate knowledge of Christ Jesus. Christians are required to "grow in the grace and knowledge of our Lord and Savior Jesus Christ" (2 Peter 3:18). Truth matters. Ideas have consequences.

God the King Is Not Pleased by Emotional Experiences Alone

What human king would be satisfied with a person who wants to stay in his kingdom for all the positive benefits provided by him, but who will not follow the king as lord? When confronted, this person might say, "I had a subjective experience when I felt that I was following you," or "I had a warm feeling in my heart that we were friends, even though my life right now shows no submission to you as king." There is a name for such nonsense: treason.

Ephesians 4:21 says that you have really learned Christ "if indeed you have heard Him and have been taught in Him, just as truth is in Jesus." Paul even uses irony for his purposes, declaring, "since you have heard about Jesus ..." Of course they had "heard about Jesus," so what is he doing? He is simply stacking the deck of his argument. He is demanding authentication and substantiation of the Ephesians' professed faith. The question from Paul is not "Have you learned Christ properly?" but "Have you learned Christ to any degree?" Emotions are not the issue at all. He is not even remotely addressing mystical, subjective experiences or feelings.

In the book of Ephesians Paul rarely uses the word "Jesus." What is the reason for placing it in 4:21? Robinson posits the following theory: "It [the name "Jesus"] rarely occurs alone; and, when it does, there is generally an express reference to the death or resurrection of our Lord ... He uses the name 'Jesus' by itself when he wishes emphatically to point to the historic personality of the Christ."[15] Believing in the historical Jesus will dramatically change the life of any pagan, Gentile, or Jew. Truths about Jesus initially taught to Christians about Christ's incarnation, perfect life, substitutionary death, and literal resurrection must flesh themselves out in their lives. Bruce states, "If they had received even the most rudimentary fragments of Christian teaching, if they knew anything at all about Christ, they would be aware that by practice and precept He had commended a way of life vastly different from the pagan way which Paul has just described."[16] Emotional experiences might follow "learning Christ," but they cannot serve as the litmus test for faith.

Remember James 2:19: "You believe that God is one. You do well; the demons also believe, and shudder." Demons have more than a simply intellectual faith; "shudder" indicates that their "faith" contains an emotional element. They are afraid; they shudder. The Greek word that James employs for "shudder" describes what happens to the hair on a dog's back when scared or fearful. In other words, if demons had hair, it would bristle because of the horror they experience knowing who the Lord God really is and what he will do for them in the future.[17] Far from being stoic about God, demons have an emotional response, but no one would consider them saved or holy. The same is true with human beings, because emotions themselves prove nothing. Emotional reactions to the gospel are great, but they are not, in and of themselves, saving. True saving faith is intellectual, emotional, and volitional.

In our day, emotions seem to rule secularism and spirituality. Hordes of people are self-described mystics who are led by subjective experiences instead of by truth, specifically, truth concerning the historical Jesus. This elevation of personal reality contributes to the church's misunderstanding of the role of emotions. Have you learned Jesus the King in a way that goes beyond an emotional experience?

God the King Is Not Pleased without Repentance

In times past, kings often subdued their enemies and did what they wished with captive soldiers. Imagine a king who, out of mercy, says, "Lay down your arms, or perish where you stand. Turn your allegiance away from your deposed, dead king and bow to me with complete loyalty and live." No soldier would dare exclaim in public, "While I will now acknowledge you as my king, I will never turn from serving my old king!"

Sadly, there is an aberrant teaching in evangelistic circles that mirrors the above response. I wish I were making up the following quote from Zane Hodges: "Thus, though genuine repentance may precede salvation (as we shall see), it need not do so. And because it is not essential to the saving transaction as such, it is in no sense a condition for that transaction. But the fact still remains that God demands repentance from all and He conditions their fellowship with Him on that."[18]

On the contrary: real repentance is the flip side of saving faith. Both must exist simultaneously. Turning from sin and turning to Christ are part and parcel of the package of saving faith.

What the Reformers (and Paul, for that matter) considered rudimentary is denied by far too many today. Thankfully, there are men like John MacArthur who will not compromise the Word of God: "Thus salvation is impossible apart from repentance … faith presupposes repentance. How can those who are mortal enemies of God (Rom. 5:10) sincerely believe in His Son without repenting? How can anyone truly comprehend the truth of salvation from sin and its consequences, unless that person also genuinely understands and hates what sin is?"[19] When God grants you entrance into His kingdom, you change your mind about almost everything, which gives way to a changed life. The Greek word from which our word "repentance" comes means "to change one's mind." Note the following Old Testament phrases that encapsulate the idea of changing our minds:

Incline your hearts to the LORD, the God of Israel. (Josh. 24:23)

Circumcise yourselves to the LORD. (Jer. 4:4)

Wash your heart from evil. (Jer. 4:14)

Break up your fallow ground. (Hosea 10:12)

They turned from their wicked way. (Jonah 3:10)

Put those Scriptures together and we realize that we must change our thinking about God and our new allegiance to our new King. Our thoughts must be different about the One to whom we give loyalty, honor, and submission; our attitude must be "Yes, Lord and King." We no longer love to do what was right in our own eyes. Because of the Holy Spirit's work, we seek first the kingdom of God (Matt. 6:33).

For those who somehow consider repentance to smack of works, the *Westminster Catechism* clearly and biblically states that "Repentance unto life is a saving grace, wrought in the heart of a sinner by the Spirit and Word of God, whereby, out of the sight and sense, not only of the danger, but also of the filthiness and odiousness of his sins, and upon the apprehension of God's mercy in Christ to such as are penitent, he so grieves for and hates his sins, as that he turns from them all to God, purposing and endeavouring constantly to walk with him in all the ways of new obedience."[20] The Catechism simply echoes Paul's understanding that, while repentance is a command, it is simultaneously a divine gift, as we see from Paul's words to Timothy: "With gentleness [correct] those who are in opposition, if perhaps *God may grant them repentance* leading to the knowledge of the truth, and they may come to their senses and escape from the snare of the devil, having been held captive by him to do his will" (2 Tim. 2:25–26).

God the King Does Not Think "Fruit-Bearing" Is Optional

When people "learn Christ," they learn about serving God and serving other Christians. To return to our example of an earthly king: How long would a subject of a king last if that subject never contributed to the kingdom? Would the king look favorably upon a citizen in his realm who defied his laws of being productive and never contributed (e.g. by paying taxes, doing good works, or feeding the poor) to the king's realm?

Surely one of the reasons why the king would allow people into his realm would be to add to his kingdom. Similarly, Paul said in Ephesians 2:10 that we are "created in Christ Jesus for good works." In other words, we are expected to be fruit-bearers in God's kingdom. God designed Christians to do the good works that God "created." Amazingly, "create" is a verb that is used exclusively of God in the Bible. He alone creates the good works, and therefore He alone gets the praise when we do them. When God graciously saves people, He also creates fruit for them "to walk in." Salvation brings a willingness in Christians to serve their new King. The Christian asks, "What would you have me do?" The old Puritan Gurnall emphatically declared, "Say not that thou hast royal blood in thy veins, and art born of God, except thou canst prove thy pedigree by daring to be holy."[21]

Far from being optional, bearing fruit is the very purpose of existence for a Christian. Don't let any member of any kingdom tell you differently.

Summary

God is King by more than name. The word "King" is not simply a title like Mister, Doctor, or President. Since God is a King, and a good and gracious King, He demands obedience. While this obedience will, at times, be wavering, immature, slow, and sinful, it will, at the end of the day, definitely be present. Why? Because when the God of the universe changes a person, that person is changed! If there is no change in a person's life, there is every reason to suspect that there has not been a change in that person's status before the holy King. Consider the following haunting words of A. W. Tozer, as you think about kings and those who commit treason against their King:

The sinner is actually a rebel against properly constituted authority. That is what makes sin, sin. We are rebels. We are sons of disobedience. Sin is the breaking of the law and we are in rebellion and we are fugitives from the just laws of God while we are sinners ... the root of sin is rebellion against law, rebellion against God. Does not the sinner say, "I belong to myself. I owe allegiance to no one unless I choose to give it!" That is the essence of sin ... Thus in repentance, we reverse that relationship and we fully submit to the Word of God and the will of God as obedient children ... We have no basis to believe that we can come casually and sprightly to the Lord Jesus and say, I have come for some help, Lord Jesus. I understand that you are the Savior so I am going to believe and be saved and then I am going to turn away and think about the other matters of lordship and allegiance and obedience at some other time in the future. I warn you, you will not get help from Him in that way for the Lord will not save those whom He cannot command. He will not divide His offices. You cannot believe on a half Christ. We take Him for what He is, the anointed Savior and Lord who is King of kings and Lord of lords.[22]

Allegiance and loyalty to the King are mandatory. You cannot remain undecided or attempt to straddle the proverbial fence. Will you submit to Him? Do you believe in Him? There is no other way to have your sins forgiven. If you are not born again, there is no time to delay. Bow to the King today!

Hymn

Lead on, O King eternal,
The day of march has come;
Henceforth in fields of conquest
Thy tents shall be our home.
Through days of preparation
Thy grace has made us strong;
And now, O King eternal,
We lift our battle song.

Lead on, O King eternal,
Till sin's fierce war shall cease,
And holiness shall whisper
The sweet amen of peace.
For not with swords loud clashing,
Nor roll of stirring drums;
With deeds of love and mercy
The heavenly kingdom comes.

Lead on, O King eternal,
We follow, not with fears,
For gladness breaks like morning
Where'er thy face appears.
Thy cross is lifted o'er us,
We journey in its light;
The crown awaits the conquest;
Lead on, O God of might.   (Ernest W. Shurtleff, 1862–1917)

Study Questions

1. When a family member or friend who has previously professed faith in Christ says that he is she is born again but has no intention of following Christ, how would you respond?

Chapter 5

2. What is the role of feelings when you analyze the assurance of your own salvation? Can feelings be deceptive? Supportive?
3. List everything in your life that has changed since God saved you. Does this list help or hinder how you view the security of God's salvation and the feelings of assurance?
4. In what respect is the Christian faith intellectual? Is it more than intellectual?
5. Is it appropriate to tell unbelievers that they must submit to King Jesus?
6. Do you follow Jesus Christ? Do you desire to follow Him? Who gave you that desire?

Notes

1 **Richard P. Belcher,** *A Layman's Guide to the Lordship Controversy* (Southbridge, MA: Crowne, 1990); **Walter Chantry,** *Today's Gospel: Authentic or Synthetic?* (Edinburgh: Banner of Truth, 1970); **Curtis I. Crenshaw,** *Lordship Salvation: The Only Kind There Is!* (Memphis: Footstool, 1994); **Kenneth L. Gentry,** *Lord of the Saved: Getting to the Heart of the Lordship Debate* (Phillipsburg, NJ: Presbyterian & Reformed, 1992); **Anthony A. Hoekema,** *Saved by Grace* (Grand Rapids: Eerdmans, 1989); **R. B. Kuiper,** *God-Centered Evangelism* (Edinburgh: Banner of Truth, 1961); **John MacArthur,** *The Gospel According to Jesus* (Grand Rapids, Zondervan, 1988); **John F. MacArthur,** *Faith Works: The Gospel According to the Apostles* (Dallas: Word, 1993); **Ernest C. Reisinger,** *Today's Evangelism: Its Message and Methods* (Phillipsburg, NJ: Craig, 1982); **A. W. Tozer,** *I Call It Heresy!* (Harrisburg, PA: Christian Publications, 1974).
2 **MacArthur,** *Faith Works*, 23.
3 **William Webster,** "Lordship Salvation: Biblical or Heretical?", available at Christian Resources: christiantruth.com/articles/lordshipsalvation.html; accessed November 2010.
4 **R. C. Sproul,** *Faith Alone* (Grand Rapids: Baker, 1995), 168.
5 *Mono* means "alone." *Erg* is the root for the word from which we get "works" or "working." God alone works in salvation. People respond with faith, but they respond because of God's working in their lives. In other words, faith is the result of salvation, not the cause. The cause of salvation is the tender mercies and sovereign grace of God.
6 **D. M. Lloyd-Jones,** *Darkness and Light: An Exposition of Ephesians 4:17–5:17* (Grand Rapids: Baker, 1982), 85.
7 **John H. Gerstner,** *The Epistle to the Ephesians* (Grand Rapids: Baker, 1958), 60.

8 **Bruce Hurt,** "Ephesians 4:17–19, Commentary," at Precept Austin: preceptaustin.org. Accessed November 2010.

9 **Leon Morris,** *Expository Reflections on the Letter to the Ephesians* (Grand Rapids: Baker, 1994), 139.

10 **Peter T. O'Brien,** *The Letter to the Ephesians* (Grand Rapids: Eerdmans, 1999), 324.

11 **James Montgomery Boice,** *Ephesians* (Grand Rapids: Baker, 1997), 160.

12 **A. Skevington Wood,** "Ephesians," in *Expositor's Bible Commentary*, vol. 11 (Grand Rapids: Zondervan, 1978), 62.

13 **Charles Hodge,** *Ephesians* (Wheaton, IL: Crossway, 1994), 153.

14 **Zane Hodges,** *Absolutely Free: A Biblical Reply to Lordship Salvation* (Grand Rapids: Zondervan, 1989), 50.

15 **J. Armitage Robinson,** *St. Paul's Epistle to the Ephesians* (London: MacMillan, 1922), 107.

16 **F. F. Bruce,** *Ephesians* (London: Revell, 1961), 93.

17 Interestingly, the Latin word for "shudder" is *horreo*, the basis for our word "horror."

18 **Hodges,** *Absolutely Free*, 146.

19 **MacArthur,** *Faith Works*, 33.

20 *Westminster Larger Catechism*, Q. 76; quoted under "Historic Church Documents" at Center for Reformed Theology and Apologetics: reformed.org. Accessed January 2011.

21 Quoted by **J. C. Ryle,** *Holiness* (Moscow, ID: Charles Nolan, 2001), 51.

22 **A. W. Tozer,** *I Call It Heresy!* Quoted under "Free Resources" at The Body of Christ: theboc.com. Accessed January 2011.

Chapter 6

Preaching: Speaking for the King

T his chapter is designed to help both pastors and laypeople to properly assess preaching and to understand what it means to "herald," or to speak, for the King. I will expand on six historical facts about heralds that directly apply to New Testament pastors and preachers. First, however, we need to ground ourselves in the sad truth that heralding the good news of our King is not tolerated by society today.

A 2008 edition of *World Magazine* reported,

Oxford University Press editors culled a number of religious and historical words from the latest edition of its *Junior Dictionary* in a move aimed at reflecting Britain's modern, multicultural, and multi-faith society. Words that got the boot included *bishop, coronation, empire, monarch, nun,* and *sin,* while new additions included *blog, broadband, celebrity, MP3 player,* and *voicemail.* Company spokeswoman Vineeta Gupta defended the company's decision, saying the size of the dictionary ("little hands must be able to handle it") limits how many words are included.[1]

Surely it will be only a matter of time before the word "preach" is banished as well. People associate preaching with moralizing, which they believe is totally unacceptable in today's secular culture. But what is truly astonishing is that even evangelicals have a hard time saying "preach" or "preacher." Instead of "my pastor preaches," people are more inclined to say, more smoothly, "my pastor talks" or "my pastor shares." Why is that? Is there anything inherently wrong with preaching? To the modern listener, the answer is "yes." Preaching does not seem to sell well with our modern, consumerist mentalities, but talks that are "relational," "empathetic," and "sensitive" fill the sanctuaries. Could this be due to the feminization of the pulpit?[2]

If we had a time machine, a useful question to ask it would be, "What did a king's herald do in the days of the Old and New Testaments?" The answer would help twenty-first-century folk understand the role of a biblical herald. With so much time having elapsed, changes are sure to have occurred, so smart Bible students force themselves to study, with proper hermeneutics, what the word "herald" meant in a land far, far away. G. P. Hugenberger, in the *International Standard Bible Encyclopedia*, gives a marvelous description of "herald," saying,

In its broadest and most general (though not the most common) use, *kerysso* describes the making of a loud, attention-getting noise or of a public oral announcement; hence it can simply be translated "proclaim." Far more common is the narrower use of *kerysso* to refer specifically to the proclaiming of a *keryx* ("herald" or "preacher"), i.e., one who speaks as a representative of another ... Typically, however, the party represented was the king himself ... Acting in his official capacity as an envoy of the king, and so bearing the official insignia of the king, the *keryx* was granted the inviolable status of the king he represented. To reject him was to reject the king who commissioned him; to harm him was to harm the king and, worse, to incur the wrath of the gods ... In contrast to the ambassador (*presbys*), who had the authority to engage in negotiations without explicit instructions, the *keryx* was required simply to deliver any message exactly as it was given to him and to return at once ... The tenth-century AD Greek lexicographer Suidas said, "a herald [*keryx*] is in time of war what an ambassador [*presbys*] is in peace." Suidas was referring to the Greek practice of sending a *keryx* into enemy territory ahead of an advancing army to warn the enemy of certain destruction unless they accepted the proffered terms of peace. In this situation the *keryx* was empowered either to accept surrender on behalf of his king or to declare war if those terms were rejected.[3]

There has scarcely been a better paragraph written on the subject and background of heralds than the above. Hugenberger is so thorough and accurate that I have used his description of a herald to form the outline of this chapter. The six truths about preachers today that are examined in this chapter find their origin in Hugenberger's research. Here I have used Hugenberger's work as a starting point for my discussion and then fleshed out his outline with more biblical data.

The King of Kings' Herald Must Proclaim, Not "Share"

Like heralds who represented human kings in times past, Bible preachers, who serve the King of kings, must proclaim, and do so forcefully. Public announcements should never be whispered. The King's message should not be delivered with a whimper. Preachers must cry out with passion, enthusiasm, and dogmatism. A. W. Pink uses the verb "thundered" when he discusses preaching, saying, "From every pulpit in the land it needs to be thundered forth that God still lives, that God still observes, that God still reigns."[4] You can feel the strength and courage exuded by biblical preaching.

It is God who must determine the actions and attitudes of the Bible preacher, not the audience, the congregation, or the secular media. Today, the work of many pastors has morphed into something other than their original, biblical job description. They unwisely prioritize their identification with their congregations above the office and responsibility of the herald. Instead of loudly proclaiming, they share, stroke, give pep talks, or act as life coaches. Do any of these descriptions remotely resemble an old-fashioned town crier who bellowed, "Hear ye, hear ye"? Public announcements are just that: they are "public" and they are "announcements." Preaching is neither private, nor is it filled with speech that is only "warm and fuzzy." Preaching tells forth a message from the King, and it speaks to people with conviction, authority, and clarity.

Just as ancient Near Eastern kings needed to disseminate their mandates and edicts throughout their kingdom, so God the King broadcasts His Word through the world via New Testament heralds. If He wished to do so, God could obviously write His Word in the sky or drop DVDs out of the clouds, but He has purposely chosen to use pastors and elders to spread His thoughts and commands by authoritative proclamation.

Kings in times past used heralds to declare, among other things, increased taxes, military duties, required attendance before themselves, arrangements for sporting tournaments, and mandates to find themselves wives from within their realms. The herald could not negotiate as an ambassador would; he would simply say, "Thus says the king." The herald had no leeway to cut, paste, alter, amend, subtract from, add to, or change the message in any way, shape, or form. Culture did not determine the mandate from the earthly king. So why are preachers swayed by those to whom they are sent to preach, instead of being compelled to honor the One who has sent them to preach? Did heralds in the past need to be more relational and less direct? Were ancient heralds required to be open to discussion and to dialogue with their hearers? The answer to these questions is an unequivocal "no!"

Ancient heralds were most certainly put in tough spots through their kings' messages. A king could be cruel, wicked, and vile, but would still have the military power and authority to unjustly exact anything from his people—yet the herald was to be faithful in delivering the king's message. Christian pastors should rejoice in the fact that they have been given a perfect and holy message, one filled with loving-kindness and righteousness—so they should proclaim it boldly.

Preaching like a herald is nonnegotiable for every pastor. To share instead of to preach is to disobey God and His Word. Frankly, it is a gross sin. Using courtroom language, Paul declares in 2 Timothy 4:1–2, "I solemnly charge you in the presence of God and of Christ Jesus, who is to judge the living and the dead, and by His appearing and His kingdom, preach the word; be ready in season and out of season; reprove, rebuke, exhort, with great patience and instruction."

The theological main point is "Preach the Word." The verb is an aorist imperative, which functions like a command with an exclamation point. Preachers must preach. They have great authority, not in and of themselves, but because they have been sent by Another. One lexicon describes Paul's word for "preach" as "announce, publicly proclaim … make known extensively … in a religious sense, denoting proclamation of a sacred message."[5] You don't find the idea of "the King suggests" here. Pleading with a "pretty-please-with-sugar-on-top" mentality is not the language of a herald of the King! Monarchs give authoritative notices. The message is to be declared in such a way that people can understand it and are compelled to obey it as something that has moral and eternal obligations. In the Bible, the word translated "preach" signifies an assertive declaration, "always with a suggestion of formality, gravity, and an authority which must be listened to and obeyed."[6]

One-way communication, although despised today as prideful and condescending, is the biblical model. Preachers should function like town criers in medieval England; these were the chief means of news communication with the people of the town, since many people could not read or write. Royal proclamations, local bylaws, announcements of market days, adverts, even sales of loaves of sugar: all were proclaimed by bellmen or criers throughout the centuries. A faithful pastor verbally "posts a notice" to the doorpost of the congregation's mind.[7]

Pastors should never be critiqued on the basis of perceived warmth, kind delivery, or whether they preach down to the people. Only God's preacher scorecard matters, and He demands doctrinal fidelity, biblical precision, and a passionate obsession for God's honor and glory to be exalted through heralding.

If you are a pastor, do you herald? If you are a member of a local church, does your pastor proclaim?

The King of Kings' Herald Represents the Only Way to Hear from the King

Since God has ordained the preaching of the gospel and of His Word as the way people understand Him today (compared with God speaking directly to Moses, directly to the Son at His baptism, or directly to prophets like Elijah who spoke for God), heralds cannot compromise their message or their methods; otherwise how else could God be heard?

Hebrews 1:1–2 says, "God, after He spoke long ago to the fathers in the prophets in many portions and in many ways, in these last days has spoken to us in His Son." The English translation of the Greek loses the original alliteration; these verses contain five Greek words that all begin with the "p" sound, which give a rolling, melodic, and soothing feel.[8] This is in stark contrast to the opening words of this epistle, words whose sound is more akin to that of a starting gun at a track meet. There is no formal greeting or address. The writer of Hebrews offers nothing that might make the readers deviate from the idea that Jesus Christ is superior to all others. Good wishes and the writer's name would hinder the author diving immediately into his great theme, Jesus Christ. As in Genesis 1:1, the writer, with no attempt to apologetically verify God's existence, explodes with a word that he will use sixty-eight times in the letter, once every seventy-three words: "God."

In earlier days, God spoke directly to forefathers like Abraham, Isaac, and Jacob. God spoke to and through prophets, from Moses to Malachi. Bit by bit, here and there, God spoke "in many portions" and "in many ways," like the Urim and Thummim, and through dreams, visions, direct speaking, still small voices, signs, and natural events. While God used to speak in part and piecemeal (there is nothing wrong with this fragmentary revelation), in Jesus Christ, God spoke fully and completely. In Jesus Christ and His apostolic messengers, God was delivering a superior revelation. Scholar Bruce is helpful as he explains, "Priest and prophet, sage and singer were in their several ways His spokesmen; yet all the successive acts and varying modes of revelation in the ages before Christ came did not add up to the fullness of what God wanted to say."[9] When Jesus spoke, it was both superior and final. God has spoken with finality and completeness in Jesus Christ. Nothing else need be said or declared. New or additional revelation is not necessary. Thankfully, God did not remain mute like some silly wooden idol. God, in these last Messianic days, spoke to us in His Son.

A recent liberal church advertising campaign championed the unbiblical slogan "God is still speaking." The meaning was not that God still communicates through His Word (which is absolutely true); rather, the churches wanted to convey that God is still giving revelation today (which is absolutely false). In other words, this catchphrase attempts to state that the canon of Scripture is still open and that God is still adding to His Word. At best, the catchphrase is ignorant, but it still impinges upon the glory of Jesus Christ, God's Son. Why? Because in these last days, God has spoken definitively and completely in His Son and His apostolic messengers. The book of Hebrews explains that God spoke to us "in His Son." The Greek has no definite article, which puts the stress upon the nature or the quality of the Son. The prophets were wonderful, but they were not God's Son. Prophets obeyed as finite and fallen creatures, but God spoke, with finality, in the One who is His Son! The woman at the well knew that the Messiah would speak in this fashion, saying to Jesus, "I know that Messiah is coming (He who is called Christ); when that One comes, He will declare all things to us" (John 4:25).

My point is this: since God does not speak to people today in dreams, still small voices, or in any other format, it is imperative that God speak through His Word and through His ordained method, namely, preaching.

Paul, using the same root word for "preacher" that he uses for "preach" in 2 Timothy 4:2, asks, "How then will they call on Him in whom they have not believed? How will they believe in Him whom they have not heard? And how will they hear without a preacher?" (Rom. 10:14). If God still spoke in visions and dreams today, Bible preaching would not be as important. If God communicated in a variety of methods, preaching would be just one of a pastor's many important tasks. But since the Word is the only way God speaks today, the Bible must be preached. Paul, in Romans, discloses the vital nature of preaching: "faith comes from hearing, and hearing by the word of Christ" (Rom. 10:17). Therefore, if preaching the good news of Jesus Christ becomes as extinct as the Tyrannosaurus rex, then, humanly speaking, God's communication to us (the gospel) will be hindered. There are no other options and no plan "B." All the eggs of the gospel are in one basket.

The King of Kings' Herald Must Bear the Official Insignia of God

An earthly king's herald had to have the right garb and livery. He needed to be recognized by the people in the kingdom as a "herald." Many times the herald bore official insignia from the king that were easily recognizable as royal. Since there was only one monarch, and there were many people in the kingdom, there were many heralds who were simultaneously dispatched, fully equipped with the king's message, fully authorized, and in full regal apparel. Whether or not the herald had a royal coat of arms or special tabards, each king would make certain that his heralds were recognizable.

In Christ's kingdom, the insignia of the King's herald are not found in clothing but in the cloak of godliness. The only livery or attire for the New Testament herald is found in 1 Timothy 3 and Titus 1. These chapters list qualifications for elders and generally describe an elder's internal, spiritual characteristics as given by God. The qualifications for the herald (New Testament elder) are the issue, not the herald's facial features, mannerisms, or pitch or tone of voice. How do we recognize a herald today? By his papers? Credentials? Letters of reference? Backwards collars? No. Listen to Paul's requirements for the elder, "God's insignia," that will make every herald immediately recognizable, especially in today's worldly and sinful culture:

An overseer, then, must be above reproach, the husband of one wife, temperate, prudent, respectable, hospitable, able to teach, not addicted to wine or pugnacious, but gentle, peaceable, free from the love of money. He must be one who manages his own household well, keeping his children under control with all dignity (but if a man does not know how to manage his own household, how will he take care of the church of God?), and not a new convert, so that he will not become conceited and fall into the condemnation incurred by the devil. And he must have a good reputation with those outside the church, so that he will not fall into reproach and the snare of the devil.

(1 Tim. 3:2–7)

For this reason I left you in Crete, that you would set in order what remains and appoint elders in every city as I directed you, namely, if any man is above reproach, the husband of one wife, having children who believe, not accused of dissipation or rebellion. For the overseer must be above reproach as God's steward, not self-willed, not quick-tempered, not addicted to wine, not pugnacious, not fond of sordid gain, but hospitable, loving what is good, sensible, just, devout, self-controlled, holding fast the faithful word which is in accordance with the teaching, so that he will be able both to exhort in sound doctrine and to refute those who contradict.   (Titus 1:5–9)

Every herald of God the King comes equipped, by God himself, with insignia or a spiritual pedigree that reflects Paul's requirements in the pastoral epistles. One particular characteristic of a biblically qualified elder is faithfulness. Heralds must be faithful to their sender, the king, or, in this case, the King. Heralds must precisely and accurately deliver the King's message so that all listening will understand the original intentions of the King.

Unfaithfulness by heralds of earthly kings sometimes resulted in death. One historical account describes Sir William Stewart, Lord Lyon King of Arms in 1567. He "only held office for 6 months after which he was arrested under charges of conspiring to kill the Regent via sorcery and necromancy, and for which he was put to death in August 1569."[10] Thankfully, God rarely executes unfaithful elders and heralds today. So many modern-day preachers have supped with modernity and have attempted to be popular with their people, but heralds must be "popular" with their King, not necessarily with their audiences. It is practically impossible to be faithful to the Lord and His Word and to simultaneously desire human applause and popularity. The apostle Paul understood the popularity tension, so he told Timothy to preach the Word and "be ready in season and out of season" (2 Tim. 4:2). Faithfulness to God's call must show itself by preaching in such a way as to "never lose your sense of urgency" (Phillips Translation) because of the King, not because of the people in the kingdom. Like a soldier who is always on his guard and who stays at his post or station, heralds are never off duty, and they must never forget who gave them their orders.

The King of Kings' Herald Must Be Obeyed

Assuming that the herald delivered the king's decree accurately, the people were required to fully obey the herald's instructions. The king would certainly punish all who indirectly rejected him by directly rebuffing his herald. Why? Because the herald was "a messenger vested with ... authority, who conveyed the official messages of kings, magistrates, princes, military commanders, or who gave a public summons or demand, and performed various other duties."[11] To reject the message of the herald was to reject the king; conversely, to accept the herald's commands was to obey the king. The people either accepted the message of the herald or they rejected it. To simply ignore the message was to reject the king.

How does this relate to a New Testament preacher? The herald of the Divine Monarch must preach with an authoritative boldness that expects obedience. After all, it is not his message that he selfishly wants people to comply with, but God's holy law. The contemporary enthrallment of preaching "as one without authority"[12] is not biblical. Al Mohler recognizes authoritative preaching: "If we have no authoritative message, why preach?"[13] The same could be said for the human herald of a temporal king: "If there is no message to be obeyed, why herald?" But the Bible is clear: the King's herald has the authority to "reprove, rebuke, [and] exhort" (2 Tim. 4:2). To "reprove" means to inform the congregation of the definition of sin. To "rebuke" attaches ownership to the sin that the herald just reproved. It convicts the offender by attaching individual culpability. To "exhort" means to come alongside and encourage people to obey.

The King of Kings' Herald Must Not Negotiate

For most of us, negotiation has its place and time, but it was and is never appropriate for a herald. To negotiate was not in the herald's job description or modus operandi. Ambassadors may be schooled in smooth and persuasive speech and the art of negotiation, but a herald's responsibility was simply to deliver the communication from the king and to do it without conciliation. Heralds could not negotiate. "Precise" and "exact" were the calling cards for the method of the herald's proclamation. We find no compromise language in Cotton Mather's words: "The great design and intention of the office of a Christian preacher is to restore the throne and dominion of God in the souls of men."[14] Heralds did not concede, compromise, or sit at the bargaining table. They simply stated the facts and never met anyone halfway.

Paul started 2 Timothy 4 with somber, courtroom language. The seriousness of his you-are-under-oath language is nearly unrivaled in Holy Writ (it is found also in 1 Tim. 5:21 and 2 Tim. 2:14). Paul said, "I solemnly charge you in the presence of God and of Christ Jesus, who is to judge the living and the dead, and by His appearing and His kingdom: preach the word" (2 Tim. 4:1). The Greek word translated "charge" is defined as follows:

To make a solemn declaration about the truth of something, testify of, bear witness to (orig. under oath) ... to exhort with authority in matters of extraordinary importance, freq. w. ref. to higher powers and/or suggestion of peril, solemnly urge, exhort, warn ... to state something in such a way that the auditor is to be impressed with its seriousness.[15]

If you are a preacher, God, the judging God who will judge you, has given you strict orders to preach. Paul on his "deathbed" was concerned that Timothy preach to others before an audience of the Trinity. Matthew Henry said that "the eye of God and Jesus Christ was upon him."[16]

Heralds pushed the consciences of their listeners so that they were forced to listen and obey. The call to obey the herald can be seen in several biblical examples. Not one of them gives any inkling of negotiation language.

- An angel: "And I saw a strong angel proclaiming with a loud voice, 'Who is worthy to open the book and to break its seals?'" (Rev. 5:2).
- A healed man: "And he went away and began to proclaim in Decapolis what great things Jesus had done for him; and everyone was amazed" (Mark 5:20).
- Nebuchadnezzar's herald: "Then the herald loudly proclaimed: 'To you the command is given, O peoples, nations and men of every language, that at the moment you hear the sound of the horn, flute, lyre, trigon, psaltery, bagpipe and all kinds of music, you are to fall down and worship the golden image that Nebuchadnezzar the king has set up'" (Dan. 3:4–5).
- God instructing Jonah to herald: "Arise, go to Nineveh the great city and cry against it, for their wickedness has come up before Me" (Jonah 1:2); "Arise, go to Nineveh the great city and proclaim to it the proclamation which I am going to tell you" (Jonah 3:2).[17]
- John the Baptist: "He said, 'I am a voice of one crying in the wilderness, "Make straight the way of the Lord," as Isaiah the prophet said'" (John 1:23).

Heralds preached for a white-flag verdict! Does your pastor herald? Do you want him to herald?

The King of Kings' Herald Must Proclaim Clemency to Those Who Surrender and Doom to Those Who Resist

The herald was often sent into hostile enemy territory, and he was required to warn the opposing military. Again, with no possibility of offering any middle ground, the king's terms were announced and made known. The terms were simple and well understood by both parties: surrender and receive mercy, or persist in aggression and have a full-scale war, which would most likely lead to the enemy's demise. This idea can be seen in

Deuteronomy 20:10: "When you approach a city to fight against it, you shall offer it terms of peace." If they accepted the offer, there was peace. If they rejected the offer, war was declared.

In a similar fashion today, the King's heralds offer divine leniency for those willing to repent and "lay down their arms." His herald also says, "If you continue in your willing rebellion, prepare to meet your eternal doom." Peace or destruction? Life or death? Heaven or hell?

Tracing the background of the meaning of the word "herald" yields insight into the message of clemency:

In the ancient world a "herald" was the person who by order of a superior made a loud, public announcement. Thus, in public games it was his function to announce the name and country of each competitor, and also the name, country, and father of the victor … The picture is beautiful. It is not the rebellious city which sends out an ambassador to sue for peace-terms, but the offended King of kings who sends his own herald to proclaim peace through a ransom, and that ransom: the blood of his own dear Son![18]

What about you? Have you surrendered, or will you persist in your insurgency?

Summary

I wonder what the next report by *World Magazine* will include. Let's pray that it is a story about how Oxford University Press does not plan to remove the words "herald" or "preach" from various dictionaries. Until then, if you are a preacher, it will be enough if you love preaching as the King loves preaching and as the King loves His preachers. If you are a layperson, it is enough to love preaching and the One who ordained preaching.

Hymn

Praise, my soul, the King of Heaven;
To His feet thy tribute bring.
Ransomed, healed, restored, forgiven,
Evermore His praises sing:
Alleluia! Alleluia!
Praise the everlasting King.

Praise Him for His grace and favor
To our fathers in distress.
Praise Him still the same as ever,
Slow to chide, and swift to bless.
Alleluia! Alleluia!
Glorious in His faithfulness.

Father-like He tends and spares us;
Well our feeble frame He knows.
In His hands He gently bears us,
Rescues us from all our foes.
Alleluia! Alleluia!
Widely yet His mercy flows.

Frail as summer's flower we flourish,
Blows the wind and it is gone;
But while mortals rise and perish
Our God lives unchanging on,
Praise Him, Praise Him, Hallelujah
Praise the High Eternal One!

Angels, help us to adore Him;
Ye behold Him face to face;
Sun and moon, bow down before Him,
Dwellers all in time and space.
Alleluia! Alleluia!
Praise with us the God of grace.   (Henry F. Lyte, 1834)

Study Questions

1. What are the essentials of expository preaching?
2. In what specific ways should you pray for your pastor(s)?
3. Do you consider your pastor to be "the preacher"? If so, what is the main function of a preacher?
4. List five duties of a pastor. What should be at the top of the list as the most important? Why?

5. What are the common mistakes made by pastoral search committees that this chapter should correct?

6. Is there any validity to having the pulpit in the center of the church sanctuary? What is conveyed to the congregation when there is no pulpit found in the building at all?

Notes

1 "The Buzz," in *World Magazine*, 23/26 (December 27, 2008), n.p.

2 I am not against femininity in any way, shape, or form; I simply appreciate femininity in women and not in men. The pulpit is the place for the man of God to boldly assert the truths of God's Word, without compromise, without dialogue, and with the full authority given to the preacher by God Himself. Understanding God as King will help all those seeking biblical clarity on this issue today.

3 **G. P. Hugenberger,** "Preach," in **Geoffrey W. Bromiley** (ed.), *The International Standard Bible Encyclopedia* (Grand Rapids: Eerdmans, 1986), 942.

4 **A. W. Pink,** *The Sovereignty of God* (Grand Rapids: Baker, 1984), 8.

5 "κηρύσσω" in **Timothy Friberg, Barbara Friberg,** and **Neva F. Miller,** *Analytical Lexicon to the Greek New Testament* (Baker's Greek New Testament Library; Grand Rapids, MI: Baker, 2000; BibleWorks, v. 8.).

6 "κηρύσσω" in **Joseph Henry Thayer,** *A Greek–English Lexicon of the New Testament* (Abridged and Revised Thayer Lexicon) (Ontario: Online Bible Foundation and Woodside Fellowship of Ontario, 1988–1997).

7 "A little-known fact is that the term 'Posting A Notice' actually comes from the act of the Town Crier, who, having read his message to the Townspeople, would attach it to the doorpost of the local Inn or Tavern"; from "History of Town Crying," Pembroke Ontario Tourism, at: pembrokeontario.com/content/living_here/town_crier.html; accessed November 2010.

8 Even if you cannot read Greek, notice the bold sections of Hebrews 1:1: **Πολυμερῶς** καὶ **πολυτρόπως πάλαι** ὁ θεὸς λαλήσας τοῖς **πατράσιν** ἐν τοῖς **προφήταις**.

9 **F. F. Bruce,** *The Epistle to the Hebrews* (NICNT; Grand Rapids: Eerdmans, 1990), 3.

10 **Leslie A. Schweitzer,** "Heralds in History in the Middle Ages and Renaissance," July 2002, at: heraldry.sca.org/laurel/heralds_history.html.

11 κηρύσσω in *Thayer's Lexicon*, *Bible Works* (CD-ROM; Norfolk: BibleWorks LLC, 1992–2003).

12 **Fred B. Craddock,** *As One Without Authority* (St. Louis: Chalice Press, 2001).

13 Al Mohler, "Expository Preaching and the Recovery of Christian Worship (Part Three)," August 11, 2005, at albertmohler.com.

14 Quoted in **John Piper,** *The Supremacy of God in Preaching* (Grand Rapids: Baker, 1993), 22.

15 Διαμαρτύρομαί in **Walter Bauer, William F. Arndt, F. Wilbur Gingrich,** and **F. W. Danker,** *A Greek–English Lexicon of the New Testament and Other Early Christian Literature* (Chicago: University of Chicago Press, 1957). Wallace says this is a "constative aorist, signifying 'a solemn or categorical command.' The stress is not 'begin an action,' nor 'continue to act.' Rather, the stress is on the solemnity and urgency of the action" (Διαμαρτύρομαί in **Daniel Wallace,** *Greek Grammar Beyond the Basics: An Exegetical Syntax of the New Testament* [BibleWorks LLC, 1996]).

16 Matthew Henry, notes on 2 Timothy 4:1, in *Matthew Henry's Commentary* (public domain).

17 In the Septuagint, "proclaim" in Jonah 3:2 comes from the exact same Greek word that is used in 2 Timothy 4:2.

18 William Hendriksen, *New Testament Commentary: Exposition of I and II Thessalonians, Timothy and Titus* (Grand Rapids: Baker, 1979), 89.

When the King Talks, We Should Listen

"When E. F. Hutton talks, people listen." If we will stop to listen to the advice of an investment firm, how much more should we heed the words of our Creator and King! Like the previous chapter, this chapter deals with God's Word being heralded by a preacher, but it focuses on the person hearing the proclamation. The premise of this chapter is that if we remember that God the King sent us our preachers/heralds, it will radically alter the way we listen to our frail, fallen pastors preach his sermons.

Modern culture roars at the top of its voice, "Don't preach to me!" This mantra reveals the culture's hatred of preaching, especially biblical preaching. Contemporary definitions of preaching betray the pessimistic views of it, usually portraying a type of negative, moralizing message that encroaches on someone's personal and private life. One of the definitions of a preacher given by an online dictionary, for example, is "somebody giving advice on morals: somebody who gives advice on morality or behavior in an irritatingly tedious or overbearing way."[1] Sadly, it seems that true proclamation of the Bible is going the way of the dodo, with "participatory learning" or "nonlinear learning" becoming the preferred form of communication, even in churches. Many congregations want multiple voices to be heard (translation: congregants themselves want to speak), with time for questions, comments, and exploration replacing what they see as one preacher's voice monopolizing "the conversation."

How would the people in a real kingdom listen to the proclamation of their king's message? Would they listen indifferently, lackadaisically, lazily, disobediently, passively, or like couch potatoes? We all know that that would not be the case; if it were, the people would not live very long in their complacent listening.

As we listen to God the King's message, we should see past the preacher.

We do not need some kind of prop or movie clip during the sermon, and we should not mind the preacher addressing us with the second person imperative "you."

Even the world knows that listening is important. Thoreau said, "It takes two to speak the truth—one to speak, and another to hear."[2] Walt Whitman echoed this, saying, "To have great poets, you must have great audiences too,"[3] and Boardman said, "The world is dying for want, not of good preaching, but of good hearing."[4] Communication breakdown regularly occurs within a society made up of inept listeners who tend to sit with their arms folded and an "impress-me" attitude.

The importance of listening to God is underscored throughout the Bible. The phrase "hear the Word of the LORD" is found twenty-eight times in the NASB. The words "listen" and "hear" are also found over three hundred times. Additional emphasis is shown by phrases such as "incline your ear" and "give attention." You will remember the common refrain, "Today if you hear his voice" (Heb. 3:7, 15; 4:7) and Jesus' words to the seven churches in Revelation: "He who has an ear, let him hear what the Spirit says to the churches" (Rev. 2:7, 11, 17, 29; 3:6, 13, 22). There is no superficial listening implied in these verses.

The following quote attributed to Spurgeon accurately summarizes the point of this chapter: "There is no worship of God that is better than the hearing of a sermon." For most worship services, listening to the sermon is the largest portion of worship. True "worship" is not only the music and singing, but also includes giving, praying, Scripture reading, baptisms, celebrating the Lord's Supper, and preaching. Since this is true, let us be determined to listen better, in a more worshipful manner. To help us in this Herculean task, let's look at four truths from James 1 that will assist us in listening to the King's message properly. We can give glory to God as we listen to a sermon, especially when we remember that the King is addressing us! Imagine the glorification of God through the hearing of a sermon!

Come to the Worship Service with an Attitude of Anticipation and Eagerness to Hear the King's Word

What is your attitude to the worship service as you drive to church? Are you bored, excited, or dutiful? James says, "This you know, my beloved brethren. But everyone must be quick to hear, slow to speak and slow to anger; for the anger of man does not achieve the righteousness of God" (James 1:19–20). "This you know" links these verses to what preceded them. James 1:18 states, "In the exercise of His will He brought us forth by the word of truth, so that we would be a kind of first fruits among His creatures." The readers had just been taught that God monergistically regenerated them by the Word and now, with that regeneration in view, James states the words of verses 19 and 20. James commanded, "Everyone must be" (using a continual command verb form) quick to listen, slow to speak, and slow to anger. The context is not about listening to just anyone, but about hearing the Word of God. Doerksen says, "The mention of regeneration through the Word fittingly introduces new thoughts concerning the Word. As the Word produces regeneration, so it is also a means of sanctification. After writing of the experience of the new birth, James continues with the challenge to live out the new life by means of the Word."[5]

We are to listen to the Word and respond to it properly, namely, with obedience. Our hearts need to be attentive and set to pursue the Word as it is proclaimed. This was especially important when people did not possess their own copies of the entire Bible. We take it for granted that we have multiple Bibles in our possession, but many in the world still do not have one copy.

Is your attitude like that of Jeremiah: "Your words were found and I ate them, and Your words became for me a joy and the delight of my heart; for I have been called by Your name, O LORD God of hosts" (Jer. 15:16)? Do you love hearing the Word more than eating food, as Job did: "I have not departed from the command of His lips; I have treasured the words of His mouth more than my necessary food" (Job 23:12)? Do you cherish God's Word more than sleep, like the psalmist: "My eyes anticipate the night, that I may meditate on Your word" (Ps. 119:148)? Again like the psalmist, do you treasure the Word more than riches: "I love Your commandments above gold, yes, above fine gold" (Ps. 119:127)? Is your attitude like that of Samuel when he said, "Speak, for Your servant is listening" (1 Sam. 3:10)? Are you like a newborn babe who longs "for the pure milk of the word"

(1 Peter 2:2)? Babies desire, crave, hanker, hunger, and ache for milk all day, every day.

The great David Livingstone, when he

started his trek across Africa … had 73 books in 3 packs, weighing 180 pounds. After the party had gone 300 miles, Livingstone was obliged to throw away some of the books because of the fatigue of those carrying his baggage. As he continued on his journey his library grew less and less, until he had but one book left—his Bible.[6]

Livingstone desired God's Word above all else! What about you? Are you quick to hear from the television, the Internet, *Newsweek*, the radio, and your favorite podcast? Do any of these things relate to eternity? Stott said that, when you listen to preaching, you are hearing about "the sinner's plight under the judgment of God, the saving action of God through the death and resurrection of Christ, and the summons to repent and believe. How can you treat such themes with cold indifference?"[7]

My favorite example of eager listening is a well-known but powerful story:

A man in Kansas City was severely injured in an explosion. Evangelist Robert L. Sumner tells about him in his book *The Wonders of the Word of God*. The victim's face was badly disfigured, and he lost his eyesight as well as both hands. He was just a new Christian, and one of his greatest disappointments was that he could no longer read the Bible. Then he heard about a lady in England who read Braille with her lips. Hoping to do the same, he sent for some books of the Bible in Braille. Much to his dismay, however, he discovered that the nerve endings in his lips had been destroyed by the explosion. One day, as he brought one of the Braille pages to his lips, his tongue happened to touch a few of the raised characters and he could feel them. Like a flash he thought, I can read the Bible using my tongue. At the time Robert Sumner wrote his book, the man had "read" through the entire Bible four times.[8]

Don't Get Angry at the Preacher when the King's Word Convicts You

Since I have never been martyred or put in jail for preaching, I can't complain very loudly about getting persecuted when I preach, but I have had people get really, really mad at my preaching. The funniest retort was given to me as I preached on the exclusivity of Jesus Christ at a Jewish rest home. Toward the end of my message a lady yelled, "Beans!" to signify her disgust at my proclamation that Jesus is the only Messiah. Another time a Roman Catholic family forbade their college student from attending the church I pastor because of my biblical discussion of Mary, the mother of Jesus. And, of course, I have received my share of "hate mail." What should our response be to biblical preaching that stings? "This you know, my beloved brethren. But everyone must be quick to hear, slow to speak and slow to anger; for the anger of man does not achieve the righteousness of God" (James 1:19–20).

Seething outbursts at the Bible's deep and penetrating conviction have no place in the congregation's attitude. Submission, not resentment or anger, is the proper response to the preaching of the Word, for "anger resides in the bosom of fools" (Eccles. 7:9). James warns his readers because man's anger at God's Word does not yield God's pleasure; rather, it raises His wrath. James obviously knew that the desire of a true Christian is for righteousness. Have you ever become mad at a Bible preacher because he taught you something out of the Bible that you had never thought of before, or because he pressed a truth to your conscience too vigorously? A better attitude would be to say, "God, please show me my sins, transgressions, and faults, so that I can repent and receive your parental forgiveness. Help me to see my sins in light of Your Son's death at Calvary!"

Come to Hear a Sermon from the King with a Prepared Heart and Soul

When people have travel plans or an exciting day planned, they will often get everything ready the night before the "big day." Clothes will be neatly set out, golf clubs will be shined, and luggage will be packed, as such preparation will surely pay off and guarantee a more successful adventure. I ask with Spurgeon,

We are told men ought not to preach without preparation. Granted. But, we add, men ought not to hear without preparation. Which, do you think, needs the most preparation, the sower or the ground? I would have the sower come with clean hands, but I would have the ground well plowed and harrowed, well turned over, and the clods broken before the seed comes in. It seems to me that there is more preparation needed by the ground than by the sower, more by the hearer than by the preacher.[9]

James gives every listener some prep work to accomplish with the help of the Holy Spirit: "Therefore, putting aside all filthiness and all that remains of wickedness, in humility receive the word implanted, which is able to save your souls" (James 1:21).

To receive the Word in a way that most glorifies the King, we need a righteous response. Just as we would quickly take off an outfit daubed with mud, so we must get rid of every vestige of moral filth in order that the Word might take root. Make a break with sin. How fast would you take off a coat that was on fire or clothes that had poison ivy all over them? James switches from clothing language ("putting aside") to an agricultural idiom ("receive the word implanted"). James would like his readers to receive the Word with open arms.

The following account does not necessarily exemplify the attitude the apostle James was describing, but it is illustrative of a man who thinks that the Bible is the solution to his problem and of his determination to "apply" the Bible:

He was one of the greatest rulers in African history and the creator of modern Ethiopia. Born in 1844, he was captured during an enemy raid and held prisoner for 10 years. Escaping, Menelik II declared himself head of the province of Shewa. He began conquering neighboring kingdoms and developed them into modern Ethiopia with himself as emperor. When Italy tried to take over Ethiopia Menekil's army met and crushed the Italians at the Battle of Aduwa. This victory, as well as his efforts to modernize Ethiopia (schools, telephones, railroads), made Menekil world-famous. The emperor had one little known eccentricity. Whenever he was feeling ill, he would eat a few pages of the Bible, insisting that this always restored his health. One day in December, 1913, recovering from a stroke and feeling extremely ill, he had the entire book of Kings torn from an Egyptian edition of the Bible, ate every page of it—and died.[10]

To receive the Word humbly and in meekness would certainly include the avoidance of critically judging the pastor and his preaching style. Spurgeon knew only too well that some people are prone to sit "over" the Word, not "under" it:

Preaching is often too much like a fiddler's playing. People come to see how it is done, and then they pass round the question, "What do you think of him?" Now, I do not care two straws what you think of me. But I do care a whole world what you think of Christ and of yourselves and of your future state.[11]

A much better attitude is to pray for your pastor and your reception of the Word. Pray for your pastor's protection, biblical fidelity, marriage and family, and time management and study time. You get the kind of sermons you pray for, so pray for your pastor! Prepare your mind with obedience and come with a desire to be more changed into the likeness of Jesus Christ.

Be Determined to Obey the King

Listening is becoming a lost art in our modern technological age. People have difficulty paying attention because of their ever-decreasing attention spans. Besides that, many today forget that the Bible, when it talks about "listening," means that we are to listen with a desire to obey. Biblical "listening" is far from a passive reception of the Word. You cannot honor the King by listening to His Word with the same attitude you have when listening to relaxing music. Listening to the Word requires work, involvement, and a mental readiness to act upon it. Deuteronomy 4:1 gives the sense of active listening: "Now, O Israel, listen to the statutes and the judgments which I am teaching you to perform, so that you may live and go in and take possession of the land which the LORD, the God of your fathers, is giving you."

James commands people not to neglect, reject, refuse, or shun the Word: "But prove yourselves doers of the word, and not merely hearers who delude themselves" (James 1:22). Instead of stressing one action ("do"), James wants the readers' whole lives to be characterized by "doing." We should not simply hear the Word, we should respond with regular obedience. The meaning is "continue to be doers of the Word until glory!" Habitually. Constantly. Like an occupation.

Fathers catch football passes from time to time with their sons in the backyard, but professional football players catch passes for a living. Make obedience a lifestyle. Think of obedience the way you think of your job. You'll understand it better if you consider the difference between the words "occasional" and "occupational." Commentator Johnstone knew the difference between "do" and "be doers," saying,

To be doers has a force of its own, distinct from that of the simple "to do" … [it] exhibits an habitual occupation … It sets before us as being real Christians persons who make the doing of the Word of God the *main* business of their lives, a business affecting, penetrating, pervading all other business and all pleasure; so that just as when you speak of an ordinary trade or profession, you say that a man is a teacher, a manufacturer, or the like, so speaking of character, those who know a Christian intimately should always be able to say of him, "He is a doer of the word of God!"[12]

If you are a Christian, you will be a doer of the Word. God's Word implores you to obey. The Bible is unlike any other book—it commands us to obey. Sheet music does not force anyone to play the piano, cookbooks do not beckon people to bake chocolate chip cookies, and your car engine manual does not force you to fix your distributor—but God's Word is living and active, and it divinely bellows, "Be doers of the Word!" God's Word appeals for you to respond. Do not ever say to your pastor, "That was a great sermon," because he might just respond with, "So what are you going to do about it?"

Tragically, the flip side of being a "doer" is being a "self-deceiver." Those who simply audit the Bible don't fool anyone but themselves. I have heard that the Scots had a slogan warning people who consumed sermons but never applied them: such people were "sermon tasters who never taste the grace of God." Run from such a grave miscalculation. The Greek word translated "delude" in James 1:22 is *paralogizomai*, and it denotes a deception by bogus or fake reasoning. Did you know that incredibly smart people can make unbelievably dumb decisions? Why? Because they are good at "reasoning" their bad choices in their own minds. Do not misjudge the gravity of obeying God's Word. No excuses are valid; they are all self-deception through erroneous reasoning. Preaching is not simply to be admired or to give you fodder for your mind, nor is its purpose to make you feel good; rather, it is a divine summons to be followed. The following Old Testament verses allow no room for auditing:

The secret things belong to the LORD our God, but the things revealed belong to us and to our sons forever, that we may observe all the words of this law.   (Deut. 29:29)

The conclusion, when all has been heard, is: fear God and keep his commandments, because this applies to every person.   (Eccles. 12:13)

Sermon listening with intent to obey is an act of worship. If you would attentively listen to the Queen of England or the President of the United States, how much more should you pay attention to the Word preached at your church? The right attitude to the preached Word is seen in Nehemiah 8:5: "Ezra opened the book in the sight of all the people for he was standing above all the people; and when he opened it, all the people stood up." They stood up to receive the Word with humility so that they might obey it. Tozer, with his usual way with words, makes us want to sprint away from disobedience:

There is an evil which I have seen under the sun ... It is the glaring disparity between theology and practice among professing Christians ... So wide is the gulf that separates theory from practice in the church that an inquiring stranger who chances upon both would scarcely dream that there was any relation between them. An intelligent observer of our human scene who heard the Sunday morning sermon and later watched the Sunday afternoon conduct of those who had heard it would conclude that he had been examining two distinct and contrary religions.[13]

The choice to listen to the King worshipfully is yours. It is your choice this Sunday. It is your choice every Sunday. I pray that you don't fall into the trap described in this little ditty, even if the preacher is particularly dry and boring:

I never see my preacher's eyes
However bright they shine—
For when he prays, he closes his,
And when he preaches, he closes mine![14]

Instead, may you, by God's grace, tremble at His Word, for He says, "My hand made all these things, thus all these things came into being ... But to this one I will look, to him who is humble and contrite of spirit, and who trembles at My word" (Isa. 66:2)!

Summary

The following two exhortations, one ancient and one new, urge you to listen to the King!

CHARLES SPURGEON: "BREAD FOR THE HUNGRY"

We should come to hear the Word, like baby birds in the nest—when the mother-bird comes with the worm, they are all stretching their necks to see which one shall get the food, for they are all hungry and want it.

And so should hearers be ready to get hold of the Word, not wanting that we should force it down their throats, but waiting there, opening their mouths wide that they may be filled, receiving the Word in the love of it, taking in the Word as the thirsty earth drinks in the rain of heaven. Hungry souls love the Word. Perhaps the "speaker" may not always put it as they may like to hear it, but as long as it is God's Word, it is enough for them. They are like people who are sitting at the reading of a will—the lawyer may have a squeaking voice, perhaps, or he mispronounces the words, but what does that matter? They are listening to see what is left to them. So is it with God's people. It is not the preacher, but the "preacher's God" that these hungry ones look to. Why, if you were very poor, and some benevolent neighbor should send you a loaf of bread by a man who had a club foot, you would not look at the foot, you would look at the bread. And so is it with the hearers of the Word—they know if they wait until they get a perfect preacher, they will get no preacher at all, but they are willing to take the man, imperfections and all, provided he brings the Master's bread. And though he be but a lad, and can bring but a few barley loaves and fishes, yet since the Master multiplies the provision, there is enough for all, and they feed to the full.[15]

JIM ELLIFF: "DULL PREACHERS"

"Dull preachers make the best martyrs," said Spurgeon. "They are so dry they burn well." Well said. My contention is that dullness in preaching is not so much in a scarcity of speaking ability of the preacher as it is in the dry-as-dust heart of the same. Ross Perot was not heard because he could speak like Charlton Heston, but because you at least knew that he believed and was exercised by what he believed enough to unload the burden. Dull hearts make dull preachers. But I must also say that dull ears can ruin the best of sermons. And dull ears are outgrowths of dull hearts also. There is nothing more devastating to a Sunday than putting both of them together. You might as well be living with Cain in the land of Nod. The preacher blows arid desert air on the people, and the people flap their eyelids shut, the dust of indifference circling up from their nodding heads. Ever been there?

Dull preachers and dull hearers infect each other. But live preaching and live listening are also contagious. I have noticed for some time that churches make the preachers and preachers make the churches. A sermon will catch on like hotcakes in the minds of the listeners when preached in a different church, while the same sermon sits like beef steak in the stomachs of the crew back home.

Let's make a pledge. Preachers, sharpen your hearts and you will get a better tongue; Church, sharpen your hearts and you will get better ears. Come ready, expectantly, with straight backs and clear eyes. Ask God for bright services, and do not fail to get whatever you need. Really pray about this. God is able to give you some morsel to feed on if you scratch for it. Then tell the pastor what you've gotten. Be specific.

Can you imagine what would happen if you got a group of the complainers together and all of you listened like you were hearing Jesus Himself? Your present pastor might die in the pulpit (which is the quick solution to your problem). He may not catch on the first week, but after a short while, he will be praying and studying and preaching like lives depended on it. Unless he is completely comatose, he will respond to that. After all, he got into this business to help people. If you are getting something, he will load on a little more. I have almost never seen a God-called preacher act any differently. They are like Pavlov's dog. Try it.[16]

Hymn

All glory, laud and honor,
To Thee, Redeemer, King,
To Whom the lips of children
Made sweet hosannas ring.

Thou art the King of Israel,
Thou David's royal Son,
Who in the Lord's Name comest,
The King and Blessèd One.

The company of angels
Are praising Thee on High,
And mortal men and all things
Created make reply.

The people of the Hebrews
With palms before Thee went;
Our prayer and praise and anthems
Before Thee we present.

To Thee, before Thy passion,
They sang their hymns of praise;
To Thee, now high exalted,
Our melody we raise.

Thou didst accept their praises;
Accept the prayers we bring,
Who in all good delightest,
Thou good and gracious King.

(Theodulph of Orleans, c.820; tr. by John M. Neale, 1851)

Study Questions

1. In what ways would Saturday night preparation (going to bed early, picking out the proper clothes, reading the passage for the sermon, etc.)

benefit believers in their Sunday morning worship? What could you do in preparation for Sunday morning worship?

2. What is the role of the father in helping his family concentrate while the pastor is delivering the sermon?

3. Does the concept taught in this chapter support the idea that the pinnacle of corporate worship is preaching (hearing from God)?

Notes

1 "Preacher," in *Encarta Online English Dictionary* (North American edn.): encarta.msn.com/encnet/features/dictionary/DictionaryResults.aspx?refid=1861737453. Accessed November 2010.

2 **Henry David Thoreau,** *A Week on the Concord and Merrimack Rivers* (Princeton, NJ: Princeton University Press, 2004), 218.

3 Cited in **Milton Hindus,** "On Whitman, Dickinson, and Readers," in *Walt Whitman Quarterly Review*, 1/2 (1983), 18; accessed from ir.uiowa.edu/cgi/viewcontent.cgi?article=1017&context=wwqr.

4 **George Dana Boardman,** cited at: thinkexist.com; accessed January 2011.

5 **Vernon Doerksen,** *James* (Everyman's Bible Commentary Series; Chicago: Moody Press, 2001), 39.

6 **Yvonne Schultz,** *Isaiah: From Darkness to Light* (Chicago: David C. Cook, 1989), 62.

7 **John R. W. Stott,** *The Message of 2 Timothy* (Grand Rapids: InterVarsity Press, 1999), 107.

8 "Read with Tongue," at: bible.org. Accessed November 2010.

9 **Charles Spurgeon,** cited by **Fred A. Malone,** "The Sovereignty of God and the Killen Massacre," in *The Founders Journal*, 7 (Winter 1992), 19. Available from founders.org/journal/fj07/fj07.pdf.

10 **Amy Wallace,** *The New Book of Lists: The Original Compendium of Curious Information* (New York: William Morrow, 2005), 484. While I am not advocating the literal consumption of the Bible, I am in full support of Christians devouring the Word—spiritually, that is—by reading and memorization.

11 **Charles Spurgeon,** "The Three Whats," in *The Metropolitan Tabernacle Pulpit*, vol. 25 (London: Passmore and Alabaster, 1880), 192.

12 **Robert Johnstone,** *A Commentary on James* (Carlisle, PA: Banner of Truth, 1977), 143.

13 **A. W. Tozer,** *The Root of the Righteous* (Harrisburg, PA: Christian Publications, 1955), 51.

Chapter 7

14 Cited by **Dr. Raymond Barber,** "I Am Ready to Preach," May 19, 2006, under "Sermon Archives," Sword of the Lord, at: swordofthelord.com.

15 C. H. Spurgeon, "Bread for the Hungry," November 10, 1861, sermon no. 418, *Metropolitan Tabernacle Pulpit*; accessed from spurgeongems.org.

16 Jim Elliff, "Dull Preachers," 1993, article available from Christian Communicators Worldwide: ccwtoday.org. Accessed November 2010.

Speaking to the King: Approaching God through Prayer

W
hat would it have been like to approach the throne of a Near Eastern King? Most twenty-first-century Christians have never asked themselves such a question or thought about the ramifications of approaching a powerful monarch. Those who lived in Bible times, however, would immediately and correctly have understood the issue and answered the query fittingly and quickly. Those living under powerful kings keenly grasped the frightening implications associated with this scenario. They knew it could be terrifying; it could be a nightmare.

Put yourself in their place. The chills would intensify as you got progressively closer. Your heartbeat would seem so loud and strong that you would wonder if anyone else could "hear" your fear. The building would seem smaller than you imagined (Near-Eastern judgment halls were purposely designed to highlight the throne by making the room seem small, which was done by extending the walls). Your eyes, with peripheral vision, would make out the shapes of lions and other fierce creatures, all designed to illustrate the king's ferocity. You would try to remember all the counsel the court advisors gave you about royal etiquette. As you finally were ushered into the presence of the king, you would abandon all thoughts of decorum or protocol; you would just pray that the king would be gracious.

But imagine this possibility. With your head down, you are quickly rushed to the foot of the throne and the courtier demands that you "state your crimes against the king." You slowly lift up your face, at which point the courtiers, to their consternation, realize that you are the king's child. The people blush with embarrassment and give every explanation to the king for their blunder. You are released, and you spring up the steps to the throne and greet your father with delight.

This scenario helps us to think about the abstract idea of how a Christian approaches God in prayer.

By nature, men are finite and not all-powerful. The most powerful human kings that ever lived still had people and things that restrained their power. What about God and His power? God the King's power is unbridled, matchless, and perfectly just. What would be the thought process of a sinful person wanting to approach God's holy throne? Would that person arrogantly saunter toward God? Would he or she rush up to God with an attitude of "Hey, pal, aren't you lucky that I'm here?" Would there be any vestige of a proud swagger? Hardly.

Approaching God is not something Christians have a right to do. Christ is the worthy One, and the redeemed sinner gladly renounces any claim on being worthy. Christians cling to Christ by grace alone and "attach" themselves to Jesus' sacrificial death in their place, through faith alone. Christians wholeheartedly believe in the bodily resurrection, a resurrection that confirmed the power and completeness of the sacrifice at Calvary. Society underestimates our sin and God's holiness and is therefore insufficiently in awe of approaching God's throne.

Jesus is the One who has turned the "No Trespassing" sign into a "Welcome" mat. His perfect life and perfect death for sinners have forever ripped open access to God. Although Adam was driven out of the Garden of Eden, believers are impelled into the heavenly places and into the good graces of God. Christians are never treated like Cain, who was figuratively vomited out of Eden into the land of Nod (Gen. 4:16). Jesus has torn down the veil in the Temple for the Jew and the Gentile alike. More than that, believers are personally escorted into the Holy of Holies to "see" God by faith.

Both Jewish and Christian traditions describe the high priest's yearly trek into the Holy of Holies, with bells on his ephod and a rope tied around his leg. As long as the bells were chiming, the people knew that the priest was still alive, not consumed by God for his personal, unrepented sin. If the bells stopped chiming, the dead body was pulled outside the Holy of Holies by the rope. Can you imagine the people standing outside the Holy Place?

The buzz of muted and muffled conversation would be everywhere. "Will he make it?" "Will his sacrifice please the Lord?" It must have been eerie. If there were seats to sit on, the people would have been right on the edge of them.

Today, Christians never need to worry whether the sacrifice was a sweet aroma to the nostrils of God. We already know that it was very pleasing to God the King, because His Son accomplished all the work given to Him to do, and He was raised from the dead for our justification (Rom. 4:25). God, who is a consuming fire, poured His holy wrath on His Son, even though the Son did not deserve it. Fill in the blank: "For Christ also died for sins once for all, the just for the unjust, so that _____." If you said or wrote, "He might bring us to God," you quoted 1 Peter 3:18 properly. Wholeness, psychological fulfillment, and fun are not the most important things in life. People need to be brought to God!

Hebrews 4 and the Throne of God the King

Let's examine Hebrews 4 to see, from a New Testament perspective, the importance and possibility of approaching God in prayer. Be prepared to be encouraged as you learn from the writer of Hebrews as he addressed his Jewish audience, an audience that would fully comprehend the difficulty of approaching a King.

Hebrews 4:16 is almost too familiar to Christians today. Many believers have memorized this verse, but few have fully appreciated it: "Therefore let us draw near with confidence to the throne of grace, so that we may receive mercy and find grace to help in time of need."

It is not that I think that few have received comfort from this verse; I just don't believe that most Christians have received all the comfort they could from it. Read the verse again. In light of this book, what jumps out at you? Do you remember stereograms? If you stared at the blurry page for a long time, a 3D image would begin to appear. Treat this verse as a verbal stereogram. What word or image protrudes as you stare at the verse or contemplate it? The word you need to concentrate upon is "grace." Context always helps. In verses 1 through 10, the author is setting out the tragedy of unbelief. He warns his readers about the danger of retreating into Judaism at the expense of believing in Jesus, the Messiah.

Therefore, let us fear if, while a promise remains of entering His rest, any one of you may seem to have come short of it. For indeed we have had good news preached to us, just as they also; but the word they heard did not profit them, because it was not united by faith in those who heard. For we who have believed enter that rest, just as He has said,
"As I swore in My wrath,
They shall not enter My rest,"
although His works were finished from the foundation of the world. For He has said somewhere concerning the seventh day: "And God rested on the seventh day from all His works"; and again in this passage, "They shall not enter My rest." Therefore, since it remains for some to enter it, and those who formerly had good news preached to them failed to enter because of disobedience, He again fixes a certain day, "Today," saying through David after so long a time just as has been said before,
"Today if you hear His voice,
Do not harden your hearts."
For if Joshua had given them rest, He would not have spoken of another day after that. So there remains a Sabbath rest for the people of God. For the one who has entered His rest has himself also rested from his works, as God did from His.   (Heb. 4:1–10)

In light of these irrevocable truths, the author says that his readers must respond. Hebrews 4:11 gives the proper reaction: "Therefore let us be diligent to enter that rest, so that no one will fall, through following the same example of disobedience."

Before we go further, we need to do a mini study on the biblical concept of throne rooms, the throne itself, and the throne of God. Each of these biblical concepts contributes to our understanding of Hebrews 4:16. Hang in there; it will be worth it!

THRONE ROOMS
In the Bible, the room that housed a king's throne is called by many names, such as the "throne hall," the "hall of judgment," or the "hall of justice." It was in this room or hall that the king sat upon his throne and governed. Judgment halls were smaller in size than you might imagine. They were small and narrow, and for a reason: all eyes needed to be on one focal point, the king on the throne.

He made the hall of the throne where he was to judge, the *hall of judgment*, and it was paneled with cedar from floor to floor. (1 Kings 7:7)

Now it came about on the third day that Esther put on her royal robes and stood in the inner court of the king's palace in front of the king's rooms, and the king was sitting on his royal throne in the *throne room*, opposite the entrance to the palace. (Esth. 5:1)

THE THRONE

We might think that today we would understand the concept of thrones better than we understand the concept of halls of judgment. Sadly, however, that is not the case. *Baker's Dictionary of Theology* educates the modern Bible student: "In a country where people usually squatted or reclined, the use of a chair was already a token of dignity."[1] A biblical example of this symbolic chair is seen when Elisha came to town. The influential woman got everything ready for him, including a chair, which would have been perceived as a tangible expression of honor:

Now there came a day when Elisha passed over to Shunem, where there was a prominent woman, and she persuaded him to eat food. And so it was, as often as he passed by, he turned in there to eat food. She said to her husband, "Behold now, I perceive that this is a holy man of God passing by us continually. Please, let us make a little walled upper chamber and let us set a bed for him there, and a table and a chair and a lampstand; and it shall be, when he comes to us, that he can turn in there." (2 Kings 4:8–10)

More than honor, chairs that served as thrones for kings were meant to convey power and majesty:

So Pharaoh said to Joseph, "Since God has informed you of all this, there is no one so discerning and wise as you are. You shall be over my house, and according to your command all my people shall do homage; only in the throne I will be greater than you." (Gen. 41:39–40)

Everything had a symbolic meaning. The chair, which denoted honor, was found in the judgment hall, conveying power. The throne also was positioned higher than anything else in the throne room, for very symbolic reasons. The following account describes Solomon's throne:

Moreover, the king made a great throne of ivory and overlaid it with refined gold. There were six steps to the throne and a round top to the throne at its rear, and arms on each side of the seat, and two lions standing beside the arms. Twelve lions were standing there on the six steps on the one side and on the other; nothing like it was made for any other kingdom.   (1 Kings 10:18–20)

Second Chronicles 9:18 adds that there was "a footstool in gold attached to the throne." Steps lined with lions have been found in ancient throne rooms in Egypt, Palestine, and Syria. Why lions? Because they were a perfect symbol of the potential wrath of the king. Proverbs 19:12 states, "The king's wrath is like the roaring of a lion." The lions, the elevated throne, and the king sitting on the throne must have made receiving a summons to see the king horrifying. It has been stated that criminals had to approach kings with knives tied under their chins so that they were forced to look the king in the eye when they received their punishment. Knees would have been knocking and teeth chattering, as "a king who sits on the throne of justice disperses all evil with his eyes" (Prov. 20:8).

GOD'S THRONE

As wild as it sounds, there is another throne described in the Bible that makes such a throne of a human king look like child's play. God, the thrice-holy God, is described in the Bible as sitting on a throne and wielding perfect justice. Read the following verses reflecting upon the awesome, transcendent God in the heavens:

Now above the expanse that was over their heads there was something resembling a throne, like lapis lazuli in appearance; and on that which resembled a throne, high up, was a figure with the appearance of a man.   (Ezek. 1:26)

In the year of King Uzziah's death I saw the Lord sitting on a throne, lofty and exalted, with the train of His robe filling the temple.   (Isa. 6:1)

Biblically speaking, thoughts about judgment must dominate our minds when we study God on His throne. His judgments are righteous and His verdicts are full of fury:

You have rebuked the nations, You have destroyed the wicked;
You have blotted out their name forever and ever.
The enemy has come to an end in perpetual ruins,
And You have uprooted the cities;
The very memory of them has perished.
But the LORD abides forever;
He has established His throne for judgment,
And He will judge the world in righteousness;
He will execute judgment for the peoples with equity.　　(Ps. 9:5–8)

I kept looking
Until thrones were set up,
And the Ancient of Days took His seat;
His vesture was like white snow
And the hair of His head like pure wool.
His throne was ablaze with flames,
Its wheels were a burning fire.
A river of fire was flowing
And coming out from before Him;
Thousands upon thousands were attending Him,
And myriads upon myriads were standing before Him;
The court sat,
And the books were opened.　　(Dan. 7:9–10)

The LORD is in His holy temple; the LORD'S throne is in heaven;
His eyes behold, His eyelids test the sons of men.
The LORD tests the righteous and the wicked,
And the one who loves violence His soul hates.
Upon the wicked He will rain snares;
Fire and brimstone and burning wind will be the portion of their cup.　　(Ps. 11:4–6)

It is one thing to analyze God's throne from the human perspective and quite another to understand it from the viewpoint of heaven itself. John, the beloved apostle, found himself in heaven and wrote, "Immediately I was in the Spirit; and behold, a throne was standing in heaven, and One sitting on the throne" (Rev. 4:2). Everything in Revelation 4 revolves around the throne of God. Eleven out of the thirteen uses of "throne" in that chapter are directly referencing God's throne, the symbol of the dominion of God's rule. Revelation 4 could be known as "the chapter of God's throne."

Combined with the picture of God's sovereignty, God's faithfulness is also seen from John's description of the throne: "And He who was sitting was like a jasper stone and a sardius in appearance; and there was a rainbow around the throne, like an emerald in appearance" (Rev. 4:3). The rainbow harks back to the first book in the Bible, Genesis, and how God faithfully promised that He would never again destroy the world with water. Now the rainbow in heaven symbolizes God's immutable fidelity to His promises.

The amazing images seem to keep piling up. How much more could a finite, sinful human being bear? These images are too solemn, too holy, and too awful. But there is more: "Around the throne were twenty-four thrones … Out from the throne come flashes of lightning and sounds and peals of thunder. And there were seven lamps of fire burning before the throne" (Rev. 4:4–5). MacArthur calls the lightning and thunder "not the fury of nature, but the firestorm of righteous fury about to come from an awesome, powerful God upon a sinful world."[2] Reminiscent of when, in Exodus 19, the Lord descended on Mount Sinai in fire to give Moses His Ten Words, the Holy Spirit here paints an incredible picture of the holy justice of God Himself.

To set the Lord apart from everything else in heaven, John depicts a sea of glass before the throne to delineate and show off the greatness of God, and he follows by emphasizing the holiness of our great God:

And before the throne there was something like a sea of glass, like crystal; and in the center and around the throne, four living creatures full of eyes in front and behind … And the four living creatures, each one of them having six wings, are full of eyes around and within; and day and night they do not cease to say, "Holy, holy, holy, is the Lord God, the Almighty, who was and who is and who is to come." (Rev. 4:6, 8)

God, whose name is "holy and awesome" (Ps. 111:9) is praised because His "eyes are too pure to approve evil" (Hab. 1:13).

What situation could be worse for a sinful human being than to approach the thrice-holy God on His throne? It is unthinkable! The effect of a sinful human being in the presence of God would be like nuclear fission. To compound the problem, the omniscient God knows the total number of the sinner's sins and the degree of their severity. This is a sure recipe for destruction—or is it?

The Good News

As we saw earlier in Hebrews 4, the writer of Hebrews was pushing his readers to stop vacillating and to fully commit themselves to the Messiah, Jesus Christ. They must not waver and then turn back to an inferior Judaism. The writer then goads his readers to enter into God's rest by demonstrating the awfulness of God's Word and how it exposes everything that the reader has ever said, done, or thought. If God's comprehensive gaze were not so inclusive, maybe they could circumvent God's holy justice; but since God's awareness is laser-like and inclusive, what person can merit access to God? Every person approaching God's throne would miserably fail the divine polygraph test. All are guilty.

Unlike every other book known to man, God's Book, His Word, is active and invasive. It penetrates. It allows no personal sin-secrets to be kept and no "sin-skeletons" to be housed in the attics of our hearts, never to be revealed, broadcast, or seen. Although people might hope to have their sins remain undiscovered, God's Scriptures are like an X-ray, piercing through all protective covering and infiltrating the conscience with a swift thoroughness. The recesses of the heart and mind are easily perceived by God. No nook or cranny can be protected from God's knowledge. Calvin knew this truth well: "There is nothing so hard or firm in a man, nothing so deeply hidden that the efficacy of the word does not penetrate through to it."[3] And the Bible is quite clear: "The word of God is living and active and sharper than any two-edged sword, and piercing as far as the division of soul and spirit, of both joints and marrow, and able to judge the thoughts and intentions of the heart" (Heb. 4:12).

From the human perspective, the picture gets bleaker and bleaker. The original readers of Hebrews must have been hyperventilating by the time they finished the next verse: "And there is no creature hidden from His sight, but all things are open and laid bare to the eyes of Him with whom we have to do" (Heb. 4:13).

Naked, without pretense, without masks or facades, each person is completely and immediately known by God. Every single thought, word, deed, event, and detail of your life is "fully and inexorably open to the gaze of God ... [and] lie[s] unexposed before him."[4] Paul similarly states, "The Lord ... will both bring to light the things hidden in the darkness and disclose the motives of men's hearts" (1 Cor. 4:5). Unlike in our modern secular culture, "this theme of complete exposure and vulnerability of all creation before God was common in Jewish theology of the era."[5] Today's culture cringes at those who reveal their gross hypocrisies. Evangelicals themselves are quite disturbed by God's Word serving as a critic of intentions. But let's examine Hebrews 4:13 more closely. Beware—you might need a defibrillator after you understand it more clearly!

The word translated "open" in Hebrews 4:13 is the Greek word *gymna*. It means "uncovered" and is used for a body that is naked or bare. From God's perspective, even if we are literally clothed, we appear completely open, naked, and exposed. God sees us as we are, without Photoshop, airbrushing, or carnival mirrors that change our appearance. Furthermore, Hebrews warns that people are "laid bare." The Greek word behind this English term is rare, used only here in the New Testament. It is a word closely attached to *trachelos*, the word we translate as "neck." If you think of a tracheotomy, the cutting of a hole in the neck to allow oxygen to flow to a person with a restricted airway, you get the idea. Could it be that God wanted his readers to understand that, before the omniscient King, people have their necks exposed—much like an animal about to be sacrificed, with head pushed away to fully reveal the jugular vein and carotid artery for a quick kill? Commentator Homer Kent states, "Whether the metaphorical use here is based upon the act of the victorious wrestler grasping his opponent's throat to render him helpless, or derives from the exposing of the sacrificial victim's throat just before the knife is thrust, is not certain."[6] What is certain is this: we do not want to be in such close contact with the holy King. God's spotlight is to be avoided by sinful man, not relished. Hordes of people today "bask in the presence of God," when they should run from such an unnerving nightmare.

Is there help to be found? Can grace make its way through holy justice? Does this King ever have mercy? Scripture says, "Therefore, since we have a great high priest who has passed through the heavens, Jesus the Son of God, let us hold fast our confession" (Heb. 4:14). Luther's words soothe us: "After terrifying us, the apostle now comforts us; after pouring wine into our wound, he now pours in oil."[7] The oil is actually a Person, the Great High Priest Himself, King Jesus. No Old Testament priest was ever given such an exalted name. Elsewhere, Jesus is called "a merciful and faithful high priest" (Heb. 2:17) and "the Apostle and High Priest of our confession" (3:1), but here in Hebrews 4:14, Jesus alone is seen as the great Mediator who will allow a condemned sinner to confidently stand before God's holy throne because of His perfect work. The original Greek in this verse is striking; "we have a great high priest" could more literally be translated "we are having a great high priest"—even at this moment in time, two thousand years later. Jesus, the Priest, passed through the heavenlies, when human priests could only pass through the Holy of Holies once per year. Jesus ascended into the heavens to find Himself at the throne of God, to forever be our Advocate.

Perhaps someone will make this objection: "That's fine and dandy, but I would rather have a human priest on earth who can identify with me than a divine mediator in heaven who is far off, aloof, and impersonal. I need someone to know my pain, struggles, and hurt!" But read on: "We do not have a high priest who cannot sympathize with our weaknesses, but One who has been tempted in all things as we are, yet without sin" (Heb. 4:15).

We must never forget that the Great High Priest is human as well as divine. He is not far away, He is close. Just as the song wonderfully states, "Jesus knows all about our struggles."[8] Jesus fully understands what you are going through because He remains the God-Man, even in heaven. Jesus is omniscient, and He is a Man who lived on this evil earth for over thirty years. Jesus is sympathetic, which Spicq says does not imply an exact sharing of experiences (Jesus never sinned), but that He is "compassionate to the point of helping."[9] As a Man, Jesus is willing to help, and, as God, He is fully able to do so.

What should be your response? The writer of Hebrews makes it clear:

"Therefore let us draw near with confidence to the throne of grace, so that we may receive mercy and may find grace to help in time of need" (Heb. 4:16).

Christians approach the throne? But the only throne ever spoken of in the Scriptures has been a throne of judgment! Yet now, because of Jesus Christ's finished work, that throne of judgment, for the first time in the Bible, is a throne of *grace*! Come with no fear of ridicule or rejection. Approach with confidence and approach regularly (a priest used to be able to approach only once per year). Approach whether you are a Jew or a Gentile (only Jews could approach before). Approach with trusting confidence rather than with fear and trembling. The Sovereign's throne is accessible to all who trust in the Messiah. In chapter 10, the writer of Hebrews similarly entreats his readers:

Therefore, brethren, since we have confidence to enter the holy place by the blood of Jesus, by a new and living way which He inaugurated for us through the veil, that is, His flesh, and since we have a great priest over the house of God, let us draw near with a sincere heart in full assurance of faith, having our hearts sprinkled clean from an evil conscience and our bodies washed with pure water. (Heb. 10:19–22)

Do not draw back—draw near. Because you can! Trouble and sin must make you run toward the King, not away from Him. Approach, don't abandon! Sinners now have, by faith alone, total and free access to the inner chamber of God. At the throne of God the King, grace is given. "Only Christianity can give sinful creatures the boldness to present themselves before God."[10]

In Ephesians 3:12 Paul echoes Hebrews 4:16, stating that, through faith in Christ alone, we may approach God with freedom and confidence. The biggest conundrum of the ages has been solved by the King Himself: How can a sinner stand in the presence of a holy God? Through the Great High Priest, Jesus the Messiah. The throne of God's judgment is now a throne of grace.

Summary

Christian, do you pray? Do you pray for as long as you want (the high priest had to move quickly)? Do you pray without fear? Do you pray even when you are sinful? Or do you pray with your fingers crossed, hoping that

God will hear you? Look to Christ. Approach. Draw near. The psalmist asked, "Who may stand in Your presence when once You are angry?" (Ps. 76:7). What is the reply? Only those clothed in the perfect obedience of Jesus Christ, those who have been completely forgiven of their sins because Jesus fully paid for each one of them! You can stand before a holy God because the Son has stood in your place.

Hymn

Before the throne of God above
I have a strong and perfect plea:
A great High Priest, whose name is Love,
Who ever lives and pleads for me.

My name is graven on His hands,
My name is written on His heart;
I know that while in heaven He stands
No tongue can bid me thence depart.

When Satan tempts me to despair,
And tells me of the guilt within,
Upward I look, and see Him there
Who made an end of all my sin.

Because a sinless Savior died,
My sinful soul is counted free;
For God, the Just, is satisfied
To look on Him and pardon me.

Behold Him there, the risen Lamb,
My perfect, spotless righteousness,
The great unchangeable I AM,
The King of glory and of grace!

One in Himself, I cannot die,
My soul is purchased by His blood,

My life is hid with Christ on high,
With Christ, my Savior and my God.   (Charitie L. Bancroft, 1863)

Study Questions

1. When praying, is one particular physical posture better than any other?
2. Do you ever think what it cost for you to have open access to the throne of grace? Try thinking about this for one minute before you begin to pray.
3. Have you ever been to visit a real throne room (whether still in use today or used in times past)? If so, what do you remember about it? (If you haven't, look for pictures of some on the Internet.)
4. What are the benefits of having a *fixed* daily time of prayer?

Notes

1   **D. H. Walters,** "Throne," in **Everett F. Harrison, Geoffrey W. Bromiley,** and **Carl F. H. Henry** (eds.), *Baker's Dictionary of Theology* (Grand Rapids: Baker, 1960), 523.

2   **John MacArthur,** *The MacArthur Study Bible* (Nashville: Thomas Nelson, 2006), 1998.

3   **John Calvin,** *Hebrews and I and II Peter,* in *Calvin's New Testament Commentaries* (Grand Rapids: Eerdmans, 1963), 53.

4   **R. Kent Hughes,** *Hebrews,* vol. 2 (Wheaton, IL: Crossway, 1993), 167.

5   **William L. Lane,** *Hebrews 1–8* (Word Bible Commentary, vol. 47a; Nashville: Thomas Nelson, 1991), 103.

6   **Homer Kent,** *The Epistle to the Hebrews* (Grand Rapids: Baker, 1972), 90.

7   **Martin Luther,** in **James Atkinson** (ed.), *Luther: Early Theological Works* (Louisville: Westminster, 1962), 99.

8   **Johnson Oatman, Jr.,** "No, Not One!", 1895.

9   Attributed to **Ceslas Spicq,** *Theological Lexicon of the New Testament,* vol. 3 (Peabody; Hendricksen, 1994), 320.

10 **Ceslas Spicq,** quoted by **Philip Edgcumbe Hughes,** *A Commentary on the Epistle to the Hebrews* (Grand Rapids: Eerdmans, 1977), 174.

The King's Sovereign Choice

"**D**o not hold in hand. Lay on ground. Light fuse. Get away. Use outdoors under adult supervision only." Instructions for fireworks and firecrackers were exciting to read as a kid. The anticipation of the explosion is more than most twelve-year-old boys can bear on a hot, humid day in July. Likewise, this chapter is highly charged and explosive. It contains discussion about a doctrine that has perplexed and confounded thousands. Get ready for the feeling of the explosion's concussion, the sound of the bang, the smell of gunpowder, and the ringing in your ears.

Everyone would agree that kings in the past, especially very powerful ones, could choose almost anything their realm could offer. Kings freely chose who would advise them, cook for them, protect them, and even who would wed them (or be in their harem as concubines). No one else decided for them. No other person in the realm had such a sweeping and total prerogative to choose. Interestingly, no peasant or serf would question the king's right to discriminate. It was taken for granted that the king would act like a king. The kingdom citizens may have disliked the king's choices or harbored feelings of resentment or envy, but they knew their king could do whatever he wanted, whenever he wanted, to whomever he wanted.

The premise of this chapter is simple. Monarchs choose their subjects. Since God is the ultimate King, God chooses His subjects too. It is amazing that what people will "allow" a human king to do, they have trouble "allowing" God to do: specifically, choosing people. The biblical term for choosing people is called "election" or "predestination." God, based on His own free will and pleasure, has chosen who will enter His holy kingdom and presence. Why do people shudder at God's unconditional election but embrace a human king's right to choose? Choosing comes with the territory of being a king.

Since the fall of Adam, people are not born into the kingdom of God, nor do they have God as their Father. Contrary to the liberal "Fatherhood of God" notions that permeate modern theology, God is not the Father of everyone. Jesus told the Jewish leaders who rejected the Messiah, "You are of your father the devil, and you want to do the desires of your father. He was a murderer from the beginning, and does not stand in the truth because there is no truth in him. Whenever he speaks a lie, he speaks from his own nature, for he is a liar and the father of lies" (John 8:44). No wonder the leaders called Jesus "demon-possessed"! Jesus directly confronted their presumed claim to "our father Abraham." A man's being born into the Jewish nation and being circumcised did not force God to become his "Father."

Before we look a little closer at the doctrine of the King's sovereign election, let's establish, from the Bible, that kings did whatever they wanted to do. We could look at extra-biblical history, but there is plenty of evidence in the Bible itself.

The Old Testament book of Esther unveils King Ahasuerus's absolute rule. Notice the rule and reign of the human king and how he, by being king, got to choose. By definition, kings are sovereign and answer to no other human. Kings do whatever they want to do.

Ahasuerus, the human king, chose the next queen based on his own pleasure:

Then the king's attendants, who served him, said, "Let beautiful young virgins be sought for the king. Let the king appoint overseers in all the provinces of his kingdom that they may gather every beautiful young virgin to the citadel of Susa, to the harem, into the custody of Hegai, the king's eunuch, who is in charge of the women; and let their cosmetics be given them. Then let the young lady who pleases the king be queen in place of Vashti." And the matter pleased the king, and he did accordingly. (Esth. 2:2–4)

Ahasuerus, the human king, chose when to see the queen:

In the evening she would go in and in the morning she would return to the second harem, to the custody of Shaashgaz, the king's eunuch who was in charge of the concubines. She would not again go in to the king unless the king delighted in her and she was summoned by name. (2:14)

Ahasuerus, the human king, crowned Esther and "made" her queen:

The king loved Esther more than all the women, and she found favor and kindness with him more than all the virgins, so that he set the royal crown on her head and made her queen instead of Vashti. (2:17)

Ahasuerus, the human king, could take the life of anyone in his kingdom:

Hathach came back and related Mordecai's words to Esther. Then Esther spoke to Hathach and ordered him to reply to Mordecai: "All the king's servants and the people of the king's provinces know that for any man or woman who comes to the king to the inner court who is not summoned, he has but one law, that he be put to death, unless the king holds out to him the golden scepter so that he may live. And I have not been summoned to come to the king for these thirty days." They related Esther's words to Mordecai. (4:9–12)

Then Esther told them to reply to Mordecai, "Go, assemble all the Jews who are found in Susa, and fast for me; do not eat or drink for three days, night or day. I and my maidens also will fast in the same way. And thus I will go in to the king, which is not according to the law; and if I perish, I perish." (4:15–16)

Then Harbonah, one of the eunuchs who were before the king said, "Behold indeed, the gallows standing at Haman's house fifty cubits high, which Haman made for Mordecai who spoke good on behalf of the king!" And the king said, "Hang him on it." So they hanged Haman on the gallows which he had prepared for Mordecai, and the king's anger subsided. (7:9–10)

So the king commanded that it should be done so; and an edict was issued in Susa, and Haman's ten sons were hanged. (9:14)

You should be convinced about the sovereign selections by Ahasuerus, who was a human king who decided temporal matters. Human kings choose. Human kings rule. Human kings decide. How much more does God, the all-powerful and completely holy King, decide? Just as Ahasuerus, the human king, would extend the golden scepter (which symbolized acceptance and favor), so, too, God the Father chooses figuratively to extend the golden scepter to anyone as He pleases. Because of Jesus Christ, believers can come to the Father ("Esther came near and touched the top of the scepter," Esth. 5:2). God, the ultimate King, brings near or banishes, based solely on His delight.

So many people have a visceral reaction to sovereign election and predestination. What about you? Does God's election of individuals for heaven make you smile? Shiver? Seethe? Submit? Herman Melville wrote *Moby Dick* because he disliked Calvinism, which includes election. Did you know that Edgar Allan Poe's *The Fall of the House of Usher* was actually a metaphor for the fall of Calvinism? To be fair to famous literature, Daniel Defoe wrote *Robinson Crusoe* as a wonderful polemic for the doctrines of grace, which includes the doctrine of election.

Maybe some people react negatively because they are wrongly defining election. Paul Enns gives a simple definition of election: "Election comes from a compound Greek verb meaning 'from' and 'to gather, pick out' and describes God's sovereign act of choosing some individuals for salvation."[1] God chooses and selects His own. God picks His spiritual bride.

It is part of God's nature and essence to choose. Yes, that's right—it is God's nature to choose; that is, electing is one of the things that makes God God. In a righteous way, God is "pro-choice" because, by His essence and nature, He chooses. God makes discriminations between hell-deserving sinners. Who God is manifests itself in what He does. "For He says to Moses, 'I will have mercy on whom I have mercy, and I will have compassion on whom I have compassion'" (Rom. 9:15). Paul, quoting Exodus 33:19, declares that God's sovereign and merciful will shows itself by God making a compassionate choice to rescue a hell-deserving sinner. As an old commentary put it, "He does not say, 'I will have mercy on none but whom I will,' but 'I will have mercy on whomsoever I will.'"[2] But did you notice that the text does not specifically state which people God will be merciful and compassionate toward? Why is this? So that all our focus will be upon the God who chooses, not upon the people whom God chooses. The Scriptures do not say, "I will have mercy on the disobedient Israelites who worshipped the calf." God wants the readers of Exodus 33 and Romans 9 to understand, by an idiom called the *idem per idem* formula,[3] that God is not influenced by an external compulsion or influence when He chooses. What God chooses to do, He does.

Instead of killing the whole nation of idolatrous calf-worshippers, God slew only 3,000 insurgents. Why? He sovereignly chose not to slay all the guilty because He is, by nature, sovereignly merciful and compassionate. A complete reading of the Old Testament account in Exodus chapters 33–34 shows us that Moses places the accent on God the King's choice. God, who by nature is sovereign, makes a devastating declaration to Moses. In the portion of Scripture below, notice the part (in italics) where God's goodness is actually shown in sovereign election:

The LORD said to Moses, "I will also do this thing of which you have spoken; for you have found favor in My sight and I have known you by name." Then Moses said, "I pray You, show me Your glory!" And He said, "*I Myself will make all My goodness pass before you, and will proclaim the name of the LORD before you; and I will be gracious to whom I will be gracious, and will show compassion on whom I will show compassion.*" But He said, "You cannot see My face, for no man can see Me and live!" Then the LORD said, "Behold, there is a place by Me, and you shall stand there on the rock; and it will come about, while My glory is passing by, that I will put you in the cleft of the rock and cover you with My hand until I have passed by. Then I will take My hand away and you shall see My back, but My face shall not be seen."

(Exod. 33:17–23)

God's goodness passes by Moses and heralds His name in a specific and particular way, namely, election. John Piper explains it this way:

God's glory and his name consist fundamentally in his propensity to show mercy and his sovereign freedom in its distribution. Or, to put it more precisely still, it is the glory of God and his essential nature mainly to dispense mercy (but also wrath, Ex. 34:7) on whomever he pleases apart from any constraint originating outside his own will. This is the essence of what it means to be God.[4]

God's decision to choose as He wills should not shock anyone. Consider that God creates human beings and they bear His image and likeness. Part of God's nature is His sovereignty; that is why humans love to pick and choose according to their own wills. Watch any group of children play Cowboys and Indians or "war" in the sandbox and you will see little image-bearers choosing who lives, who dies, who the heroes are, and who they themselves will be. Why is it that what people love in themselves (sovereign choice), they detest in God?

Seven Election Truths from Ephesians that Describe God the King

There are a plethora of books that marvelously teach the doctrine of election.[5] But we should proceed straight to the one passage in the New Testament which rises to the greatest height in teaching the simple, yet, for some, shocking truth about God's free choice. Let's do a cursory overview of Ephesians 1:1–6 and discover several lessons about election. A quick, high-altitude view of this passage will yield spiritual nuggets of gold that produce joy and exaltation. My goal is for you to celebrate the fact that God the King chooses!

THE KING'S ELECTION IS FOR ALL CHRISTIANS, NOT JUST FOR THE "SUPER MATURE"

Imagine you could ask the people on the highways and byways of an ancient kingdom this question: "When did you learn about your king and his ability and right to choose a new queen, determine the tax levels, or decide to go to war with another kingdom?" Information like this would be so ingrained into the warp and woof of the people who lived in the days of the Bible that this question would surely strike them as humorous. But we live in a different time, culture, history, and part of the world. And we are bombarded by democracies, republics, and "one-man–one-vote" ideologies. Part and parcel to living under a monarch in Bible times was acknowledging that kings were sovereign. Why is choice so strange to most evangelicals today?

A contributing factor to the average Christian's misunderstanding of election is that many pastors are afraid to teach it. They muse, "I'd better not cause any trouble," "I'm more concerned about 'saving souls,'" or "I think I'll teach election when the saints are more mature." Professor James Daane echoes this observation: "Sermons on election are so rare that even a regular churchgoer may never hear one ... No other doctrine has been so central in theology and so ignored in the pulpit."[6] When was the last time you heard a sermon on election or an extended sermon series on predestination?

To whom did the apostle Paul write these words: "He chose us in Him before the foundation of the world, that we would be holy and blameless before Him. In love He predestined us to adoption as sons through Jesus Christ to Himself, according to the kind intention of His will" (Eph. 1:4–5)? Was Paul addressing only seminary students, the elder board, older believers, or the extremely curious? No. Ephesians 1:1 gives the inspired answer: "Paul, an apostle of Christ Jesus by the will of God, to *the saints* who are at Ephesus and who are faithful in Christ Jesus." Paul was writing from prison to the saints, the holy ones, men and women who had been "set apart" by God. Every Christian is a saint. Mature or recently saved, all Christians are regularly designated "saints" by biblical authors.

The letter to the Ephesians made its way through Ephesus and many other cities (most scholars consider Ephesians to be a "circular letter"). Paul did not begin his letter by saying, "Here is some milk, since you are just theological babies," "I have something that only the super-mature should read," or "New Christians, please skip this difficult doctrine of election—just go directly to chapter 2 and do not get too caught up in this divisive, complicated doctrine." No, Paul wanted all Christians to know about unconditional election. You need to know about God's election too. Calvin grasped the gravity of not teaching election the same way Paul did:

Scripture is the school of the Holy Spirit, in which, as nothing is omitted that is both necessary and useful to know, so nothing is taught but what is expedient to know. Therefore we must guard against depriving believers of anything disclosed about predestination in Scripture, lest we seem either wickedly to defraud them of the blessing of their God or to accuse and scoff at the Holy Spirit for having published what it is in any way profitable to suppress ... But for those who are so cautious or fearful that they desire to bury predestination in order not to disturb weak souls—with what color will they cloak their arrogance when they accuse God indirectly of stupid thoughtlessness as if he had not foreseen the peril that they feel they have wisely met?

Whoever, then, heaps odium upon the doctrine of predestination openly reproaches God, as if he had unadvisedly let slip something hurtful to the church.7

Did God the Holy Spirit make a mistake in placing sovereign election in the opening chapter of Ephesians? Such thinking sadly betrays the large chasm between the Bible's view of election and the position many of today's evangelical churches hold. If you are a Bible teacher, you need to teach this doctrine. If you are a parent, do you teach election to your children? This doctrine is not "meat" for the ultra-mature; it is for all to understand. The King of kings chooses His subjects, and evidence of this abounds throughout the Bible.

THE KING'S ELECTION STIMULATES RATHER THAN SQUASHES PRAISE
If you lived in a kingdom under a brutal dictator, and a foreign king conquered your land, personally brought you into his kingdom, took you into his court, bought you expensive clothes, and fed you from his royal kitchen, would you complain? Of course not! Jubilation would be in order. Words of praise and thanksgiving would gush from your mouth. There would never be a dull moment, especially as you reflected upon your old king and kingdom. I doubt that you would call your new king "unfair" for not bringing every citizen into his palace.

The same is true for God's election. He rescued you from the kingdom of darkness and brought you into His kingdom. Election elicits praise. Like a tea kettle about to whistle when the water is at a boil, your heart and soul should be ready to cry out with admiration and thankfulness because of the Spirit's work in your heart. The Baptist pastor Spurgeon would agree; he stated,

Whatever may be said about the doctrine of election, it is written in the Word of God as with an iron pen, and there is no getting rid of it; there it stands. To me, it is one of the sweetest and most blessed truths in the whole of Revelation; and those who are afraid of it are so because they do not understand it. If they could but know that the Lord had chosen them, it would make their hearts to dance for joy.8

Paul extols God the Father for election when he bursts forth with,

"Blessed be the God and Father of our Lord Jesus Christ, who has blessed us with every spiritual blessing in the heavenly places in Christ, just as He chose us in Him" (Eph. 1:3–4). Praise for election even preceded praise for redemption for sins by Christ (1:7–12) and the sealing work of the Holy Spirit (1:13–14). Do you praise God for election, or are you influenced by preachers who attribute election to Calvin and spew out lies about how "predestination sends people to hell"?

Did you know that, as Calvin grew in grace, he moved the doctrine of election in His *Institutes of the Christian Religion* from the Theology Proper section (the formal study of God and His attributes) to the Ecclesiology section (the doctrine of the church)? Why did he do that? Because our view of God determines how we praise Him! The church needs this doctrine in order to properly grasp the great mercy of God. Then we must respond with praise. We need to sing of election, using words like those expressed in this well-known hymn:

Come, Thou fount of *every* blessing,
Tune my heart to sing Thy grace;
Streams of mercy, never ceasing,
Call for songs of loudest praise.   (Robert Robinson, 1758; emphasis added)

The Greek word translated "blessed" in Ephesians 1:3 is related to our word "eulogy." Paul celebrates the grace of God because He chose him. In a very Jewish style, called a *berakah* (blessing), Paul speaks well of God. In the New Testament, this word "blessed" is used only of God. Paul, at this point, had been saved for about twenty-five years, yet he still burst out in praise to God. The experience on the Damascus road was unforgettable and it changed him forever. From killer to eulogizer! In the Greek, Ephesians 1:3–14 is actually one sentence, with only one verb, the implied verb "be." That one sentence consists of 202 Greek words that all scream the blessings of God (the Father's electing, the Son's redeeming, and the Holy Spirit's sealing) and are meant to be internalized by us and then mimicked as we too praise God. Paul's purpose is captured brilliantly by Calvin: "The lofty terms in which he extols the grace of God toward the Ephesians, are intended to rouse their hearts to gratitude, to set them all on flame, to fill them even to overflowing with this disposition."⁹ Have you lost the memory of God's elective love for you? Stott challenges you: "Nobody can read it [this passage in Ephesians] without being moved to wonder and worship, and challenged to consistency of life."¹⁰

EVERY CHRISTIAN MUST BELIEVE IN THE KING'S ELECTION

Think about the following scenario. In the past, a king selected a woman to be his bride, the queen, and, in so doing, he passed over two hundred other ladies who had primped themselves and tried to look as beautiful as possible. Today, many people in the kingdom cannot believe that their king would have said "no" to any of the other young ladies because they know him to be a king of great love. They get mad and say, "I don't believe that the king did this!" Some citizens begin to research in the annals of history in order to prove that this did not happen. To their surprise, all the ancient scrolls confirm what their king did: he chose one queen and passed over the rest.

Does this sound implausible? Unfortunately, the parallels with the doctrine of election with God as the King are all too evident. The underlying issue is not that people are professing, "I don't believe this doctrine," but that they're actually saying, "I can't believe it" or "I don't want to stomach it."

One option for people who can't make themselves believe the free selection by the King is to redefine the words "choice," "election," and "selection" so that they seem more palatable. My grandma once thought that my flu symptoms could be cured by a teaspoon of whiskey. To get me to swallow it, however, she first scooped the teaspoon into the sugar bowl before pouring cheap whiskey over it. I don't know if I was healed, but I do know that my throat and esophagus sure burned! When Grandma later asked if I felt better, I'm sure I lied and said, "I feel fine now," thus preventing another round of "the medicine." This is similar to how people treat the doctrine of election.

But hard truths must not be softened by the sugar of redefinition. Why do people today redefine election? Because it is found in every book of the Bible. Instead of submitting to this humbling doctrine, people rise up against it and actually place themselves above the Bible by redefining

God's Word. Such pragmatism does not change the situation—it merely assuages the conscience. The truth does not change! Instead of unconditional election, they have a "conditional" election, which is more of a "post-destination" than a "pre-destination." That is to say, in predestination, God chooses "pre" (before) He sets the "destiny" of a person. In what I term "post-destination," God sees what will happen, or what happened in time, "post" (afterwards), and then He chooses based upon that knowledge. Therefore, conditional election is better termed "post-destination." Spurgeon, always the wordsmith, weighs in on those who want to discard unconditional election: "Can you, O Rejector, cast [election] out of the Bible? Can you take the penknife of Jehudi and cut it out of the Word of God? Would you be like the women at the feet of Solomon and have the child cut in halves that you might have your half? Is it not here in Scripture?"[11]

Just as a human king has the right to choose people for himself and his desires, so the Bible teaches that God has the right, as Creator, to choose. Paul asks rhetorically, "Or does not the potter have a right over the clay, to make from the same lump one vessel for honorable use and another for common use?" (Rom. 9:21). God picks out sinners just as He picked out the nation of Israel from among hundreds of other nations. Israel alone received God's favor. Israel was God's "*favor*-ite."

You have a choice: to believe or to disregard the Bible's description of election.

THE KING'S ELECTION TOOK PLACE "BEFORE THE FOUNDATION OF THE WORLD"
Paul's praise starts with the rehearsal of God's election. Which type of election would stimulate more praise: one whereby God chooses the sinner because the sinner has first chosen God, or one whereby God chooses the sinner even though the sinner is God's enemy and has no spiritual resources to save him- or herself? Ephesians 1:4 clearly tells us when the election was made: "He chose us in Him before the foundation of the world."

What could a sinner do or say to oblige God to save him or her? What does a sinner deserve? Not grace and salvation, but holy justice and righteous wrath. "John Newton used to tell a whimsical story, and laugh at it, too, of a good woman who said, in order to prove the doctrine of election, 'Ah! sir, the Lord must have loved me before I was born, or else He would not have seen anything in me to love afterwards.'"[12] There may be many who want to dance around this verse, but the Bible is replete with the language of election before time began, to the utter exclusion of any teaching about foreseen faith:

But we should always give thanks to God for you, brethren beloved by the Lord, because God has chosen you from the beginning for salvation through sanctification by the Spirit and faith in the truth. (2 Thes. 2:13)

Therefore do not be ashamed of the testimony of our Lord or of me His prisoner, but join with me in suffering for the gospel according to the power of God, who has saved us and called us with a holy calling, not according to our works, but according to His own purpose and grace which was granted us in Christ Jesus from all eternity. (2 Tim. 1:8–9)

All who dwell on the earth will worship him, everyone whose name has not been written from the foundation of the world in the book of life of the Lamb who has been slain. (Rev. 13:8)

The beast that you saw was, and is not, and is about to come up out of the abyss and go to destruction. And those who dwell on the earth, whose name has not been written in the book of life from the foundation of the world, will wonder when they see the beast, that he was and is not and will come. (Rev. 17:8)

God chose people before time began, before they did anything good or bad. Electing people before the foundation of the world ensures that salvation is all of God and not due to human works, deeds, or merit. Calvin said, "The very time of election shows it to be free; for what could we have deserved, or in what did our merit consist, before the world was made?"[13] Praise is the only response to such election. Self-congratulation is the only alternative.

ELECTION BY GOD THE KING IS NOT BASED ON ANYTHING FORESEEN IN THOSE CHOSEN

God chooses people for His own reasons, not because of anything found in those chosen. Unlike King Ahasuerus, who chose his queen because of her beauty and appeal, God picks people for His own reasons. God never chooses people because of who they are or what they will do. Ephesians 1:4 says that God chose us "that we would be holy and blameless before Him." Notice that the text does not say that God chose us "*because* we are holy and blameless."

It is the opposite that is true: God chose us when we were unholy and blameworthy. God knew every sin that you would ever commit, He knew all the skeletons that would be in your sin closet, and yet, if you are a Christian, He still chose you. Calvin is reported to have said, "When God elects us, it is not because we are handsome." Man-centered "election"-teachers instruct their followers with the following type of reasoning: God looks down the corridor of time and chooses people on the basis of a foreseen faith. Such reasoning elicits back-patting, not praise to God. Is that what the apostle Paul says?

For even the most downcast, this truth of election should revolutionize our praise and thankfulness. For many, the grasping of the truth of election is like a real "second blessing." My charismatic friends get super excited about speaking in tongues, or in what they call "the second blessing." I want you, the reader, to be just as excited about this radical truth about God and His nature. Unlike the portrayal of God as a deist, who winds things up in the universe and watches them unfurl, the Bible shows God to be controlling and ruling His universe exactly the way He wants to, and it obeys Him. God the King saves sinners by Himself, for Himself, to delight Himself, consulting only Himself and "answering" only to Himself. Wow.

GOD'S ELECTION IS VERY LOVING

The loudest and most raucous complaint levied against the doctrine of unrestricted and free election is that "it is not loving." Human kings pick their subjects or wives often because of lust or to affiliate themselves with other rival countries (for peace), but they rarely choose people out of a pure *agape* love. Contrary to all chants and shouts, however, the Bible simply but clearly says, "In love He predestined us" (Eph. 1:4–5). The coldest-hearted Christians can have their hearts enflamed with joy by knowing that God loves them. God's motivation for predestination was love. When others state the opposite of this truth, they massacre God's Word. The phrase "in love" "expresses God's attitude to his people when he foreordained them for adoption into his family."[14] God predestined individual people for the same reason He chose Israel: "because the LORD loved you" (Deut. 7:8). One writer challenges any opponent: "Any interpretation of this mysterious doctrine that detracts from the love of God is rightly suspect."[15]

Frankly, the sixth *sola* of the Reformation could easily have been *sola amāre* (through love alone). And God's love is far from impersonal and arbitrary. God personally relates to individuals as sons and daughters, and His love is inextricably tied to His goodness, His unsearchable wisdom, and His sovereignty.

GOD'S ELECTION IS VERY PERSONAL

Ask any child adopted into a loving family if his or her new parents are impersonal and cold. Ask adopted children if they feel like robots as they live lavishly in their new houses, with two loving parents. God's loving predestination yields adopted sons and daughters: "He predestined us to adoption as sons through Jesus Christ to Himself" (Eph. 1:5). Because of election, we can heartily sing the hymn "A Child of the King" (see end of chapter). Who complains about the couple who adopts only one child out of a dirty orphanage?

But the imagery of adoption here is even richer. Often in ancient times, adults were adopted by a childless couple or individual so that they might pass on their wealth and heirlooms. Usually, such an individual was a trusted friend or servant. This is behind Abram's complaint to God that Eliezer of Damascus would inherit his estate. Octavian's claim to power in ancient Rome was based on the fact that he was Julius Caesar's heir, and that everything that had belonged to Caesar belonged to him. This is the imagery that is behind the term here: we become, in effect, heirs to whom God has promised the greatest riches through Christ. We have the status of sons and heirs in the household, and we receive the riches of God's grace abundantly poured out upon us.[16]

Predestination gives sinners all the privileges of their new position of "child." God, in the language of an adoptive legal proceeding in the Roman

Empire, adopts sinners into His family. With this adoption, all claims of the former family were released and the child had full rights as a family member, complete with an inheritance. Old debts were no longer binding because the adopted child had a different name than the one that was on the collector's list. Packer famously explained, "If you want to judge how well a person understands Christianity, find out how much he makes of the thought of being God's child, and having God as his Father. If this is not the thought that prompts and controls his worship and prayers and his whole outlook on life, it means that he does not understand Christianity yet."[17] Additionally, we only rightly understand Christianity when we realize that God the Father is also God the King, who chooses freely.

Summary

Sometimes, when I was a kid, a firecracker would explode in my hands. The burning sensation, with the concomitant redness, was highly memorable! I hope the following story clinches this chapter's discussion with something memorable.

Whitecross cites the story of King William III and Bishop Burnet. The prelate affected to wonder, "How a person of his Majesty's piety and good sense could so rootedly believe the doctrine of absolute predestination." The king replied, "Did I not believe absolute predestination, I could not believe in a Providence. For it would be most absurd to suppose, that a Being of infinite wisdom would work without a plan; for which plan, predestination is only another word."[18]

Hymn

My Father is rich in houses and lands,
He holdeth the wealth of the world in His hands!
Of rubies and diamonds, of silver and gold,
His coffers are full, He has riches untold.

I'm a child of the King,
A child of the King:
With Jesus my Savior,
I'm a child of the King.

Chapter 9

My Father's own Son, the Savior of men,
Once wandered on earth as the poorest of them;
But now He is pleading our pardon on high,
That we may be His when He comes by and by.

I once was an outcast stranger on earth,
A sinner by choice, an alien by birth,
But I've been adopted, my name's written down,
An heir to a mansion, a robe and a crown.

A tent or a cottage, why should I care?
They're building a palace for me over there;
Though exiled from home, yet still may I sing:
All glory to God, I'm a child of the King.

(Harriet E. Buell, 1877)

Study Questions

1. Is there any greater joy than knowing that God has chosen you freely? Meditate on this thought.

2. When adopted children mature, how grateful would they be toward their generous parents? Should you, a child adopted by God the Father, be even more joyous? In what ways?

3. Why do many Christians avoid the topic of election? Should they? Give reasons for your answer.

4. Is it wrong for parents to adopt only one child in an orphanage? What obligation are the parents under toward the children they did not adopt? How is this related to God's election/adoption?

Notes

1 **Paul Enns,** *Moody Handbook of Theology* (Chicago: Moody, 2008), 710.

2 **Robert Jamieson, A. R. Fausset, David Brown,** "Romans 9," in *Commentary Critical and Explanatory on the Whole Bible*, cited at Bible Study Tools, at: biblestudytools.com/commentaries/JamiesonFaussetBrown. Accessed November 2010.

3 **John Piper,** *The Justification of God: An Exegetical and Theological Study of Romans 9:1–23* (Grand Rapids: Baker, 1993), 62. Piper says, "By leaving the action unspecified the force of this

idiom is to preserve the freedom of the subject to perform the action in whatever way he pleases. By simply repeating the action without adding any stipulations the *idem per idem* formula makes clear that the way the action is executed is determined by the will of the subject within the limits of prevailing circumstances … He is stressing that there are no stipulations outside his own counsel or will which determine the disposal of his mercy and grace."

4 Ibid. 100.

5 See, for example: **Loraine Boettner,** *The Reformed Doctrine of Predestination* (Phillipsburg, NJ: P & R, 1991); **Edwin Palmer,** *The Five Points of Calvinism* (Grand Rapids: Baker, 1996); **James Boice** and **Phillip Ryken,** *The Doctrines of Grace: Rediscovering the Evangelical Gospel* (Wheaton, IL: Crossway, 2009); **R. C. Sproul,** *Chosen By God* (Carol Stream, IL: Tyndale House, 1994).

6 Quoted in **Michael Horton,** *Putting Amazing Back into Grace* (Grand Rapids: Baker, 2002), 73.

7 **John Calvin,** *Institutes of the Christian Religion*, book 3 (Louisville: Westminster John Knox Press, 1960), 925–926.

8 **Charles Spurgeon,** "The Beloved Pastor's Plea for Unity," August 6, 1893, sermon 2320, in *Spurgeon's Sermons*, vol. 39. Available from Christian Classics Ethereal Library, at: ccel.org.

9 **John Calvin,** *Calvin's Commentaries*, vol. 41: *Galatians and Ephesians*; from Christian Classics Ethereal Library, at: ccel.org. Accessed February 2011.

10 **John Stott,** *The Message of Ephesians* (Downers Grove, IL: InterVarsity Press, 1979), 15.

11 **Charles Spurgeon,** "Unconditional Election," sermon, September 2, 1855, in *The New Park Street Pulpit*, vol. 1, nos. 41–42; available from Spurgeon Gems and Other Treasures of God's Truth, at: spurgeongems.org.

12 **Charles Spurgeon,** "A Defense of Calvinism," the Spurgeon Archive, at: spurgeon.org. Accessed November 2010.

13 **John Calvin,** quoted by **R. Kent Hughes,** *Ephesians: The Mystery of the Body of Christ*, vol. 49 (Wheaton, IL: Crossway, 1990), 23.

14 **Peter O'Brien,** *Letter to the Ephesians* (Pillar New Testament Commentary; Grand Rapids: Eerdmans, 1999), 100.

15 **A. Skevington Wood,** in **Frank E Gaebelein** (ed.), *The Expositor's Bible Commentary* (CD-ROM; Grand Rapids: Zondervan, 2006).

16 **Barry Hofstetter,** "Perspectives on Predestination," Center for Reformed Theology and Apologetics, at: reformed.org/calvinism. Accessed November 2010.

17 **J. I. Packer,** *Knowing God* (Downers Grove, IL: InterVarsity Press, 1993), 201.

18 **Jonathan Gerstner,** *Theology for Everyman* (Morgan, PA: Soli Deo Gloria, 1997), 45.

Worship of the King

Who gets all the attention in today's society? Sports stars? Musicians? Politicians? The wealthy? Corporate executives? In the days of monarchies and kings in the past, no one other than royalty would have been vying for the attention of the crowds. They were at the top of the food chain when it came to awareness, notice, interest, and "people watching." There was, in essence, no competition when it came to kings. Even in the UK today, when the Queen walks into any room in any city for any function, every head turns her way. How much more attention does the King of kings, God Himself, deserve?

You are a worshipper. Your real goal is to be a biblical worshipper. Worship cannot be merely audited nor be an elective for the Christian. Christians must pay God homage and recognize Him for who He is by ascribing worth to His name.

The main Greek word behind our word "worship" is *proskuneo*. Its origin stems from a word meaning "to kiss with reverence," which signifies stooping or bending low to kiss. You might see in your mind's eye how a person would kneel down and then kiss a king's hand or foot. Signs of respect denote proper submission and honor. For God Himself, however, external worship is not sufficient, for He requires worship "in spirit and in truth." Put another way, "going through the motions" before God the King simply will not suffice.

Worship wars, music debates (traditional hymns vs. contemporary songs), and every other ecclesiological dispute could be virtually solved if we remembered that God is *the* King and that He is the only Audience that matters in worship. The focus needs to be on the One who has "worth" ("worth" was the ancient root word in "worth-ship," or "worship"). When people today move the spotlight and the center of attention away from the Lord and His Word, they move it toward themselves and end up saying dumb things like, "I didn't like the music," "The sermon was too long," "The hymns were boring," or "New means bad." Immaturity and ignorance manifest themselves in self-centeredness and thinking that worship is about getting, not giving. Frankly, human monarchs were not at all impressed by those in their realm who received an audience with them but then wanted the meeting to be about themselves. The following comments sound rather stupid: "I didn't like the king's throne"; "I thought the carpet wasn't royal enough"; "The trumpeters signifying the king's entrance weren't playing my style of music"; "The meeting with the king was too long." Can you imagine a person telling a king, "I don't like drums in your court"? It's silly, stupid, short-sighted, asinine. Yet this is very common today—not before human kings, but before God the King Himself.

When someone gets the privilege of performing in front of a king or queen, he or she must be schooled in proper protocol, especially observing the etiquette that shuns speaking of self. Telling the king what you prefer, what you like, and what you feel, will end the meeting with royalty rather quickly. You must go to serve the king and give him your undivided concentration. If you understand that God is King, it will help you to perceive worship biblically and to actually worship better.

This chapter addresses the influence that knowing God as King should have on personal and corporate worship for the Christian. All of us, as finite and fallen creatures, can slip into worship that is rote, dull, listless, and simply goes through the motions, paying lip service to God. The words of Psalm 95, on which this chapter focuses, will realign our minds to what God says worship should be like, so that we can steer clear of anything that would resemble "worship" which God has not ordained. We need this reminder, because

The tendency is to exalt what is human and diminish what is divine. Even in evangelical circles, we find increasingly attractive a view of God in which God is one of us, as it were, a partner in the unfolding drama of life. But lost in much of this contemporary evangelical theology is the full omniscience, omnipotence, splendor, greatness, supremacy, rulership and unqualified lordship of God.[1]

Conversely, could it be that, if true worship increased, it would, in and of itself, correct many of the church's problems of ministry, evangelism, hospitality, and love? Yes; better worship is the remedy to the current problems of the church. If we look back to 1969, even the title of one of A. W. Tozer's books seems prophetic: *Worship: The Missing Jewel*. Let's discover what Psalm 95 says about real worship and ask the Lord to help us implement what we learn in our lives as individuals and as churches, so that our worship is not "missing" anything!

Psalm 95 addresses God as King explicitly only once (v. 3), but every verse oozes with an implicit royal motif. This psalm provides a needed biblical refresher course in worshipping the King.

It is important to know that Psalms 95 through 100 are united by the theme of worship or praise. Psalm 95 serves as the invitation to praise, "striking the keynote,"[2] as Leupold says, or notifying the reader that Psalm 95, as well as the next several psalms, is rich with the language of worship and praise to God. It is for this reason that many Western and Eastern churches have used Psalm 95 as a "call to worship," to commence the corporate worship service. Cumming wrote about "the extraordinary use of it in the Church. In the Church prayer-books, and in the 'Sarum use,' as it is called, it is, and has been since the 4th century, part of the public service every Lord's Day, in thousands upon thousands of churches."[3] Such a psalm will teach us today much about real worship.

Psalm 95 commands its readers to worship God the King. It starts, "O come, let us sing for joy to the LORD, let us shout joyfully to the rock of our salvation" (v. 1). The King deserves enthusiastic praise. This verse is an invitation to convene worship, and it is an imperative. Leupold helps us understand the Hebrew verbs:

The verbs that are employed urge men to use more than tame terms and methods of praise … Tepid praise defeats its own purpose. In the Old Testament, Temple worship may often have been characterized by a vigor and forcefulness that we are strangers to. The Oriental nature is more inclined toward a certain demonstrativeness than we are.[4]

Our worship should not be based on our feelings; it should not be lackadaisical; it should not be about seeing our friends or assuaging our consciences. Worship involves placing our focus upon the King. Worship ascribes honor to the King as the highest priority of our lives. The psalmist implores us to approach God, no matter what our circumstances are:

whether they are full of trials, financial difficulties, or anything else. Come! Don't think horizontally, but "come" and worship the King. But *how* should we come to worship the King? Psalm 95 gives four ways.

With Joyful Singing (v. 1)

When Psalm 95:1 says, "Let us sing for joy to the LORD," the Hebrew nuance is "to give a ringing cry of exultation or praise." Sadly, the English translation is too bland. It is like Mexican food without spices and peppers. Its real meaning is to cry out jubilantly, with or without musical instruments. Pagans sing loudly to their false gods, so sing with all your heart to the only King! It is your heart that is the issue, not the musical style.

Do you ever see people scream at the tops of their voices at professional sports games? They are full of vigor and conviction, their hearts fully set on their team. In a similar way we must fully focus our hearts on the King when we worship. John Wesley captures the essence of Psalm 95:1 perfectly:

Above all sing spiritually. Have an eye to God in every word you sing. Aim at pleasing him more than yourself, or any other creature. In order to do this attend strictly to the sense of what you sing, and see that your heart is not carried away with the sound, but offered to God continually; so shall your singing be such as the Lord will approve here, and reward you when he cometh in the clouds of heaven.[5]

In corporate worship, we address the Lord. We sing for Him. We sing joyfully to Him. Like a horse with blinders on it, we must have tunnel vision for the Lord, not caring if others see or hear us. Is your voice bad? Sing anyway. Can you not read music? Sing in spite of that. Do you get weird looks from others when you sing? Disregard them. Come and sing, with your focus on the King. If you were in the presence of a human king 2,500 years ago, you would not be concerned at all with the actions and reactions of other people.

With Joyful Shouting (v. 1)

Psalm 95:1 declares, "Let us shout joyfully," meaning "raise a loud shout with joy." The Hebrew can signify loud battle-alarm shouts, the screams of triumph over enemies in battle, trumpets sounding, or, in this context, shouting with intense excitement because of the greatness of the Lord. The psalmist yearns for his readers to burst forth with praise to God. All attention is funneled toward God. Just as a magnifying glass concentrates all the sun's rays into a hot focal point, so too must our worship be condensed and centered upon the King Himself. Barnes calls this kind of worship "animated."[6] This command deals with loudness and decibels. Since God is the "rock of our salvation," let us sing with a holy joy! We cannot worship the King with the same passive attitude we have when we watch television. We cannot worship according to the slogan "Moderation in all things." The King deserves singing that is not indifferent, halfhearted, or apathetic. Remember that Jesus spits out lukewarm worshippers (Rev. 3:16).

With Thanksgiving (v. 2)

Those entering the presence of the King with downcast countenances and grumbling spirits indicate their contempt for life in the King's great and generous kingdom. In your worship, give a public acknowledgment of God's wonderful grace. Be thankful for who He is and what He has done. Spurgeon insisted that we only worship when we

remember [God's] great goodness to us and cheerfully confess it. Our worship should have reference to the past as well as to the future; if we do not bless the Lord for what we have already received, how can we reasonably look for more. We are permitted to bring our petitions, and therefore we are in honour bound to bring our thanksgivings.[7]

In times past, people could be killed by a king because they showed sadness in his presence. Remember the fear the cupbearer Nehemiah felt before King Artaxerxes?

So the king said to me, "Why is your face sad though you are not sick? This is nothing but sadness of heart." Then I was very much afraid. I said to the king, "Let the king live forever. Why should my face not be sad when the city, the place of my fathers' tombs, lies desolate and its gates have been consumed by fire?" Then the king said to me, "What would you request?" So I prayed to the God of heaven. (Neh. 2:2–4)

The king's attitude was, "This person should be happy to be in my court, but his/her sadness reflects poorly on me." As forgiven men and women, we ought to be the most thankful people of all.

With Joyful Shouts and Psalms (v. 2)

This joyful shout is the same as the earlier "joyful shouting" above. Repetition conveys emphasis. The question we must ask ourselves is, "Does this 'joyful shouting' even remotely describe my attitude and actions in worship?"

For the benefit of those wondering whether this kind of worship is bordering on the "charismatic," let us examine the second call to worship found in the psalm, in verse 6: "Come, let us worship and bow down; let us kneel before the LORD our Maker." Here is a "balancing effect": the psalmist now adds soberness to the excited shouting. This command "come" is not from the same Hebrew word found in verse 1. Here the imperative means "enter" or "engage." While Christians are not Old Testament priests, every believer has been placed, by God, into His New Covenant priesthood (1 Peter 2:5, 9). The implication of Psalm 95 for us is clear. Just as priests had to enter the tabernacle with reverence, so, too, we must worship Jesus the King with awe and respect. Tozer says, "We have lost our spirit of worship and our ability to withdraw inwardly to meet God in adoring silence."[8] In this psalm, we have moved from enthusiastic praise to bowing low with quietness and humility. Worshipping the King may include a fever-pitched exuberance, but it must also include an "on-your-face" prostration. Interestingly, when William Carey arrived at the mission church in Tranquebar, India, he saw Psalm 95:6 inscribed there.[9] This verse set the tone for Carey's fruitful ministry for years to come.

The verse gives us more insight into reverence: "Come, let us worship and bow down, let us kneel before the LORD our Maker." We are to "bow down," just as we would before a monarch or king. Every knee must bow before the King. Second Chronicles 7:3 lends the same idea to worship: "All the sons of Israel, seeing the fire come down and the glory of the LORD upon the house, bowed down on the pavement with their faces to the ground, and they worshiped and gave praise to the LORD, saying, 'Truly He is good, truly His lovingkindness is everlasting.'" The worship of the King must include contrite breast-beating, figuratively speaking. Humility recognizes our true state and the true nature of the King. Reflection on the difference between what we deserve and what we have received leads to worship.

Five Reasons to Worship God

Psalm 95 states, in wonderfully poetic fashion, five reasons to worship the King. Each reason drives deeper the fact that worship must be theocentric: centered and focused on God the King alone. God Himself is the only focus, or audience, of our worship. He is the object of the worshipper. God, the thrice-holy One, and His glory must be our motivation. The right questions to ask about worship are: "Was God pleased?" "Was the Son of God honored and exalted?" When God is not the object of our worship, someone else fills His place, and it is almost always ourselves: "How do I feel?" "What did I get from the service?" "What did the unbelievers think?" These questions betray anthropocentric, consumerist, faux worship. Never approach the design of a worship service with the thought "Let's take a survey of what the neighborhood is looking for in a church," "What would an unbeliever like?" or "What would attract 'seekers'?" Instead, remember to ask questions like "Was the King honored in what we said, thought, and sang?" and "How did the King react to our worship?"

Lest we forget, although Psalm 95 is strikingly vertical in its focus of worship (i.e. toward God), it assumes that there will be horizontal implications; that is, that God-centered worship finds its place in corporate worship. The phrase "let us" is found four times in verses 1–2, indicating a communal, shared manner of worship. Individualistic solo worship, while important for personal and private devotions, is not the emphasis in Psalm 95. The community must come together to declare the greatness and worth of Yahweh. Let us now examine the five reasons this psalm gives for worshipping God.

BECAUSE HE IS GREAT

The first reason to worship God is because "the LORD is a great God" (v. 3). He is so vastly superior to any other being that He must be worshipped. Psalm 99:2–3 echoes this call to worship the Lord for His greatness: "The

LORD is great in Zion, and He is exalted above all the peoples. Let them praise Your great and awesome name; Holy is He." While man is finite, fallen, and frail, God is great, marvelous, and awesome. For Christians this side of Calvary, we recognize that the greatest thing God did was to redeem us from our sins. Paul said, "But may it never be that I would boast, except in the cross of our Lord Jesus Christ, through which the world has been crucified to me, and I to the world" (Gal. 6:14). To Paul, it was incredible, unbelievable, that God should have saved him. Paul boasted in the awful cross because Jesus turned its shame into glory. Any deviation from this kind of worship turns into "Muhammad Ali worship"—that is, "I am the greatest." Remember your sins and the doom that awaited you before God forgave you in Christ Jesus, then remember your great Savior, your great salvation, and you will praise Him with earnestness!

BECAUSE HE IS ABOVE ALL GODS
The second reason given for worshipping is that the Lord is "a great King above all gods." While the psalmist knew that there are no other real "gods," he poetically highlighted the truth of God's superiority by using a fake foil: a false, lifeless idol. Come up with a god and, no matter what you can devise for that god, Yahweh will be greater and far above him or her. No matter what god you can conceive, the real God is far greater. In fact, one of the reasons why I believe the Bible is because it portrays a truly awesome God, a God no one could ever make up. God is so much more than a localized god. Instead, He is great and above all other gods, powers, or dominions. Barnes stated this truth in this fashion: "This does not mean that he is a great ruler of all other gods, as if they had a real existence, but that he is king or ruler far above all that were worshipped as gods, or to whom homage was paid. Whoever, or whatever, was worshipped as God, YAHWEH was supreme over all things."[10] Who could possibly be as worthy as the King of Israel?

BECAUSE HE IS SOVEREIGN
God should be worshipped because He is the God "in whose hand are the depths of the earth, the peaks of the mountains are His also" (Ps. 95:4). Everything is under the control and dominion of God. God owns all things,

including the mountains. He is not merely a localized deity of the valley, but He rightfully owns everything and every place absolutely. The "depths of the earth" are ruled by God, in contrast to the false gods, who dwell only on forbidden "high places" (see, for example, Lev. 26:30; Num. 33:52; 1 Kings 3:2). You can bore into the center of the earth and God rules there. You might not be able to see some places, but God sees and controls them all. From the peaks of the mountains to the depths of the earth, God owns and rules the whole earth as King. From Mt. Everest, at 29,000 feet above sea level, to the Dead Sea's 1,300-foot depth below sea level, God utterly rules.

Spurgeon's words elicit praise for the Sovereign King:

He is the God of the valleys and the hills, the caverns, and the peaks. Far down where miners sink their shafts, deeper yet where lie the secret oceans by which springs are fed, and deepest of all in the unknown abyss where rage and flame the huge central fires of earth, there Jehovah's power is felt, and all things are under the dominion of his hand. As princes hold the mimic globe in their hands, so does the Lord in very deed hold the earth.[11]

BECAUSE HE IS THE CREATOR

Psalm 95:5 continues, "The sea is His, for it was He who made it, and His hands formed the dry land." God the King can actually *create*, out of nothing. Human kings can *rearrange*, out of something, but they cannot make things *ex nihilo* (out of nothing). From the Red Sea to the Mediterranean, God created the oceans. From wet seas to dry land, God is the Maker and Former. To draw forth proper praise for such a King, the psalmist says, "Simply look at God's handiwork!" God made everything and is sovereign over what He made. Remember the kids' song "He's Got the Whole World in His Hands"? We rightly praise people for their craftsmanship in wood, for their sculpting abilities (for example, Michelangelo's *David*), or for their musical skill, but how much more should praise be given to the King of heaven!

BECAUSE HE IS CLOSE TO HIS PEOPLE

Far too many kings would "hole" themselves up in their castles and protected palaces. They were far removed from *hoi polloi*, the common people, for many reasons: maybe through fears of safety or out of pride, or because they were following the counsel of their court advisors. Many kings, over time, became increasingly distant from their subjects. Is this the way God the King is?

When theologians discuss God they often place all God's attributes under the overarching categories of "transcendence" and "immanence." "Transcendence" focuses upon God's otherness, His being different from human beings. Transcendent attributes, for example, include His holiness, sovereignty, and omnipotence. God is over His people as Sovereign and Creator. "Immanence," on the other hand, emphasizes the closeness of God to His creation. It relates to God's compassion, patience, and forbearing love of His people. God's immanence is most strikingly seen in the incarnation of Jesus Christ, "God with us." Psalm 95:7 depicts God as Israel's personal God: "For He is our God, and we are the people of His pasture and the sheep of His hand." God is Lord, Creator, and Sovereign King, yet He is a close Father, Friend, and Shepherd. Such an intimate King must be worshipped.

Good shepherds know their sheep because they are close to them. Far from being a stoic, Islamic-kind-of fatalistic "god" who is only transcendent, King Jesus is personally close to His sheep. Jesus said, "I am the good shepherd, and I know My own and My own know Me" (John 10:14). In Psalm 95, with covenant language, God is called "our God." Words like these remind us of 2 Samuel 7:24: "For You have established for Yourself Your people Israel as Your own people forever, and You, O LORD, have become their God." Personal. Close. Intimate. Immanent. Compassionate. Caring. Not just a King, but a Shepherd King.

What earthly king cares for his subjects as God the King compassionately cares for His sheep? Isaiah 40:11 echoes this praise-promoting verity: "Like a shepherd He will tend His flock, in His arm He will gather the lambs and carry them in His bosom; He will gently lead the nursing ewes." Such care and provision must draw forth praise and worship of the divine King. "Man may dismiss compassion from his heart, but God never will."[12] Every Christian has Jesus the King as his or her compassionate, providing Shepherd, who is close to His people and "knows all about our struggles."[13]

The Often-Overlooked Warning to Worship Properly

I can't do what I criticize others for doing, that is, skip the last verses of Psalm 95. They give a bare-knuckled wallop to man-centered, ill-motived worship:

Today, if you would hear His voice,
Do not harden your hearts, as at Meribah,
As in the day of Massah in the wilderness,
When your fathers tested Me,
They tried Me, though they had seen My work.
For forty years I loathed that generation,
And said they are a people who err in their heart,
And they do not know My ways.
Therefore I swore in My anger,
Truly they shall not enter into My rest.   (vv. 7–11)

Now we can see why people want to avoid these closing verses of the psalm! The contrast with verses 1–7 could not be starker. From exalting praise to one of the most solemn warnings in all of Holy Writ, the change of disposition should get our attention and demand our worshipful obedience.

God the King desires more than singing, praise, and the performance of other sacred rituals: He demands reverent obedience to His Word. God's sheep follow Him as the Shepherd King. The theme is simple, yet devastating: improper worship yields a hardened heart, a heart despised by God. Obedience is critical for worship. God does not include any comfort to those who disobey His commands. Israel is the example of what *not* to do. Spurgeon describes this psalm in this way: "It has about it a ring like that of the church bells, and like the bells it sounds both merrily and solemnly, at first ringing out a lively peal, and then dropping into a funeral knell as if tolling at the funeral of the generation which perished in the wilderness."[14] Worship is faulty on Sunday if the worshipper has been disobedient Monday through Saturday.

Why do modern "worship" conferences rarely promote obedience? Shouldn't more books discussing worship include the exhortation to conform to the King's Word? Compliance and submission form the period at the end of the worship-sentence. Israel should serve as a perpetual reminder to avoid complaining against God's providence, testing God, presuming on His goodness, and not trusting in Him. Forty years in the wilderness were summed up at Massah and Meribah, as Israel did everything but submit worshipfully. We don't want God to "loathe" our worship, do we? God has cared for us so wonderfully, and our response must be respectful obedience. And, as the psalmist says, "Today"!

Summary

Worship is all about God the King. Deviations to the left or right in worship cause trouble of catastrophic proportions. God must be the *only* concern of the worshipper.

Forget what others are doing or thinking in worship. A story about the Italian poet Dante Alighieri says that he did not kneel at the right moment in worship. "His enemies hurried to the bishop and demanded that Dante be punished for his sacrilege. Dante defended himself by saying, 'If those who accuse me had had their eyes and minds on God, as I had, they too would have failed to notice events around them, and they most certainly would not have noticed what I was doing.'"[15] What other people are doing in worship should never be a consideration. Be taken up with the greatness of the King and His marvelous works.

Some people say that they get "bored" during corporate worship. Boredom reveals a major problem that must be addressed, but it is not with the worship leader, the hymns, or any temporal part of the service; it is with the worshipper him- or herself. Boredom in worship reveals a problem of focus. If the object of worship is God, boredom cannot exist. MacArthur, with surgeon-like precision, identifies the real culprit in "boring worship":

If you get bored in church, may I suggest to you that it's not a commentary on the sermon—it's a commentary on your heart! Even if the sermon isn't particularly worth listening to, the chance to pick up some truths about God that come through, and then to meditate on them, should be the most exhilarating time of your life. If you're uninterested or indifferent, it's not a commentary on the sermon, it's a commentary on you.[16]

What reason is there for not delighting in and admiring the greatness of God? Is there anyone greater, more awesome, or more wonderful? Redeemed sinners ought to gush with wonder and explode with joy, knowing that the King stooped low to serve them by sending His Son to die in their place, completely forgiving them of their sins. The response to what God has done is worship. William Temple said, "To worship is to quicken the conscience by the holiness of God; to feed the mind with the truth of God; to purge the imagination by the beauty of God; to open up the heart to the love of God; to devote the will to the purpose of God."[17]

Hymn

All hail the power of Jesus' Name! Let angels prostrate fall;
Bring forth the royal diadem, and crown Him Lord of all.
Bring forth the royal diadem, and crown Him Lord of all.

Let highborn seraphs tune the lyre, and as they tune it, fall
Before His face Who tunes their choir, and crown Him Lord of all.
Before His face Who tunes their choir, and crown Him Lord of all.

Crown Him, ye morning stars of light, who fixed this floating ball;
Now hail the strength of Israel's might, and crown Him Lord of all.
Now hail the strength of Israel's might, and crown Him Lord of all.

Crown Him, ye martyrs of your God, who from His altar call;
Extol the Stem of Jesse's Rod, and crown Him Lord of all.
Extol the Stem of Jesse's Rod, and crown Him Lord of all.

Ye seed of Israel's chosen race, ye ransomed from the fall,
Hail Him Who saves you by His grace, and crown Him Lord of all.
Hail Him Who saves you by His grace, and crown Him Lord of all.

Hail Him, ye heirs of David's line, whom David Lord did call,
The God incarnate, Man divine, and crown Him Lord of all.
The God incarnate, Man divine, and crown Him Lord of all.

Sinners, whose love can ne'er forget the wormwood and the gall,
Go spread your trophies at His feet, and crown Him Lord of all.
Go spread your trophies at His feet, and crown Him Lord of all.

Let every tribe and every tongue before Him prostrate fall
And shout in universal song the crownèd Lord of all.
And shout in universal song the crownèd Lord of all.

O that, with yonder sacred throng, we at His feet may fall,
Join in the everlasting song, and crown Him Lord of all,
Join in the everlasting song, and crown Him Lord of all!

(Edward Perronet, 1726–1792; last verse added by John Rippon in 1787)

Study Questions

1. In what way, or ways, can the worship of God help someone avoid idolatry? How can the worship of Jesus Christ assist a person who is "worshipping" a false god?

2. Do you trust your elders for the planning of the worship service, song selection, sermon title, and so on? In what ways is it necessary for the congregation to submit regarding their leaders' choices in these matters?

3. Is everything you need to know about worship found in the Bible? How does this protect the worshipper?

4. Who gave you your voice, and why? Should you sing wholeheartedly? What would you say to someone who said that he or she was "too shy" to sing at a worship service?

5. If you are a father, do you require your children to sing in the Sunday worship service? If not, why not?

Notes

1 **Thomas R. Schreiner** and **Bruce A. Ware,** *Still Sovereign* (Grand Rapids: Baker, 1995, 2000), 11.

2 **H. C. Leupold,** *Exposition of Psalms* (repr.; Grand Rapids: Baker, 1979), 675.

3 **J. Elder Cumming,** *The Psalms: Their Spiritual Teaching* (London: Religious Tract Society, 1920), 30.

4 **Leupold,** *Exposition of Psalms*, 676.

5 **John Wesley,** quoted under the "Topic" of "Singing," at quoteland.com. Accessed November 2010.

6 **Albert Barnes,** *Notes, Critical, Explanatory, and Practical, on the Book of Psalms*, vol. 3 (New York: Harper & Brothers, 1869), 36.

7 **C. H. Spurgeon,** commentary on Psalm 95:2, *The Treasury of David*, vol. 4 (New York: Funk & Wagnalls, 1883), 318.

8 **A. W. Tozer,** *The Knowledge of the Holy* (San Francisco: Harper & Row, 1961), 6.

9 Cited in **Herbert Lockyer, Sr.,** *Psalms: A Devotional Commentary* (Grand Rapids: Kregel, 1993), 343.

10 **Barnes,** *Notes*, 37.

11 **Spurgeon,** *Treasury of David*, 318.

12 **William Cowper,** *The Works of William Cowper* (New York: Robert Carter & Brothers, 1851), 598.

13 **Johnson Oatman, Jr.,** "No, Not One!", 1895.

14 **Spurgeon,** *Treasury of David*, 317.

15 From *Today in the Word*, March 10, 1993; cited under "Worship," at: sermonillustrations.com. Accessed November 2010.

16 **John F. MacArthur,** "True Worship—Part 7," sermon preached 1985; cited on Bible Bulletin Board, at: biblebb.com/files/MAC/TWCH7.HTM. Accessed November 2010.

17 **William Temple,** *The Hope of a New World* (Whitefish, MT: Kessinger, 2005), 30.

The Return of the King

The subject of this chapter serves as a fitting conclusion to our study of God as King and the practical implications of His rule. The return of Jesus Christ, the King of kings, is not just the conclusion of this book; it will also inaugurate the conclusion of human history on earth. Time is linear, not cyclical. There is an end to everything, a real conclusion.

God the King will return one day. He has promised it. Should His return make any difference to our lives now? Another way to ask this question is: Why study prophecy? Students who study the end times need to do more than learn about what will happen in the future; they also need to be busy working on their holiness. Warren Wiersbe hit the nail on the head when he said, "It is unfortunate when people run from one prophetic conference to another, filling their notebooks, marking their Bibles, drawing their charts, and yet not living their lives to the glory of God."[1] All eschatology (the study of the end times) needs to be ethical— that is, it should change the way we live. A powerful connection exists between our daily conduct and our view of Jesus Christ's return. Hope in the future drives godly living in the present. The apostle John said, "Now, little children, abide in Him, so that when He appears, we may have confidence and not shrink away from Him in shame at His coming" (1 John 2:28).

In this chapter, we will study the imminent return of Jesus Christ, as revealed in Revelation 19. The description of the triumphant Messiah, the King Jesus, should propel us to live lives worthy of our calling.

Triumphal Processions

Revelation 19 must be understood in light of Roman triumphal processions. These processions, formal celebrations given to conquerors, were the highest honor Rome could grant its heroes. Revelation 19 displays Jesus Christ as King, Judge, and General. A study of this chapter of Revelation highlights the folly of T. S. Eliot's notions of the end of the world: "This is the way the world ends, not with a bang but a whimper."[2] According to Scripture, quite the opposite is true.

In biblical days, parades were not considered the "warm-up" or the appetizer to the main course: they were the main event. Roman victory parades were called "triumphs." They were impressive and full of splendor. The closest thing to a victory parade that I have attended was the Los Angeles Lakers' basketball team parade through downtown Los Angeles. Magic Johnson was far from a literal general who crushed real opponents on the battlefield.

So spectacular was a triumph that people would declare, "If you have never seen a triumph, you haven't seen anything at all!" The last of the 350 recorded triumphs was held for Belisarius, but we need to realize that another triumph is coming, one with more pomp and circumstance than we could ever imagine! It is hard for the typical evangelical today to stomach Revelation 19 because our days are ruled by the imaginary "God of only love." However, Revelation 19 could be summarized by Exodus 15:3: "The LORD is a warrior; the LORD is His name." Breathtaking verses await us.

Since most people do not understand the cultural and historical backdrop to Roman triumphs, they do not adequately grasp Revelation 19. Sir William Ramsey has brilliantly described the triumphs as

a solemn procession in which a victorious general entered the city [Rome] in a chariot drawn by four horses ... passing in state along the Via Sacra, ascended the Capitol to offer sacrifice in the temple of Jupiter ... and was the cherished object of ambition to every Roman general. A triumph might be granted for successful achievements either by land or sea ... After any decisive battle had been won, or a province subdued by a series of successful operations, the Imperator forwarded to the senate a laurel-wreathed dispatch containing an account of his exploit. If the intelligence proved satisfactory the senate decreed a public thanksgiving ... After the war was concluded the general with his army repaired to Rome, or ordered his army to meet him there on a given day, but did not enter the city. A meeting of the senate was held without the walls, usually in the temple of Bellona or Apollo, that he might have an opportunity of urging his pretensions in person, and these were then scrutinized and discussed with the most jealous care. [Certain] rules and restrictions were for the most part rigidly enforced, although the senate assumed the discretionary power of relaxing them in special cases.[3]

Jesus' Triumphal Entry

With this historical background in mind, let us turn our attention to the triumph of Jesus Christ. When Jesus rode into Jerusalem on what we now refer to as Palm Sunday, it was not the real "triumphal entry." The true triumph will occur when Jesus returns, an event which is described to us by God in Scripture, specifically in Revelation 19. The picture in this chapter of Christ's return has been described by scholars as "one of the grandest"[4] and "one of the most graphic pictures of the second coming of Christ to be found anywhere in Scripture."[5] One author eloquently captures the heart and body's response to this passage: "How the heart thrills and the pulses bound as we read this description of the descending Christ of God and His saints."[6] Wilbur Smith, with some overstatement, said, "This paragraph has always seemed to me almost too overwhelmingly glorious for exposition."[7] I disagree with the anti-exposition notion, but I agree that Revelation 19 is glorious. Don't read the following verses too quickly. In fact, read them out loud for full effect.

And I saw heaven opened, and behold, a white horse, and He who sat on it is called Faithful and True, and in righteousness He judges and wages war. His eyes are a flame of fire, and on His head are many diadems; and He has a name written on Him which no one knows except Himself. He is clothed with a robe dipped in blood, and His name is called The Word of God. And the armies which are in heaven, clothed in fine linen, white and clean, were following Him on white horses. From His mouth comes a sharp sword, so that with it He may strike down the nations, and He will rule them with a rod of iron; and He treads the wine press of the fierce wrath of God, the Almighty. And on His robe and on His thigh He has a name written, "*King of kings*, and Lord of lords."
(Rev. 19:11–16)

In a book written to "reveal" Jesus Christ, Revelation 19 is the pinnacle of the unveiling of the Messiah King. This description of Jesus is stunning, stirring, and chilling. And it is drenched with the dew of the language of royalty. In this chapter we see that Jesus Christ comes in glory with His saints as the King of kings to complete His victory and to establish His rule. The Lion of the tribe of Judah descends (Rev. 5:5) to execute the victory He purchased at Calvary. Lenski comprehends the significance of the King's return: "The reason that Christ is here pictured as the King descending for battle is due to the fact that now all the previous imagery of battle is to be completed, and because this vision reveals the final defeat of the beast, and the whole antichristian power."[8]

Revelation 19:11 says, "And I saw heaven opened, and behold, a white horse, and He who sat on it is called Faithful and True, and in righteousness He judges and wages war." The heavens are, without words of caution, torn asunder, and the Greek signifies that they remain open. There have already been sounds from heaven: "After these things I heard something like a loud voice of a great multitude in heaven, saying, 'Hallelujah! Salvation and glory and power belong to our God'" (v. 1). Now a visual image is given. What do we see coming out of heaven? Whom do we see?

Let's examine ten brushstrokes of the portrait of the triumphant Messiah that are designed for us to better understand Revelation 19 and to spur us to live lives that are honoring to our returning King.

The King Rides on a Horse of Triumph

Verse 11 says that Jesus rides out of heaven on a white horse. This horse is very symbolic: it captures the ideas of holiness and sure victory. Jesus is no longer riding a humble donkey; instead he comes on an animal of warfare. White chargers were the horse of choice for generals and kings in times past. Keener elucidates: "White horses were usually considered the best … Such horses were appropriate mounts for rulers, important officials, and conquerors entering Rome in triumph."[9] No white flags of surrender are raised; rather, the One who rode into Jerusalem as meek and lowly now blazes to earth. Revelation 1:7 says of this day, "Behold, He is coming with the clouds, and every eye will see Him, even those who pierced Him; and all the tribes of the earth will mourn over Him. So it is to be. Amen."

The King Fulfills His Promise to Triumph

The only real "promise keeper" is called "Faithful and True" (19:11). Full exoneration of His Word comes at this moment. Jesus is absolutely trustworthy and completely true, and, therefore, so is His Word. The original language stresses that these attributes are habitual or continual. Jesus is always faithful, always true. His character demands it. He is no deceiving dragon or false prophet. He told His disciples that He would "come again" (John 14:3), and now He returns to vindicate His followers and smash the blasphemers. God's divine "layaway plan" is due. "Sin now and pay later" is only temporary: the time for "pay now" has arrived. In a world dominated by unfaithfulness and lies, Jesus is faithful and true. The following Scriptures emphasize that fact:

O LORD God of hosts, who is like You, O mighty LORD?
Your faithfulness also surrounds You.   (Ps. 89:8)

Your lovingkindness, O LORD, extends to the heavens,
Your faithfulness reaches to the skies.   (Ps. 36:5)

The LORD's lovingkindnesses indeed never cease,
For His compassions never fail.
They are new every morning;
Great is Your faithfulness.   (Lam. 3:22–23)

The King's Triumph Is Righteous

Many today struggle with the concept of a "just war." Revelation 19 reveals a war that all Christians, even pacifists, will affirm as just. The text says, "In righteousness He judges and wages war" (v. 11). God's judgment is always just and righteous. With God, there are no hung juries, bribed jurors, partial judges, or anything else that would prevent justice. Revelation 19:2 and 16:7 describe God's judgments as "true and righteous." This war will, in fact, be a world war, the final world war, the real war to end all wars. Jesus is coming back with a vengeance.

The King's Eyes Demand Triumph

John paints the image of Jesus' return in dreadful terms, writing, "His eyes are a flame of fire" (v. 12). The King knows all and sees all. Like a piercing

X-ray, the gaze of Jesus is awful and penetrating. Robert Thomas describes the language used: "The biblical force of this simile is sometimes that of fierceness against adversaries. It can also convey the notion of penetrating vision and the associated idea of supernatural intelligence in regard to what is seen."[10] Described mainly in the context of judgment, Jesus' vision allows no one and nothing to escape His omniscient view. People may attempt to hide their sins and attitudes, but Jesus will not be distracted or repelled. With royal fury, God's judgment, at His return, will be exhaustive. Seiss declares,

To judge rightly he must see through and through, search all depths, look beneath all masks, penetrate all darkness and try everything to its ultimate residuum ... which likewise tells of the fierceness of his wrath against his enemies ... It is an eye-flame of Omniscient perception and out-breaking indignation and wrath, which seizes and unmans the foe before he feels the sword.[11]

With bone-chilling terror, John MacArthur adds,

When first He came, His eyes sparkled with tenderness and joy as He gathered little children to Himself, as He expressed His love to the poor and the needy. His eyes glowed with compassion as when a single look on guilty Peter melted Peter's heart and made him weep bitterly. His eyes were filled with tears as He looked over the city of Jerusalem and wept. And as He shed tears from those same eyes at the grave of Lazarus. But the day is coming when those eyes flash with fire, when they are penetrating burning eyes, probing the darkest recesses of every human soul and purging and purifying with judgment. To judge rightly He has to see everything. He has to sound the depths of every heart. He has to see behind every mask, under every facade. It is the flaming vision of righteous omniscience and anger.[12]

The King's Crowns Demonstrate Triumph

John's vision reveals that "on His head are many diadems" (v. 12). Diadems and crowns are universal emblems for sovereignty and rule. No longer wearing a crown of thorns, Jesus returns as royalty. The dragon and beast adorn themselves with crowns (12:3; 13:1), but these crowns are sinfully commandeered. Jesus, with "many" diadems to signify intensity, wears crowns that denote His ultimate rule. Paul proclaims in 1 Corinthians 15:24 that Jesus will eventually destroy "all rule and all authority and power." King David put the crown of the defeated Ammonite king on his head, in addition to his own crown, to signify a greater rule (2 Sam. 12:30). Similarly, "When Ptolemy entered Antioch, he set two crowns upon his head, the crown of Asia and the crown of Egypt" (1 Macc. 11:13). "The accumulation of crowns expresses accumulated victory and dominion."[13] Jesus, with multiple crowns, is King indeed.

The King's Name Reveals His Authority to Triumph

Revelation 19:12 states, "He has a name written on Him which no one knows except Himself." Who can ultimately and intimately know God unless He first purposes to reveal Himself? Finite, fallen minds cannot conceive of Jesus the King. Morris concurs: "Christ's person can never be completely understood by his creation. It is possible that there is another thought. Those who practiced magic believed that to know the name gave power over him whose name it was. John may well be saying that no one has power over Christ. He is supreme. His name is known only to himself."[14] Scholars have called this the "unknowability" of Jesus, which denotes a mystery and incompleteness on behalf of the human beholding God. In Eastern culture, the superior could withhold his name from the inferior, but not the other way around (see Gen. 32:29; Judg. 13:18). The implications here are obvious. Jesus said, "All things have been handed over to Me by My Father; and no one knows the Son except the Father; nor does anyone know the Father except the Son, and anyone to whom the Son wills to reveal Him" (Matt. 11:27). Jesus, the superior One, cannot be known unless He first makes Himself known. No one can hold anything "over His head."

The King's Robe Displays Triumph

The truly awesome imagery continues. Revelation 19:13 says, "He is clothed with a robe dipped in blood." Imagine what that will look like. Perhaps we can anticipate massive bloodshed. Wall said, "The battle's outcome is apparent even before it is waged."[15] Jesus, the warrior King, is going to slaughter His adversaries and obliterate every foe. His robe is literally "baptized" in blood. Christ's victory is as good as accomplished.

Listen to an early "battle hymn" that has direct implications for our understanding of Revelation 19:13:

Who is this who comes from Edom,
With garments of glowing colors from Bozrah,
This One who is majestic in His apparel,
Marching in the greatness of His strength?
"It is I who speak in righteousness, mighty to save."
Why is Your apparel red,
And Your garments like the one who treads in the wine press?
"I have trodden the wine trough alone,
And from the peoples there was no man with Me.
I also trod them in My anger
And trampled them in My wrath;
And their lifeblood is sprinkled on My garments,
And I stained all My raiment.
For the day of vengeance was in My heart,
And My year of redemption has come.
I looked, and there was no one to help,
And I was astonished and there was no one to uphold;
So My own arm brought salvation to Me,
And My wrath upheld Me.
I trod down the peoples in My anger
And made them drunk in My wrath,
And I poured out their lifeblood on the earth."   (Isa. 63:1–6)

Revelation 19:15 continues this theme, saying, "He treads the wine press of the fierce wrath of God, the Almighty." Every enemy of God must drink this lethal potion. God, with ease, will crush every unrepentant sinner. Just as the grape juice sloshes upon the wine treader's garment, so too will the blood of Christ's enemies splash onto Jesus' robe. Nothing in this passage speaks of any saving work. Judgment, not salvation, is the focus here. In the midst of a white backdrop—with a white horse, saints clothed in white, and white clouds—the only "non-white" color is dark-red blood.

The King's Name Confirms His Power

John continues, "His name is called The Word of God" (v. 13). John's Gospel similarly stated, "In the beginning was the Word, and the Word was with God, and the Word was God. He was in the beginning with God. All things came into being through Him, and apart from Him nothing came into being that has come into being. In Him was life, and the life was the Light of men" (John 1:1–4). Why is Jesus called "The Word of God" in both the Gospel of John and here in the book of Revelation? Jews would principally have associated this language with Genesis 1, where God powerfully spoke the world into existence by a word. Jesus would thus be seen as the powerful God. Additionally, when Jews thought of a "word," they would think of "something concrete, something much closer to what we would call an event or a deed. A word spoken was a deed done. What happens when God speaks? The answer is that the thing spoken by God is instantly done. God said, 'Let there be light: and there was light' (Gen. 1:3)."[16] Jesus, as the Word, makes things happen immediately and effectively. He is active. Mounce is helpful: "In Hebrew thought a word is not a lifeless sound but an active agent that achieves the intention of the one who speaks (Gen. 1:3, 7, 9)."[17]

The King's Sword Wields Triumph

"From His mouth comes a sharp sword, so that with it He may strike down the nations" (v. 15). Using deadly force, Jesus judges with precise deathblows. Jesus is lethal. Different swords were used in Bible times. The particular sword here "indicates a long Thracian sword or one unusually large and longer than most swords. Here [it is] used symbolically to represent a sharp instrument of war with which Christ will smite the nations and establish His absolute rule."[18] With a sickle-like stroke, Jesus metes out righteous judgment to the nations (Isa. 11:4). Ponder the horror of being on the receiving end of such ferocity. Paul says, "The Lord Jesus will be revealed from heaven with His mighty angels in flaming fire, dealing out retribution to those who do not know God and to those who do not obey the gospel of our Lord Jesus" (2 Thes. 1:7–8).

The King's Iron Scepter Destroys Triumphantly

Lastly, Jesus "will rule them with a rod of iron" (v. 15). This "rule" is not benign government, but a destructive rule (see vv. 17–21). Mounce affirms,

To rule with an iron scepter means to destroy rather than to govern in a stern fashion. The shepherd not only leads his flock to pasture but defends the sheep from marauding beasts. His rod is a weapon of retaliation. The Messiah's rod is a scepter of iron; that is, it is strong and unyielding in its mission of judgment.[19]

Jesus, the warrior King, rules. Psalm 2:9 describes God the Son breaking His enemies "with a rod of iron, You shall shatter them like earthenware." The carnage will be incredible.

Then I saw an angel standing in the sun, and he cried out with a loud voice, saying to all the birds which fly in midheaven, "Come, assemble for the great supper of God, so that you may eat the flesh of kings and the flesh of commanders and the flesh of mighty men and the flesh of horses and of those who sit on them and the flesh of all men, both free men and slaves, and small and great." And I saw the beast and the kings of the earth and their armies assembled to make war against Him who sat on the horse and against His army. And the beast was seized, and with him the false prophet who performed the signs in his presence, by which he deceived those who had received the mark of the beast and those who worshiped his image; these two were thrown alive into the lake of fire which burns with brimstone. And the rest were killed with the sword which came from the mouth of Him who sat on the horse, and all the birds were filled with their flesh. (Rev. 19:17–21)

Summary

Jesus wins, and He wins decisively. After all, "on His robe and on His thigh He has a name written, 'King of kings, and Lord of lords'" (Rev. 19:16). John wonderfully portrays Jesus as the King. When a mighty general would ride his horses, the wind might blow his robe back and expose his thigh. Here, at obvious eye level, the name of Jesus is written. Everyone will know who this King Jesus is: the name under the streaming robe leaves no doubt. Who can escape this fact? No one; it is made manifestly obvious.

Jesus is the "King of kings, and Lord of lords," a name which reveals His total and complete sovereignty. Why the double name? Moffatt gives good insight: "The doubling of the name ... was a practice of the Persians and Parthians to emphasize the supremacy of their royalties."[20] No Caesar or human king can ever claim such a title. The rider can only be Jesus Christ, the God-Man.

These will wage war against the Lamb, and the Lamb will overcome them, because *He is Lord of lords and King of kings*, and those who are with Him are the called and chosen and faithful. (Rev. 17:14)

I charge you in the presence of God, who gives life to all things, and of Christ Jesus, who testified the good confession before Pontius Pilate, that you keep the commandment without stain or reproach until the appearing of our Lord Jesus Christ, which He will bring about at the proper time—He who is the blessed and only Sovereign, *the King of kings and Lord of lords*; who alone possesses immortality and dwells in unapproachable light, whom no man has seen or can see. To Him be honor and eternal dominion! Amen. (1 Tim. 6:13–16)

Knowing that Jesus will return soon, how should you live?

Hymns

The King shall come when morning dawns,
And light triumphant breaks;
When beauty gilds the eastern hills,
And life to joy awakes.

Not as of old a little child
To bear, and fight, and die,
But crowned with glory like the sun
That lights the morning sky.

Chapter 11

O brighter than the rising morn
When He, victorious, rose,
And left the lonesome place of death,
Despite the rage of foes.

O brighter than that glorious morn
Shall this fair morning be,
When Christ, our King, in beauty comes,
And we His face shall see.

The King shall come when morning dawns,
And earth's dark night is past;
O haste the rising of that morn,
The day that aye shall last.

And let the endless bliss begin,
By weary saints foretold,
When right shall triumph over wrong,
And truth shall be extolled.

The King shall come when morning dawns,
And light and beauty brings:
Hail, Christ the Lord! Thy people pray,
Come quickly, King of kings.

(Author unknown; tr. from Greek by John Brownlie, 1907)

Rejoice! Rejoice! our King is coming!
And the time will not be long,
Until we hail the radiant dawning,
And lift up the glad new song.

Oh, wondrous day! oh, glorious morning,
When the Son of Man shall come!
May we with lamps all trimmed and burning
Gladly welcome His return!

Rejoice! Rejoice! our King is coming!
And the time will not be long,
Until we hail the radiant dawning,
And lift up the glad new song.

With joy we wait our King's returning
From His heavenly mansions fair;
And with ten thousand saints appearing
We shall meet Him in the air.

Oh, may we never weary, watching,
Never lay our armor down
Until He come, and with rejoicing
Give to each the promised crown.   (Ira D. Sankey, 1888)

Study Questions

1. If you are not already a Christian, will you bow your knee in submission to the King who is certain to return to judge all sinners?

2. Does the study of Revelation 19 make you want to read all of the Book of Revelation? What is stopping you?

3. Does the soon return of Jesus affect the way you plan for your future? What about planning the next year? Month? Week? Day? Hour?

4. Do you have joy knowing the end of history? In light of Revelation 19, explain how Christians should be the most joyful people on the earth.

5. Does Revelation 19 decrease or increase your anxiety or fear regarding what might happen in the world, for example, in China or the Middle East?

Notes

1 **Warren Wiersbe,** *The Bible Exposition Commentary: New Testament,* vol. 2 (Colorado Springs: Cook Communications Ministries, 2001), 466.

2 **T. S. Eliot,** "The Hollow Men" (1925).

3 **William Ramsay,** "Triumphus," in **William Smith** (ed.), *A Dictionary of Greek and Roman Antiquities* (London: John Murray, 1875), 1163–1167.

4 **J. A. Seiss,** *The Apocalypse: Lectures on the Book of Revelation* (Grand Rapids: Zondervan, 1957), 434.

5 **John F. Walvoord,** *The Revelation of Jesus Christ* (Chicago: Moody, 1973), 274.

6 **Henry Ironside,** *Revelation* (1920; Grand Rapids: Kregel, 2004), 186.

7 **Wilbur M. Smith,** in **Everett Harrison** and **Charles F. Pfeiffer** (eds.), *The Wycliffe Bible Commentary* (Chicago: Moody Press, 1971), 1091.

8 **R. C. H. Lenski,** *The Interpretation of St. John's Revelation* (Minneapolis: Wartburg Press, 1943), 550.

9 **Craig S. Keener,** *Revelation* (NIV Application Commentary; Grand Rapids: Zondervan, 2000), 453.

10 **Robert L. Thomas,** *Revelation 1–7: An Exegetical Commentary* (Chicago: Moody, 1992), 101.

11 Seiss, *The Apocalypse*, 436.

12 **John MacArthur, Jr.,** "The Glorious Return of Jesus Christ—Part 2," sermon on Revelation 19:11–16, 2002, cited at: biblebb.com/files/mac/66-71.htm. Accessed November 2010.

13 Seiss, *The Apocalypse*, 436.

14 **Leon Morris,** *The Book of Revelation: An Introduction and Commentary* (Tyndale New Testament Commentaries; Carlisle: Send the Light, 1987), 223.

15 **Robert W. Wall,** *Revelation* (New International Bible Commentary, vol. 18; Peabody, MA: Hendricksen, 1991), 230.

16 **James Montgomery Boice,** *Foundations of the Christian Faith: A Comprehensive and Readable Theology* (Downers Grove, IL: InterVarsity Press, 1986), 299.

17 **Robert H. Mounce,** *The Book of Revelation* (The New International Commentary on the New Testament; Grand Rapids: Eerdmans, 1977), 354.

18 **Walvoord,** *The Revelation of Jesus Christ*, 277.

19 **Mounce,** *The Book of Revelation*, 355.

20 **James Moffatt,** *A New Translation of the Bible, Containing the Old and New Testaments* (Grand Rapids: Kregel, 1995), 2.391.

My goal in writing this book was to introduce you to the overwhelming biblical data (overwhelming by sheer volume and by the feeling it induces because God is so awesome) that supports the notion that a proper view of God must include seeing Him as the King. So the question is simple: Do you think about God as King?

The concept of God, the ultimate Monarch, has so captured me that I would love to change the name of my church to "Christ the King," or something close. It might protect me from getting spiritual Alzheimer's disease and forgetting this great truth about God. Don't put this on the mental shelf that says, "I have mastered this subject." Ask God to let the doctrine master you. Be determined to remember that God is the King.

We are all guilty of the death of a king: we have committed regicide. Regicide is the deliberate killing of a king (the Latin word *regis* means "king" and *cida* means "killer"). However, if you are a Christian, your sins are what the King of kings, Jesus Christ, bore on His body at Calvary. God the Father justly poured out His wrath upon His beloved Son, not because Jesus sinned, but because God was treating the Messiah *as if He had sinned*, even though He was sinless. What an amazing demonstration of the infinite love of God! You deserved death but the Son was your gracious substitute! Aren't you thankful that God is a King who truly loves His people? Could there be a greater love from a king? Eternal praise is the proper response from you.

If you are not a Christian, your only hope is the mercy and clemency of the King whom you have offended by your sin and lack of faith. Your sins shout, "I will not have this King rule over me!" Your sins are malicious attempts to murder your royal Creator. What is the punishment for a person who tries to kill a king? In ancient times, the hand that tried to kill a human king was burned with fire before the criminal was dismembered—alive. You have earned worse. You have merited an afterlife in the Lake of Fire. Your only hope of rescue is found in the triune God who has provided atonement to satisfy His just law, yet allows the guilty to be redeemed from their sin. The risen Savior must be believed. God's Word demands that you repent and believe in the Son of God, the King.

Call out to God for mercy. Wonderfully, God the King is also God the Savior. Read Charles Spurgeon's insights into the King who saves sinners so that He receives all the glory—and cry out to this King for deliverance.

On the Father's part, thus run the covenant. I cannot tell you it in the glorious celestial tongue in which it was written: I am fain to bring it down to the speech which suiteth to the ear of flesh, and to the heart of the mortal. Thus, I say, run the covenant, in ones like these: "I, the Most High Jehovah, do hereby give unto my only begotten and well-beloved Son, a people, countless beyond the number of the stars, who shall be by him washed from sin, by him preserved, and kept, and led, and by him, at last, presented before my throne, without spot, or wrinkle, or any such thing. I covenant by oath, and swear by myself, because I can swear by no greater, that those whom I now give to Christ shall be for ever the objects of my eternal love. Them I will forgive through the merit of the blood. To these will I give a perfect righteousness; these will I adopt and make my sons and daughters, and these shall reign with me through Christ eternally." … The Holy Spirit also, as one of the high contracting parties on this side of the covenant, gave his declaration: "I hereby covenant," saith he, "that all whom the Father giveth to the Son, I will in due time quicken. I will show them their need of redemption. I will cut off from them all groundless hope, and destroy their refuges of lies. I will bring them to the blood of sprinkling; I will give them faith whereby this blood shall be applied to them, I will work in them every grace; I will keep their faith alive; I will cleanse them and drive out all depravity from them, and they shall be presented at last spotless and faultless." This was the one side of the covenant, which is at this very day being fulfilled and scrupulously kept." … He [Christ] thus declared, and covenanted with his Father: "My Father, on my part I covenant that in the fullness of time I will become man. I will take upon myself the form and nature of the fallen race. I will live in their wretched world, and for my people I will keep the law perfectly. I will work out a spotless righteousness, which shall be acceptable to the demands of thy just and holy law. In due time I will bear the sins of all my people. Thou shalt exact their debts on me; the chastisement of their peace I will endure, and by my stripes they shall be healed. My Father, I covenant and promise that I will be obedient unto death, even the death of the cross. I will magnify thy law, and make it honorable. I will suffer all they ought to have suffered. I will endure the curse of thy law, and all the vials of thy wrath shall be emptied and spent upon my head. I will then rise again. I will ascend into heaven; I will intercede for them at thy right hand; and I will make myself responsible for every one of them [surety] that not one of those whom thou hast given me shall ever be lost, but I will bring all my sheep of whom, by thy blood, thou hast constituted me the shepherd—I will bring every one safe to thee at last."[1]

Note

1 **Charles Spurgeon,** "The Blood of the Everlasting Covenant," sermon 277 in *The New Park Street Pulpit*, vol. 5; accessed from spurgeon.org.

Enthronement Psalms

Several psalms have been designated "enthronement psalms" because they reveal God, specifically Yahweh, as King. God the King is seen as ascending His throne and exerting power over everything, from creation to the nation of Israel. Whether calling this group of psalms "enthronement psalms" is proper—that is, whether it is a biblical category of psalms—we are not certain. However, what is true is that in Psalms 47, 93, 96, 97, 98, and 99, Yahweh is either explicitly called "King" or God is alluded to as King through royal language or motifs.

Keith W. Whitelam shows that, in the enthronement psalms, Yahweh is King "by virtue of his victory over the forces of chaos as represented by the primeval waters (Ps 93:3–4)."[1] The divine King is powerful and able to grant Israel safety (Ps. 47:3–4, 8–9; 97:3, 7, 9; 98:2; 99:1–2). But more than being a King, He is also Judge (Ps. 96:10–13; 97:2, 8; 98:9; 99:4).

It is worth reading the psalms to consider God as King, noting the aspects below:

- God is the King of the earth: Psalm 47
- The Lord is clothed with majesty: Psalm 93
- A call to worship the Lord, the righteous Judge: Psalm 96
- The Lord's power and dominion: Psalm 97
- A call to praise the Lord for His righteousness: Psalm 98
- Praise to the Lord for His fidelity to Israel: Psalm 99

Note

1 **Keith W. Whitelam,** "King and Kingship," in **D. N. Freedman** (ed.), *The Anchor Bible Dictionary* (New York: Doubleday, 1996), 4:40.

The Gospel of Matthew: "Behold Your King"

M atthew's Gospel clearly portrays Jesus as the King. Matthew wants his readers to understand Jesus as the divine King and to render total allegiance to Him. Since Jesus is the only absolute Monarch, we must give homage to Him.

S. Lewis Johnson describes the theme of the book of Matthew as the "presentation of the King and His kingdom to the nation (of Israel) in fulfillment of the OT prophecy."[1] If you had to summarize the entire book of Matthew by one of its verses, the summary verse would be Matthew 21:5: "Say to the daughter of Zion, 'Behold your king is coming to you, gentle, and mounted on a donkey, even on a colt, the foal of a beast of burden.'"

With this in mind, read the book of Matthew with a focus on Christ's kingship. The following outline of Matthew stresses this theme in the book:

Chapter 1: The King's Pedigree
Jesus is not an impostor, hence the royal genealogy showing Him to be the Son of David.

Chapter 2: Treachery and Intrigue Surround the King
Herod the usurper and would-be assassins try to kill the child King.

Chapter 3: The King's Forerunner
John the Baptist, the holiest man alive, heralds the King's arrival.

Chapter 4: The King's Challenger
The King's throne is challenged by Satan.

Chapters 5–7: The King's Manifesto
The Sermon on the Mount requires internal obedience.

Chapters 8–9: The King's Power

Jesus' power is demonstrated by compassionate healings and the casting-out of demons.

Chapter 10: The Delegation of the King

The Twelve are summoned, equipped, and sent.

Chapters 11–15: The Rejection of the King

The King is rejected and dire consequences follow.

Chapters 16–20: The Instruction by the King

Jesus instructs His disciples on who He is and His impending death.

Chapter 21: The Coronation of the King

The King enters Jerusalem ("Hosanna to the Son of David").

Chapter 22: Clashes with the King

Chapter 23: The King Rejects the Sinful Leadership of His People

Chapters 24–25: The King Predicts Judgment and His Return (The Olivet Discourse)

Chapters 26–27: The King's Substitutionary Self-Sacrifice

"And above His head they put up the charge against Him which read, 'THIS IS JESUS THE KING OF THE JEWS'" (27:37).

Chapter 28: The King's Ultimate Proof of His Deity—The Resurrection

Notes

1 **S. Lewis Johnson,** "The Argument of Matthew," *Bibliotheca Sacra*, 112/146 (April 1955), 144–153.

"That's My King"
by Dr. S. M. Lockridge[1]

The Bible says
He's the King of the Jews
He's the King of Israel
He's the King of Righteousness
He's the King of the Ages
He's the King of Heaven
He's the King of Glory
He's the King of Kings
and He is the Lord of Lords

Now that's my King!
David says
The Heavens declare the glory of God
And the firmament showeth His handiwork
No means of measure can define His limitless love
No far seeing telescope can bring into visibility the coastline of His shoreless supply
No barriers can hinder Him from pouring out His blessing

He's enduringly strong
He's entirely sincere
He's eternally steadfast
He's immortally graceful
He's imperially powerful
He's impartially merciful

That's my King!
He's God's Son
He's the sinners' Savior
He's the centrepiece of civilization

He stands alone in Himself
He's august
He's unique
He's unparalleled
He's unprecedented
He's supreme
He's preeminent
He's the loftiest idea in literature
He's the highest personality in philosophy
He's the supreme problem in higher criticism
He's the fundamental doctrine in true theology
He's the cardinal necessity of spiritual religion

That's my King!
He's the miracle of the age
He's the superlative of everything good that you choose to call Him
He's the only one able to supply all of our needs simultaneously
He supplies strength for the weak
He's available for the tempted and the tried
He sympathizes and He saves
He guards and He guides
He heals the sick
He cleansed the lepers
He forgives sinners
He discharges debtors
He delivers the captives
He defends the feeble
He blesses the young
He serves the unfortunate
He regards the aged
He rewards the diligent
And He beautifies the meek

Do you know Him?
My King is the key of knowledge

He's the wellspring of wisdom
He's the doorway of deliverance
He's the pathway of peace
He's the roadway of righteousness
He's the highway of holiness
He's the gateway of glory
He's the master of the mighty
He's the captain of the conquerors
He's the head of the heroes
He's the leader of the legislators
He's the overseer of the overcomers
He's the governor of governors
He's the prince of princes
He's the King of Kings
And He's the Lord of Lords

That's my King
That's my King!
My King
His office is manifold
His promise is sure
His life is matchless
His goodness is limitless
His mercy is everlasting
His love never changes
His word is enough
His grace is sufficient
His reign is righteous
His yoke is easy
and His burden is light
I wish I could describe Him to you
He's indescribable
He's indescribable
He's incomprehensible
He's invincible

He's irresistible
I'm trying to tell you
The heaven of heavens cannot contain Him
Let alone a man explain Him
You can't get Him out of your mind
You can't get Him off of your hands
You can't outlive Him
And you can't live without Him
The Pharisees couldn't stand Him
but they found out they couldn't stop Him
Pilate couldn't find any fault in Him
The witnesses couldn't get their testimonies to agree
And Herod couldn't kill Him
Death couldn't handle Him
And the grave couldn't hold Him

That's my King!
He always has been
And He always will be
I'm talking about
He had no predecessor
and He'll have no successor
There was nobody before Him
and there'll be nobody after Him
You can't impeach Him
and He's not going to resign

That's my King!
Praise the Lord
That's my King
Thine is the Kingdom
And the power
And the glory
The glory is all His
Thine is the Kingdom

And the power
And the glory
Forever
And ever
And ever
And when you get through with all of the forevers
Then
Amen

Note

1   "That's My King!" at: thatsmyking.wordpress.com/words. Accessed February 2011.

"The Unconquerable King" by C. H. Spurgeon[1]

At the end of the days I Nebuchadnezzar lifted up mine eyes unto heaven, and mine understanding returned unto me, and I blessed the most High, and I praised and honoured him that liveth for ever, whose dominion is an everlasting dominion, and his kingdom is from generation to generation: and all the inhabitants of the earth are reputed as nothing: and he doeth according to his will in the army of heaven, and among the inhabitants of the earth: and none can stay his hand, or say unto him, What doest thou? (Daniel 4:34–35)

No one has ever numbered Nebuchadnezzar with the Prophets, or believed his language to be inspired. We have before us simply a statement made by an uninspired man, after passing through the most extraordinary experience. He had been among the greatest and proudest of men—he suddenly fell into the condition of a grass-eating ox, by losing his reason. And upon being restored, he acknowledged publicly the hand of the Most High. I should not have taken his language as my text if it had not happened to be, as it is, a most correct and vigorous statement of sublime doctrines which are clearly stated by the Holy Spirit in different parts of Scripture.

It is a singular instance of how, when God comes to deal with men in afflicting providences, He can make them clearly see many great Truths concerning Himself, and can constrain them to express their convictions in identically the same way as they would have done if His own Spirit had dictated the terms. There are certain parts of the Divine Character which even the unspiritual man cannot avoid seeing. And after passing through certain processes of suffering and humiliation, the man is compelled to add his witness to the testimony of God's Spirit with regard to the Divine Character.

Every single word that Nebuchadnezzar here utters can be backed up and supported by undoubtedly inspired words of men sent of God to proclaim infallible Truth. We shall not, therefore, need to answer the objection that our text is simply the statement of Nebuchadnezzar—we grant that it is so—but we shall show as we proceed that Babylon's humbled monarch herein has spoken most correctly and accurately—and in full accordance with the testimony of other parts of Scripture.

Before I conduct your minds to a close consideration of the text, I must make one remark. Many of you will very naturally suppose that the chapter read during this service, the hymns and the sermon, were all intended to have reference to a certain great political event reported in the papers of last night [the surrender of Napoleon to the King of Prussia]. But please observe that your supposition will be unfounded, for my text was fixed upon yesterday morning, before any sort of news had reached me, and the service would have been the same if that event had not occurred. So that anything strikingly suggestive in the choice of the passage may be looked upon, if you will, as denoting the guidance of God's Spirit, but must not be imputed to any intentional reference on my part.

We will now come first to consider the doctrinal instruction of the text. Secondly, we would learn the practical teaching of it. And thirdly, we would exhibit the spirit suitable after the contemplation of such a subject.

1. First, then, let us turn to the text, and consider *the doctrinal instruction* here given to us. We have here plainly stated the doctrine of the eternal Self-Existence of God. "I blessed the Most High, and I praised and honoured him that liveth for ever." If this word needed to be confirmed we would refer you to the language of John in the Book of the Revelation, where we find him describing, in the fourth chapter, at the ninth and tenth verses, the living creatures and the four and twenty elders as giving glory and honor and thanks, "to him that sat on the throne, who liveth for ever and for ever."

Better still, let us hear the witness of our own Redeemer, in the fifth of John's gospel, at the twenty-sixth verse, where he declares that, "the Father hath life in himself." My Brethren, you need not that I marshal in array a host of confirmative passages, for the eternal Self-Existence of God is taught throughout the Scriptures, and is implied in that name which belongs only to the true God, Jehovah, "I Am that I Am," where, note that it is not "I was," which would imply that in some measure or respect he had ceased to be,

Nor is it "I will be," which would intimate that He is not now what He will be, but I AM, the only Being, the root of Existence, the Immutable, and Eternal One. "We," as a venerable Puritan observes, "have more of nothing than of being," but it is God's prerogative to BE. He alone can say, "I am God, and beside me there is none else." He declares, "I lift up my hand to heaven, and say I live for ever." He is the One only underived, Self-Existent, Self-Sustained Being. Let us know of a surety that the Lord God whom we worship is the only Being who necessarily and from his own nature, Exists.

No other being could have been but for his Sovereign will, nor could it continue were that will suspended. He is the only light of life, all others are reflections of his beams. There must be God, but there was no such necessity that there should be any other intelligences. In all the future God must Be, but the necessity for the continuance of other spirits lies in His will and not in the very nature of things. There was a time when the creatures were not. They came from Him as vessels from the potter's wheel. They all depend upon Him for continuance, as the streamlet on the fountain whence it flows.

And if it were His will, they all would melt away as the foam upon the water. That immortality of spirits implied in such passages as Matthew 25:46, "These shall go away into everlasting punishment: but the righteous into life eternal," is the result of His own resolve to make spirits whose duration should be eternal. And though He will never withdraw the endowment of immortality which He has bestowed, yet the reason for eternal existence is not in the *beings*, but entirely in Himself, for essentially, "He only hath immortality":

"He can create and He destroy."

All that is, whether material or intellectual, if so it had pleased God to ordain, might have been as transient as a sunbeam and have vanished as speedily as the rainbow from the cloud. If anything now exists of necessity, that necessity sprang from God, and still depends upon the necessity of Divine Decree.

God is independent—the only being who is so. We must find food with which to repair the daily wastes of the body. We are dependent upon light and heat, and innumerable external agencies—and above all we are primarily dependent upon the outgoings of the Divine power towards us. But the I AM is Self-Sufficient and All-Sufficient.

"He sits on no precarious throne,
Nor borrows leave to be."

He was as glorious before He made the world as He is now. He was as great, as blessed, as Divine in all His attributes before sun and moon and stars leaped into existence as He is now. And if He should blot all out as a man erases the writing of his pen, or as a potter breaks the vessel he has made, He would be none the less the supreme and ever-blessed God.

Nothing of God's Being is derived from another, but all that exists is derived from Him. Ye hills and mountains, ye seas and stars, ye men and angels, ye heavens and ye Heaven of heavens—ye minister nothing to Him who made you—ye all stand up together in existence flowing from your Creator. God ever liveth in this respect, that He undergoes no sort of change. All His creatures must, from their constitution, undergo more or less of mutation. Of them all it is decreed, "They shall perish, but thou shalt endure: yea, all of them shall wax old like a garment; as a vesture shalt thou change them, and they shall be changed: but thou art the same, and thy years shall have no end."

Our life is made up of changes. From childhood we hasten to youth, from youth we leap to manhood, from manhood we fade into old age. Our changes are as many as our days. "The creature" is, indeed, in our case, "made subject to vanity." Lighter than a feather, more frail than the flower of the field, brittle as glass, fleeting as a meteor, tossed to and fro like a ball, and quenched as a spark—"Lord, what is man?" There cometh to us all in the time appointed the great and ultimate change in the which the spirit is separated from the body—to be followed by another in which the divided manhood shall be reunited. But with God there are no changes of this or any other kind. Hath He not declared, "I am God, I change not"?

God is essentially and evermore pure Spirit, and consequently undergoes no variableness nor shadow of a turning. Of none of the creatures can this be said. Immutability is an attribute of God only. The things created were once new—they are waxing old—they will become older still. But the Lord hath no time, He dwelleth in eternity. There is no moment of beginning with the Eternal, no starting point from which to calculate age. From of old He was the Ancient of Days, "from everlasting to everlasting thou art God."

Let your mind retreat as far as its capacities will allow into the remote past of old eternity, and there it finds Jehovah alone in the fullness of His glory. Then let the same thought flash forward into the far-off future, as far as unreined imagination can bear it, and there it beholdeth the Eternal, unchanged, unchangeable. He works changes and effects changes, but He Himself abides the same. Brethren, let us worship Him with words like these:

"Thy throne eternal ages stood,
Ere seas or stars were made;
Thou art the Ever-living God,
Were all the nations dead.

"Eternity with all its years
Stands present in thy view;
To thee there's nothing old appears;
Great God! there's nothing new.

"Our lives through various scenes are drawn,
And vex'd with trifling cares,
While thine eternal thought moves on
Thine undisturb'd affairs."

That He lives forever is the result, not only of His essential and necessary Self-Existence, of His independence, and of His unchangeableness, but of the fact that there is no conceivable force that can ever wound, injure, or destroy Him. If we were profane enough to imagine the Lord to be vulnerable, yet where is the bow and where the arrow that could reach Him on His throne? What javelin shall pierce Jehovah's buckler? Let all the nations of the earth rise and rage against God, how shall they reach His throne? They cannot even shake His footstool.

If all the angels of Heaven should rebel against the Great King, and their squadrons should advance in serried ranks to besiege the palace of the Most High, He has but to will it, and they would wither as autumn leaves, or consume as the fat upon the altar. Reserved in chains of darkness, the opponents of His power would forever become mementos of His wrath. None can touch Him. He is the God that ever liveth. Let us who delight in the living God bow down before Him, and humbly worship Him as the God in whom we live and move, and have our being.

In our text we next find Nebuchadnezzar asserting the everlasting dominion of God. He saith, "Whose dominion is an everlasting dominion, and his kingdom is from generation to generation." The God whom we serve not only exists, but reigns. No other position would become Him but that of unlimited Sovereignty over all His creatures. "The most high God, possessor of heaven and earth, hath prepared his throne in the heavens, and his kingdom ruleth over all." As David said so, we say also, "Thine, O Lord, is the greatness, and the power, and the glory, and the victory, and the majesty: for all that is in the heaven and in the earth is thine; thine is the kingdom, O Lord, and thou art exalted as head above all." "The Lord sitteth upon the flood; yea, the Lord sitteth King for ever."

The Lord is naturally the Ruler of all, but who shall pretend to rule over Him? He is not to be judged of man's finite reason for he doeth great things which we cannot comprehend. Amazing is the impertinence of man, when the creature dares to sit in judgment on the Creator! His character is not to be impugned or called in question. Only the boundless arrogance of our pride would so dare to insult the thrice holy God. "Be still, and know that I am God," is a sufficient reply to such madness. The Lord's place is on the Throne, and our place is to obey. It is His to govern, ours to serve—His to do as He wills, and ours, without questioning, to make that will our constant delight. Remember, then, that in the universe God is actually reigning.

Never let us conceive of God as being infinitely great, but not exerting His greatness—infinitely able to reign—but as yet a mere spectator of events. It is not so. The Lord reigneth even now. Though in one sense we pray, "Thy kingdom come," yet in another we say, "Thine is the kingdom, and the power, and the glory, for ever and ever." The Throne of the universe is not vacant, nor its power in abeyance. God doth not hold a bare title to kingship—He is actually King. The government is upon His shoulders, the reins of management are in His hands. Even at this hour He speaks to the sons of men, "See now that I, even I, am he, and there is no god with me: I kill, and I make alive; I wound, and I heal: neither is there any that can deliver out of my hand."

Before your very eyes He has fulfilled His word (Luke 1:51, 52). Events appear to fly at random like the dust in the whirlwind, but it is not so. The rule of the Omnipotent extends over all things at all times. Nothing is left to its own chance hap, but in wisdom all things are governed. Glory be unto the Omnipresent and Invisible Lord of all!

This Divine kingdom appeared very plainly to the once proud monarch of Babylon, to be an everlasting one. The reign of the Ever-Living extends as other kingdoms cannot, "from generation to generation." The mightiest king inherits power and soon yields his scepter to his successor. The Lord hath no beginning of days nor end of years—predecessor or successor are words inapplicable to Him. Other monarchies stand while their power is unsubdued, but in an evil hour a greater power may crush them down. There is no greater power than God—yea, there is no other power but that which proceeds from God, for "God hath spoken once; twice have I heard this; that power belongeth unto God"; hence his monarchy cannot be subdued, and must be everlasting.

Dynasties have passed away, dying out for lack of heirs, but God the Ever-Living asks none to succeed Him and to perpetuate His name. Internal corruptions have often blasted empires which stood aloft like forest trees, defiant of the storm—at the core the tree was rotten, and ere long, weakened by decay—it tottered to its fall. But the infinitely Holy God has no injustice, error, partiality, or evil motive in the government of His affairs—everything is arranged with spotless holiness, unimpeachable justice, unvarying fidelity, untarnished truth, amazing mercy, and overflowing love. All the elements of His kingdom are most conservative, because radically right. There is no evil leaven in the council chamber of Omniscience, no corruption on the Judgment Seat of Heaven. Hence "his throne is established in righteousness" (Psalm 47:8). Because His Throne is holy we rejoice that it can never be moved.

Pause here, dear Hearer, and let your soul's eye behold again this view of things. God has reigned from the first day, God shall reign when days are gone. Everywhere He is the reigning God—reigning when Pharaoh said, "Who is Jehovah, that I should obey him?" as much as when Miriam took her timbrel, and said, "Sing unto the Lord, for he hath triumphed gloriously"; reigning when Scribe and Pharisee, Jew and Roman, nailed His Only Begotten Son to the Cross, as much as when the angelic cohorts shouted in triumph, "Lift up your heads, O ye gates, and be ye lift up, ye everlasting doors, that the King of Glory may come in."

He is reigning amid all the calamities which sweep the globe as much as He shall be in the halcyon days of peace. Never is the Throne vacant, never is the scepter laid aside. Jehovah is always King, and shall be King forever and forever. Oh, happy subjects, who have such a Throne to look to! Oh, blessed children, who have such a King to be your Father! You, as a royal priesthood, may feel your royalties and your priesthoods both secure for this unconquerable King sitteth securely on His Throne. Your monarch has not yielded up His sword to a superior foe. You have not to search for another leader. In the Person of His dear Son He walks among our golden candlesticks, and holds our stars in His right hand. He keepeth Israel, and never slumbers nor sleeps.

But we must hasten on. Nebuchadnezzar, humbled before God, uses, in the third place, extraordinary language with regard to the nothingness of mankind. "All the inhabitants of the earth are reputed as nothing." This is Nebuchadnezzar, but his words are confirmed by Isaiah, "Behold the nations are as a drop of a bucket," the unnoticed drop which remains in the bucket after it has been emptied into the trough, or the drip which falls from it as it is uplifted from the well—a thing too inconsiderable to be worthy of notice. "And are counted as the small dust of the balance." As the dust which falls upon scales, but is not sufficient to affect the balance in any degree whatever.

"Behold, he taketh up the isles as a very little thing." Whole archipelagos He uplifts as unconsidered trifles. This triple kingdom of ours [Great Britain] He reckons not only to be little, but "a very little thing." The vast island of Australia, the gems of the Pacific, the nations of the Southern Ocean, all these He handles as children lift their toys. "All nations before him are as nothing; and they are counted to him less than nothing, and vanity." So if Nebuchadnezzar goes far, Isaiah, inspired of the Spirit, goes farther; the one calls the nations "nothing," and the other "less than nothing" and "vanity."

You will find the passage in the fortieth of Isaiah, at the fifteenth and seventeenth verses. Now mark the force of each word, "all the inhabitants of the earth," not some of them only, not the poor ones among them, but the rich, the kings, the wise, the philosophers, the priests—all put together—"are as nothing." What an assembly would there be if all the nations could be gathered together! An impressive spectacle rises before my vision! One had need possess an eagle's wing merely to pass over the mighty congregation. Where could a plain be found which could contain them all? Yet all of them, saith the text, are "as nothing."

Now, observe they are so in themselves, for concerning all of us who are gathered here it is certain that there was a time when we were not—we were then in very deed "nothing." At this very moment, also, if God wills it, we may cease to be, and so in a step return to nothing. We are nothing in ourselves, we are only what He chooses to allow us to be, and when the time comes and it will be a very short time, so far as this world is concerned, we shall be nothing. All that will remain of us among the sons of men will be some little hillock in a cemetery or a country Churchyard, for we shall have no part in anything which is done under the sun.

Of what account at this day, my Brethren, are all the antediluvian millions? What are the hosts of Nimrod, of Shishak, of Sennacherib, of Cyrus? What reeks the world of the myriads who followed the march of Nebuchadnezzar, who obeyed the beck of Cyrus, who passed away before the eye of Xerxes? Where are the generations which owned the sovereignty of Alexander, or the legions which followed and almost adored the eagles of the Caesars? Alas! even our grandsires, where are they? Our sons forewarn us that we must die. Have they not been born to bury us? So pass the generations like the successive series of forest leaves. And what are they but at their best estate, "altogether vanity"?

The nations are nothing in comparison with God. As you may place as many ciphers as you like together, and they all make nothing, so you may add up as many men, with all their supposed force and wisdom, as you please, and they are all nothing in comparison with God. He is the Unit. He stands for All in All, and comprehendeth all. And all the rest are but so many valueless ciphers till His Unity makes them of account. Here let me remind you that every man who is spiritually taught of God is made to feel experimentally on his own account his own utter nothingness. When his inner eye, like that of Job, beholdeth the Lord, he abhors himself, he shrinks into the earth, he feels he cannot contrast or compare himself with the Most High even for a single second.

"Great God, how infinite art thou!
What worthless worms are we!"

is the verse which naturally leaps to the lip of any man who knows himself and knows his God.

Spiritually, our nothingness is very conspicuous. We were nothing in our election—"Ye have not chosen me, but I have chosen you." "The children being not yet born, neither having done any good or evil, that the purpose of God according to election might stand, not of works, but of him that calleth." "It is not of him that willeth, nor of him that runneth, but of God that showeth mercy." We were nothing in our redemption. We contributed nothing to that price which Jesus paid—"I have trodden the winepress alone; and of the people there was none with me." We are nothing in our regeneration—can the spiritually dead help the blessed God to quicken them? "It is the Spirit that quickeneth, the flesh profiteth nothing." "We are his workmanship, created anew in Christ Jesus." We shall, when we get to Heaven, make it part of our adoration to confess that we are less than nothing and vanity, but that God is All in All. Therefore shall we cast our crowns at His feet, and give Him all the praise forever and ever.

"The inhabitants of the earth are as nothing." It is a wonderful expression, and you see I do not attempt to expound it or any part of the text. I rather repeat words of the same meaning with the text by way of illustration. Before me is a great deep, and who shall fathom it? I would not darken counsel by words without knowledge. If there were an ant's nest somewhere in a farmer's estate, and suppose he had ten thousand acres of land, that ant's nest would bear some portion, though a very small one, to the ten thousand acres of land. It could not be so strictly said to be as nothing as the whole world can when compared with God.

This round earth bears a very insignificant proportion to the vast creation of God, even to that which is revealed to us by the telescope. And we have reason to believe that all which can be seen with the telescope—if indeed it be a mass of worlds, and all inhabited—is but as a pin's prick compared with the city of London, to the far-reaching universe. If it be so, and your mind were capable of compassing the entire creation of God, yet it would be only as a drop of a bucket compared with God Himself who made it all, and could make ten thousand times ten thousand as much, and then be but at the beginning of His power.

This world, then, bears no such proportion to the Lord as an ant's nest to the estate of ten thousand acres. Now if the farmer wishes to till the soil, it is not at all probable that he will take any cognizance whatever of that ant's nest in the arrangement of his affairs. And in all probability will overturn and destroy it. This proves the insignificance of the emmet, and the greatness of man as compared with ants. But as it involves a degree of forgetfulness or overlooking on the farmer's part, the ants are great enough to be forgotten—but the nations are not great enough even for that. If it were possible for the farmer to arrange without difficulty all his plans so that without disturbing his proceedings, every bird, emmet, and worm should be cared for in his scheme, how great then would he be compared with the ants!

And this is just the case with the Lord—He so arranges all things that apparently without effort the government of Providence embraces all interests, wrongs none, but yields justice to all. Men are so little in the way of God that He never finds it needful to perpetrate an injustice even on a single man, and He has never caused one solitary creature to suffer one unnecessary pang. Herein is His greatness, that it comprehends all littlenesses without a strain—the glory of His wisdom is as astonishing as the majesty of His power, and the splendors of His love and of His Grace are as amazing as the terror of his Sovereignty. He may do what He wills, for none can stay Him. But He never wills to do in any case aught that is unjust, unholy, unmerciful, or in any way inconsistent with the perfection of His matchless Character. Here let us pause, and worship. I at least must do so. For my soul's eyes ache, as though I had been gazing at the sun.

We turn now to the next sentence, which reveals the Divine power at work sovereignly. "He doeth according to his will in the army of heaven, and among the inhabitants of the earth." This is easy to understand in reference to the celestial host, for we know that God's will is done in Heaven—we devoutly pray that it may yet be done on earth after the same fashion. The angels find it their Heaven to be obedient to the God of Heaven. Under the term "army of heaven" is comprehended fallen angels who were once numbered with that band, but were expelled from Heaven for their rebellion.

Devils unwillingly, but yet of necessity, fulfill the will of God. "Whatsoever the Lord pleased, that did he in heaven, and in earth, in the seas, and all deep places." When we read in the text that on earth God's will is done, we see that it is so in a measure among the righteous whose renewed hearts seek after God's glory. But the Truth goes further, for that will is also accomplished in the *unrighteous*, and by those who know Him not. Yea, in those whose will is determined to oppose Him—still in some way unknown to us the will of God is still achieved (Proverbs 19:21; Acts 4:27, 28).

I can understand a man taking so many pieces of wood and arranging them just as he pleases, nor can I see any very remarkable skill in so doing. But the miracle of Divine Glory lies in this—that He has made men free agents, has endowed them with a will, with which will He never interferes except according to the laws of mind. That He leaves them absolutely free to do what they will, and they will universally of themselves to do contrary to His will. And yet, such is the magnificent strategy of Heaven, such is the marvelous force of the Divine mind, that despite everything, the will of God is done!

Some have supposed that when we believe with David, in Psalm cxv, that God hath done whatsoever He hath pleased, we deny free agency, and of necessity moral responsibility also. Nay, but we declare that those who would do so are tinctured with the old captious spirit of him who said,

"Why doth he yet find fault, for who hath resisted his will?" And our only answer is that of Paul, "Nay, but O man, who art thou that repliest against God?" Can you understand it, for I cannot—how man is a free agent, a responsible agent, so that his sin is his own willful sin and lies with him and never with God—and yet at the same time God's purposes are fulfilled, and His will is done even by demons and corrupt men?

I cannot comprehend it, but without hesitation I believe it, and rejoice so to do. I never hope to comprehend it. I worship a God I never expect to comprehend. If I could grasp Him in the hollow of mine hand, I could not call Him my God. And if I could understand His dealings so that I could read them as a child reads his spelling book, I could not worship Him. But because He is so infinitely great I find Truth here, Truth there, Truth multiform. And if I cannot compress it into one system—I know it is all clear to him—and I am content that He should know what I know not.

It is mine today to adore and obey—by-and-by when He sees fit I shall know more and adore better. It is my firm belief that everything in Heaven, and earth, and Hell, will be seen to be, in the long run, parts of the Divine Plan. Yet never is God the Author or the accomplice of *sin*—never is He otherwise than the Hater of sin and the Avenger of unrighteousness. Sin rests with *man*, wholly with man, and yet by some strange overruling force, Godlike and mysterious, like the existence of God, His supreme will is accomplished. Observe how the two truths combine in practice, and are stated in the same verse in reference to our Lord's crucifixion, in Acts 2:23—"Him, being delivered by the determinate council and foreknowledge of God, ye have taken, and by wicked hands have crucified and slain."

Now, to deny this Truth because we cannot understand it, were to shut ourselves out of a great deal of important knowledge. Brethren, if God does not rule everywhere, then something rules where He does not, and so He is not Omnipresently supreme. If God does not have His will, someone else does, and so far that someone is a rival to God. I never deny the free agency of man, or diminish his responsibility, but I dare never invest the free will of man with Omnipotence, for this were to make man into a sort of God, an idolatry to be loathed.

Moreover, admit *chance* anywhere, and you have admitted chance everywhere, for all events are related and act on one another. One cog of the wheel of Providence disarranged or left to Satan, or man's absolute freedom apart from God, would spoil the whole machinery. I dare not believe even sin itself to be exempted from the control of Providence, or from the overruling dominion of the Judge of all the earth. Without Providence we were unhappy beings. Without the universality of the Divine power, Providence would be imperfect, and in some points we might be left unprotected and exposed to those evils which are, by this theory, supposed to be beyond Divine control. Happy are we that it is true, "the Lord doeth as he wills in the army of heaven, and among the inhabitants of the earth."

Let us now consider the fifth part of the text—"None can stay his hand, or say unto him, What doest thou?" I gather from this that God's fiat is irresistible and unimpeachable. We are told by some annotators that the original has in it an allusion to a blow given to a child's hand to make him cease from some forbidden action. None can treat the Lord in that manner. None can hinder Him, or cause Him to pause. He has might to do what He wills. So also says Isaiah—"Woe unto him that striveth with his Maker! Let the potsherd strive with the potsherds of the earth. Shall the clay say to him that fashioneth it, What makest thou? or thy work, He hath no hands?"

Man is powerless, then, to resist the fiat of God. Usually he does not know God's design, although he blunderingly thinks he does—often in opposing that apparent design he fulfills the secret design of God against his will. If man did know God's design, and should set himself with all his might against it, yet as the chaff cannot resist the wind, as it is not possible for the wax to resist the fire, so neither can man effectually resist the absolute will and Sovereign good pleasure of the Most High. Only, here is our comfort—it is right that God should have this might, because He always uses His might with strictest rectitude. God cannot will to do anything unjust, ungenerous, unkind, ungodlike.

No laws bind Him as they bind us, but He is a Law to Himself. There is "Thou shalt," and "Thou shalt not," for me, for you—but who shall put "Thou shalt" to God, or who shall say, "Thou shalt not"? Who shall attempt to be legislator for the King of kings? God is Love. God is Holiness. God is the Law. God is Love, and doing as He wills, He wills to love. God is Holy, and doing as He wills, He wills holiness, He wills justice, He wills truth. And though there were raised a thousand questions as to how is this just? How is that loving? How is that wise? The one sufficient answer is:

"God is his own interpreter
And he will make it plain."

O sons of men, it is not for me to unriddle the enigmas of the Infinite, he shall explain Himself. I am not so impertinent as to be His apologist, He shall clear Himself. I am not called to vindicate His character. "Shall not the Judge of all the earth do right?" What folly to hold up a candle to show the brightness of the sun! How much more foolish to attempt to defend the thrice holy Jehovah! Let Him speak for Himself if He will deign to contend with you. If you do but hear His thunders, how you tremble! When His lightnings set the heavens on fire, how amazed ye are! Stand ye forth, then, and question Him if you dare.

If you are at sea in a storm, when every timber of your vessel creaks, when the mast is broken, when the mariners stagger like drunken men, when overhead is the horrible tempest, and the thundering voice of God in the tempest, and all around you the howling winds, then ye cease your cavillings, and cry unto Him in your trouble. Act ye then this day as you would do in such a case, for ye are equally in His hands (Psalm 99:1, 5; 100:3, 4). Thus have I tried to set forth the doctrine of the text.

2. Now, very briefly, consider its *practical instruction*. I think the first lesson is how wise to be at one with Him! As I bowed before the majesty of this text in my study, I felt within my soul, "Oh, how I long to be perfectly at one with this infinitely mighty, glorious, and holy God. How can I dare to be His enemy?" I felt then if I had not yielded before, I must yield now, subdued before Him. I would that any of you who are not doing His will would give up your hopeless rebellion. He invites you to come. He might have commanded you to depart. In His infinite sovereignty He has appointed Christ Jesus to be the Savior of men. Come and accept that Savior by faith.

How encouraging this is to those who are at one with God! If he be on our side, who shall be against us? "The Lord of Hosts is with us, the God of Jacob is our refuge." We ought to be of the same mind as that believing woman who, during an earthquake, was observed to be very happy. Everybody else was afraid—houses were falling, towers were rocking, but she smiled. And when they asked her why, she replied, "I am so glad to find that my God can shake the world. I believed he could, and now I see that he can."

Be glad that you have One to trust in to whom nothing is impossible, who can and will achieve His purposes. My heart feels that she would give Him the power if He had it not, and if it were all mine. I would leave all power in His hands even if I could remove it. "Great God, reign thou supremely, for there is none like unto thee." "The Lord reigneth; let the earth rejoice; let the multitude of isles be glad thereof." How joyful this thought ought to be to all holy workers! You and I have enlisted on the side of God and of His Christ, and, though the powers against us seem very strong, yet the invincible King will surely put them to the rout ere long.

Romanism, idolatry, infidelity—these all appear mighty things. And so seem those pots fresh from the potter—a child thinks them to be stone. But when the Lord Jesus smites them with the rod of iron, see how the potsherds fly! This shall He do ere long. He will lift the might of His terrible arm and bring down His iron rod! Then shall it be seen that the Truth of God as it is in Jesus must and shall prevail.

How this should help you that suffer! If God does it all, and nothing happens apart from God, even the wickedness and cruelty of man being still overruled by Him, you readily may submit. How graciously and with what good face can you kiss the hand which smites you! The husband is gone to Heaven, God took him. The property has melted, God has permitted it. You were robbed, you say—well, think not so much of the second cause, look to the great *first* cause. You strike a dog, he bites the stick. If he were wise, he would look at you who use it.

Do not look at the second cause of the afflictions, look to the great first cause. It is your God who is in it all, your Father God, the Infinitely good. Which would you desire to have done on earth, your will or God's will? If you are wise, you say, "Not my will, but thine be done." Then accept the ways of Providence. Since God appoints them, accept them with grateful praise. Herein is true sacrifice to God when we can say, "Though he slay me, yet will I trust in him." We have received good at His hands, and we have blessed Him—heathen men and publicans might have done that. But if we receive evil and still bless Him, this is Divine Grace, this is the work of His Holy Spirit.

If we can bow before His crushing strokes, and feel that if the crushing of us by the weight of His hand will bring Him honor, we are content. This is true faith. Give us Grace enough, O Lord, never to fail in our loyalty, but to be thy faithful servants even to sufferings' bitterest end. Oh, to have the mind thus subjected to God! Some kick at the doctrine of Divine Sovereignty, but I fear it is because they have a rebellious, unhumbled spirit. Those who feel obedient to God cannot have God cried up too much, cannot yield Him too absolute an authority. Only a rebellious child in a house wishes the father to be tied by rules and regulations. No, my Father must do right, let Him do what He wills!

3. What is *the right spirit* in which to contemplate all this? The first is humble adoration. We do not worship enough, my Brethren. Even in our public gatherings we do not have enough worship. O worship the King! Bow your heads now—bow your spirits, rather, and adore Him that liveth forever and ever. Your thoughts, your emotions—these are better than bullocks and he-goats to be offered on the altar—God will accept them. Worship Him with lowliest reverence, for you are nothing, and He is All in All. Next let the spirit of your hearts be that of unquestioning acquiescence. He wills it! I will do it or I will bear it. God help you to live in perfect resignation.

Next to that, exercise the spirit of reverent love. Do I tremble before this God? Then I must seek more Grace that I may love Him as He is. Not love Him when my thoughts have diminished Him of his splendor, and robbed Him of His Glory, but love Him even as an absolute sovereign, for I see that sovereignty exercised through Jesus Christ, my Shield and His Anointed. Let me love my God and King, and be a courtier, happy to be admitted near His Throne, to behold the light of the Infinite Majesty.

Lastly, let our spirit be that of profound delight. I believe there is no doctrine to the advanced Christian which contains such a deep sea of delight as this. The Lord reigns! The Lord is King forever and ever! Why, then all is well. When you get away from God, you get away from peace. When the soul dives into Him, and feels that all is in Him, then she feels a calm delight, a peace like a river, a joy unspeakable. Strive after that delight this morning, my Beloved, and then go and express it in your songs of praise.

If you are alone this afternoon, any of you, and not engaged in service, be sure to bless and magnify your God. Lift up your hearts in His praise, for "whoso offereth praise glorifieth God." May the Lord bring us all, through faith in Jesus Christ, into harmony with this ever-blessed and ever-living God, and unto Him be praise and glory forever and forever. Amen.

Notes

1 Delivered on September 4, 1870 at the Metropolitan Tabernacle; sermon no. 949 in *Metropolitan Tabernacle Pulpit*, vol. 16 (1870); accessed from spurgeongems.org/vols16-18/chs949.pdf. Scripture quotations are from the King James Version.

Jesus Christ: the prince of preachers
Learning from the teaching ministry of Jesus

MIKE ABENDROTH

176PP PAPERBACK

978–1–84625–108–5

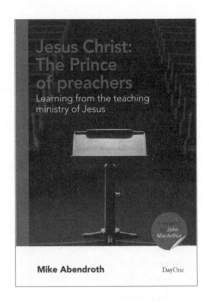

Jesus Christ:
The Prince
of preachers
Learning from the teaching
ministry of Jesus

John
MacArthur

Mike Abendroth   DayOne

Since preaching is God's ordained means of disseminating truth, it is vital that Bible teachers preach well and congregations listen well. This study of Jesus Christ's preaching will assist both the preacher and the congregation in their quests to honor the Lord with their respective responsibilities in worship.

While there are many definitions and descriptions of preaching today, preaching like Jesus must be the unchanging standard for all who dare teach the Bible. Preaching fads come and go, yet the manner and method of the Lord's preaching is always relevant, right, and worthy to be emulated.

What you win them with is what you win them to. Preaching is God's way of proclaiming the foolishness of the gospel to the weak and despised, all to His own glory. The world will always despise preaching, but when the church likewise questions God's wisdom and starts using alternatives, a major problem exists. Abendroth calls his readers back to the pre-eminence of preaching through the example of the Lord Himself. Encouraging and challenging.
JAMES WHITE, AUTHOR OF SCRIPTURE ALONE, PULPIT

CRIMES, THE GOD WHO JUSTIFIES, *AND* THE KING JAMES ONLY CONTROVERSY.

Mike Abendroth was born in Omaha, Nebraska. He was saved by God's intervening grace in 1989. After his father died, he bought a study Bible and began reading it beginning with Genesis. He graduated from The Master's Seminary (M. Div., 1996) and became the pastor of Bethlehem Bible Church, West Boylston, Massachusetts (1997). Mike has been married to Kimberly for 18 years and has three daughters and one son. He has been preaching expository sermons on a weekly basis for 15 years. One of Mike's passions is teaching men to teach the Bible expositionally. He is an Adjunct Professor of Theology at the Southern Baptist Theological Seminary, where he teaches homiletics.